Constituting Old Age
in Early Modern English Literature,
from Queen Elizabeth
to *King Lear*

Constituting Old Age

in Early Modern English Literature,
from Queen Elizabeth
to *King Lear*

CHRISTOPHER MARTIN

University of Massachusetts Press
Amherst & Boston

ISBN 978-1-55849-973-7 (paper); 972-0 (hardcover)

Set in Adobe Garamond Pro
Printed and bound by The Maple-Vail Book Manufacturing Group

Library of Congress Cataloging-in-Publication Data

Martin, Christopher, 1957–
Constituting old age in Early Modern English literature, from Queen Elizabeth to King Lear /
Christopher Martin.
p. cm. — (Massachusetts studies in early modern culture)
Includes bibliographical references and index.
ISBN 978-1-55849-973-7 (pbk. : alk. paper) — ISBN 978-1-55849-972-0 (hardcover : alk. paper)
1. English literature—Early modern, 1500–1700—History and criticism.   2. Old age in literature.
3. Aging in literature.   4. Intergenerational relations in literature.   I. Title.
PR428.O43M37 2012
820.9'354—dc23
2012031169

British Library Cataloguing in Publication Data
A catalogue record for this book is available from the British Library.

*Publication of this book has been supported by a generous grant from
the Center for the Humanities in the College of Arts & Sciences at Boston University.*

for

LORRAINE MARTIN

auld lang syne

Metaphors, like epithets, must be fitting, which means that they must fairly correspond to the thing signified: failing this, their inappropriateness will be conspicuous: the want of harmony between two things is emphasized by their being placed side by side. It is like having to ask ourselves what dress will suit an old man; certainly not the crimson cloak that suits a young man.

ARISTOTLE, *Rhetoric* 3.2

Contents

Acknowledgments   xi

1. Age, Agency, and Early Modern Constitutions   1

2. Elizabeth I's Politics of Longevity   30

3. Out to Pasture: The Bucolic Elder in Spenser, Sidney, and Their Heirs   64

4. Sexuality and Senescence in Late Elizabethan Poetry: "Old Strange Thinges"   100

5. "Confin'd to Exhibition": *King Lear* through the Spectacles of Age   137

Epilogue: Figures of Retire   176

Notes   185

Index   215

Acknowledgments

Over the course of this project's leisurely evolution, I have enjoyed numerous opportunities to air my ideas as they took shape. My thanks to the various organizing committees of the 2003 "Elizabeth R" quatercentenary conference, the Sixteenth Century Studies Conference, the John Donne Society conference, and the Boston University Lectures in Criticism Series, and to all those in attendance who responded thoughtfully to the tentative notions I then put forward. Two of these presentations went on to see early publication. A portion of Chapter 2 appeared as "The Breast and Belly of a Queen: Elizabeth after Tilbury," in *Early Modern Women: An Interdisciplinary Journal* 2 (2007), a publication of the Center for the Humanities (University of Miami) and Arizona Center for Medieval and Renaissance Studies (©Arizona Board of Regents for Arizona State University). Another section of Chapter 4 appeared as "Fall and Decline: Confronting Lyric Gerontophobia in Donne's 'The Autumnall,'" in *John Donne Journal* 26 (2007). I thank the editors of these journals for permission to reprint. In particular, my gratitude goes to Professors Ilona Bell and Adele Seeff, who offered kind moral and practical support, at short notice, when it was most needed; I hope this study offers some small return on their good collegiality. Toward its crucial final stages, the book benefited from a full year's leave funded by the Boston University Center for the Humanities, enabling timely completion of the manuscript. I'm grateful.

The exemplary manner of the University of Massachusetts Press's editorial board has kept the publication process a congenially encouraging one at every turn. The anonymous readers' generous and pointed recommendations, coupled with a relaxed willingness to grant me the extra time needed to accommodate these suggestions, made for the most rewarding kind of professional experience. Whatever shortcomings remain in the final product, the argument is decidedly stronger for their good direction.

Down the stretch, Bruce Wilcox graciously sped things along with remarkable facility. It was a delight working with Barbara Folsom, whose expert copyediting skills refreshed the manuscript throughout, helping me especially to dodge patches of stylistic quaintness to which I'd grown deaf; her own amicable style and humor kept this last revisionary phase both enjoyable and instructive. I likewise thank Carol Betsch and Mary Bellino for the friendly efficiency with which they saw the book into final production. I also take pleasure in the chance once again to express my warmest appreciation to Arthur F. Kinney, founder and series editor of Massachusetts Studies in Early Modern Culture, for his consistent receptivity, guidance, and support, from which so very many of us in the field have benefited over the space of his long and distinguished career.

On the home front, heartfelt thanks to my wife, Lydia Martin, for her quiet support throughout the time this book has developed, and for all the thirty-seven years of love and companionship I've known in her company; I have no greater ambition than to grow old together with her. Finally and especially, I acknowledge my big sister, Lorraine Martin, for teaching me early on how important it is to take full advantage of all our years. Amid my otherwise provincial and parochial upbringing, her example as a woman who struck out to explore Hawai'i before its statehood, land marlin off the coast of Mexico, and crash voodoo rituals in Haiti showed what it meant to pursue experience aggressively. Eighty-five years old as I write this, she continues to do things her own way, and there's no truer legacy than that. I'm happy to be able to dedicate this book about late life, with much love, to her.

Constituting Old Age

in Early Modern English Literature,
from Queen Elizabeth
to *King Lear*

CHAPTER ONE

Age, Agency, and
Early Modern Constitutions

T HIS BOOK EXPLORES the radical, perhaps unparalleled, experience of subjectivity that old age obliges, through a survey of literary and political expression during roughly the last quarter-century of Elizabeth I's reign. At root, the complex psychological tensions that this material discloses are themselves encapsulated in the folk wisdom driving Timothe Kendall's epigram of 1577 on the peculiar attitude we harbor toward late life:

> Eche one doeth seeke and wishe for age, all while it is awaie:
> And fewe doe come for to be olde, whiche for olde age doe praie.
> When age yet comes, eche doeth it lothe, and all doe it detest:
> So still we lothe our present state, deming the absent best.[1]

The bland moralizing that Kendall indulges in his final line does not obscure the depressing truth he expresses. Much of the indignity we come to fear and endure with the passing of time has to do with our own readiness to participate in gerontophobic "decline narratives" reinforcing a pernicious "decline ideology" that Margaret Morganroth Gullette has recently anatomized.[2] If it lacked the capacity to theorize matters of age and identity in quite the fashion that we are only now coming to realize, early modernity nonetheless intuited and subtly interrogated our paradoxical regard for the late life we fantasize. Far more than simply another instance of human fickleness or perversity, the ambivalence we feel about old age taps into some of the profoundest human apprehensions and hopes. The remarkable sophistication the period brings to this awareness empowers its literature, as I intend to demonstrate, in significant though underappreciated ways. To reclaim more fully the extent of its achievement, we need to reckon with how its representations charted and challenged received presuppositions about what it means to grow old.

While English culture of course had turned its attention sporadically to matters of senescence earlier in the period and became increasingly self-conscious about the subject of old age as the seventeenth century wore on, the intervening period on which I focus affords an uncommonly rich target for evaluation. Historians have long recognized the fierce generational strife that reached a fever pitch during Queen Elizabeth I's last decades and informed so many aspects of her political and cultural milieu. As Anthony Esler established in his benchmark study, over these years a spirit of "mutual distrust and enmity" had developed to the point where "The older generation became the first enemy of the ambitious leaders of the younger generation; and for twenty years the institutional cards were stacked against youth, until the death of the Queen cleared the board."[3] Although Esler's speculation that "To some extent, certainly, the flowering of Elizabethan literature at the end of the sixteenth century was a generational phenomenon" stands as something of a given, the notion goes largely unexamined.[4] At the nerve center of power, Elizabeth herself provided an iconic yet kinetic spectacle of age. However hostile or inured to the reality of female executive authority her subjects would grow over the course of her protracted reign, their imaginations were ultimately as stimulated by her longevity as they were by her gender, even as she reconstructed her own self-image to meet the contingencies of senescence.[5]

The period's developing vocabulary speaks directly to an emergent rethinking of the relationship between age, the body, and social context that distinguishes this pivotal cultural moment; for it is during the middle of the sixteenth century that our word *constitution* first turns inward to find its modern application as the "Physical nature or character of the body in regard to healthiness, strength, vitality, etc." (*OED,* 5a). Before this, the English term had looked instead to external bodies of laws and regulations formulated by social consensus or other agents of "superior authority," especially "civil or ecclesiastical" (*OED,* 3a). We may be tempted to dismiss this lexical development as unexceptional, one more symptom of a larger, well-documented shift toward subjectivity characterizing early modernity. The new inflection marks less of an innovation than a belated recovery of the Latin *constitutio*'s prevailing sense of a bodily disposition or nature. Moreover, it only displaces or expands the English *complexion,* already established to indicate a body's humoral makeup.[6] Yet the ambiguity or even ambivalence that "constitution" comes to encompass in the period uniquely marks the interface between competing interior and exterior realities along which contemporary self-awareness locates itself. Sensitized to a physical constitution that conditions identity independent of socially constituted, generic definitions, the individual is left to negotiate a more circumspect self-image. As the following chapters collectively document, in late Tudor England this agon plays out vigorously in cultural constructions of old age. Disinclined to nod in passive acquiescence at the plight stereotypically assigned to old age or the casually duplicitous response to this that Kendall abstracts, the subjects whose work I discuss all reimagine longevity's implications with a bold inquisitiveness enabled and encouraged by their distinct historical moment.

But what, we must first ask, did longevity in fact mean to a sixteenth-century English audience? Two contemporary texts offer a useful starting point, even as they capture the question's daunting complexity. Best remembered as a potential source for Jaques's "ages of man" set piece in *As You Like It,* Chapter 17 of Thomas Fortescue's compendium *The Foreste* (1571)—a translation via the French of Pedro Mexia's Spanish original *Silva de varia lecion* (1542)—neatly and precisely delineates the seven stages of a life course. Fortescue marks the inception of "our sixte Age, in Latine called not unproperly *Senectus*" placidly enough at fifty-five, a time of retirement "provokinge men to leave all toyle and travayle, seekinge a quiet life from sweate and payne." Lasting until age sixty-eight, this period of repose nonetheless yields to the far grimmer specter of a "Seventh and laste" phase which "continueth fully twentie yeeres, ending at the ende of eighty and eighte, which very fewe in our Age, either reache or attaine to." In this bitter time of decrepitude, "wee lyve alone and solitarye: nowe also growe on us, payne, griefe, sorowe, thoughte, sicknesse, unreaste, disdeigne, and anguishe." Charged with "perpetual annoy," the rare individual who approaches this terminus has little to anticipate save a reversion to the habits of "Babes or Suclinges," known in "the foure firste yeeres" of existence.[7]

Although obviously drawn to the structured precision of his model (if not to the bleak fate it irrevocably promises), the author simultaneously admits a telling hesitancy to invest in this or any of the other patterns he catalogues, which as plausibly partition life into three, four, five, six, or even ten stages.[8] The very assortment of possibilities instead issues in his professed confusion and wary disclaimer: "But here consideringe these variable opinions, I know not where, moste safely to arrest my selfe, neither may any man geve assured determination, as wel for diversitie of complexions, and dispositions of menne, as also that wee inhabite divers Landes and Countries, . . . by meanes whereof and of the semblable, man either sooner or later altering, becommeth at times differente, olde and decrepite" (pp. 48r–v). Fundamentally, "complexion" inheres as a critical factor, thwarting the neatness of numerical boundaries as it potentially unsettles even the most flexible of external formulations.

As if to venture a pointed rejoinder to Fortescue's calculations, William Harrison takes the opportunity to distinguish his own nation from other "Landes and Countries" in the extended prefaces he contributed to Holinshed's *Chronicle* of 1577 and 1587. For the official record, he proudly observes that the Elizabethan citizenry enjoyed long existences and left good-looking corpses:

> With us (although our good men care not to live long but to live well) some do live an hundred years, very many unto fourscore; as for threescore, it is taken but for our entrance into age, so that in Britain no man is said to wax old till he draw unto threescore. . . . These two are also noted in us (as things appertaining to the firm constitutions of our bodies), that there hath not been seen in any region so many carcasses of the dead to remain from time to time without corruption as in Britain, and that after death, by slaughter or otherwise, such as remain unburied by four or five days together are easy to be known and discerned by their friends and kindred. . . . In like sort the comeliness of our living bodies do continue from middle age (for the most) even to the last gasp, specially in mankind. And albeit that our women, through bearing of children, do after forty begin to wrinkle apace, yet are they not commonly so wretched and hard-favored to look upon in their age as the Frenchwomen and divers of other countries.[9]

However tainted by nationalist chauvinism and sheer ebullience, Harrison's claims betray in earnest how unmistakably integral elder figures were to the British self-awareness he champions. Fortescue's "complexions" graduate into the sturdy "constitution" enabling survival well beyond "threescore," which characterizes a social membership Harrison finds distinctively worthy of commemoration. As such, the passage helps corroborate the notion Pat Thane sets forth, that "there were significant numbers of visibly 'old' people in most 'past' communities, whatever their chronological ages, and they had a strong presence in public conscience."[10]

Interestingly, demographic evidence available in the records that came to be kept with increasing regularity and responsibility over the course of the century reveals Harrison's basic assertions to be significantly less extravagant than they may at first sound. Between the years 1541 and 1606, census numbers gauge the population over age sixty as ranging from 7.21 to 8.67percent.[11] These figures remained constant, moreover, not only through the virtual population explosion England experienced in the second half of the 1500s but well beyond, into the first decades of the twentieth century.[12] Other indicators flesh out these statistics, reaffirming an endurance into later life across the social spectrum. Steven R. Smith, for instance, notes that "of the 118 persons listed in *Who's Who in History, 1485–1603*, and whose ages at death could be determined, . . . 42.4% lived to sixty, though approximately one-third survived to the age of seventy."[13] At the opposite end of the social scale, John Howes reports in his *Familiar and Frendely Discourse* of 1582 that, of the 2,100 London indigent "which requyred present relefe" surveyed during the reign of Edward VI, 400 were listed as "aged persons."[14] As Thane again concludes, "The percentage of the population of pre-industrial England and Wales aged 60 and over was not small by modern standards. . . . [L]ife may often have been 'nasty and brutish,' but it was not unduly 'short.'"[15]

Statistical evidence unfortunately has not always helped to illuminate our understanding of senescence in early modernity. We now commonly recognize that the period's high rate of infant mortality skewed the numbers to project a misleading picture of an "average" thirty-five-year lifespan, where actually "Those who survived the hazardous earlier years of life in medieval and early modern England had a respectable chance of living at least into what would now be defined as middle age—that is, their late forties or fifties—and often for longer still. . . . Even in medieval times the death of someone in their later thirties was not regarded as 'timely' or normal."[16] This impression of old age's "early" threshold nonetheless dies hard, supported (for instance) by Creighton Gilbert's discussion, in his pioneering article "When Did a Man of the Renaissance Grow Old?" (1967), of how Erasmus, Vasari, and even Michelangelo—who lived to be almost ninety—all seemed to regard forty as elderly.[17] While Henry of Valois and Philip Sidney, both around the age of twenty, regarded the English queen in her late thirties and early forties as superannuated, we shall see that she emphatically did not share their outlook.

As my frequent recourse to its findings already suggests, Pat Thane's authoritative *Old Age in English History* has, since its publication in 2000, proven instrumental for any fresh approach to the topic. The book's transformative impact on the field derives not least from its cogent and sensible diagnoses of the logistical difficulties burdening the subject, especially the various, often conflicting, criteria for defining senescence reliably in this or any other era: "'Old age' may be defined chronologically, by birth-date; functionally, in terms of fitness to perform certain tasks; biologically, in terms of physical fitness and other physical characteristics; or culturally, in terms of everyday perceptions and definitions of old age."[18] Thane's splendid synthesis and rethinking of an academic concern that saw its first stirrings only in the middle of the last century reaches well beyond her specific attention to English traditions to organize an essential foundation for continued debate about the topic broadly. As important, the book confirms that "old age" indeed has its "histories," ones that can be recorded.[19]

Valuable in its own right, Thane's historical research takes on an even greater urgency when viewed against the conspicuous neglect that old age has suffered at the hands of humanities scholars. Late to emerge as an orchestrated discipline, age studies have been slower still to find extended application to fields of cultural and literary criticism. Despite Anne Wyatt-Brown's proper insistence in 1992 that "literary gerontology" has "come of age," fifteen years would pass before the *Journal of Aging, Humanities, and the Arts* that she edits with Dana Burr Bradley took shape to provide a prominent critical forum for cross-disciplinary conversation.[20] Book-length treatments of old age in literature remain relatively few.[21] It comes as no surprise that one of the strongest studies to appear in the wake of Thane's work, Helen Small's *The Long Life* (2007), originates in a thorough survey and assessment of Western philosophy's startling reluctance throughout its history to address senescence in the concerted fashion we find in Cicero's anomalous *De senectute*.[22]

Given our enduring Burckhardtian notion of early modernity as an epoch when conceptions of selfhood definitively emerged, we can easily recognize how profoundly vexed yet utterly essential to our fuller understanding of the period an investigation of age and identity becomes.[23] This evident point further spotlights the unfortunate belatedness of period specialists to devote sustained critical attention to the subject. Gilbert's early inquiry blazed an important trail but provoked little response; almost a decade later, Keith Thomas's British Academy lecture "Age and Authority in Early Modern England" (1976) enabled a more coordinated and applied investigation of the nominal privileges and practical hardships facing senescence in Tudor and Stuart records, though it likewise remained an isolated discussion.[24] In the 1980s, Georges Minois's ambitious *History of Old Age: From Antiquity to the Renaissance* touched down in the sixteenth century, but its sweeping assertions about the bleakness of aged experience that blighted Western outlooks often proved too tendentious to garner wide subscription.[25]

Apart from the relevant sections of Thane's book and the essays she edited with Lynn Botelho as *Women and Aging in British Society since 1500* (2001), it was 2003 before a day-long session of four panels at the Renaissance Society of America conference in Toronto reaffirmed the topic's critical centrality to the field.[26] The meetings were themselves symptomatic of an important shift, suggested by the scholarly productivity in the field that we have just begun to witness in the wake of Erin J. Campbell's edited *schrift* of the conference's wide-ranging papers.[27] Philip Sohm's examination of the visual record in his *The Artist Grows Old: Arts and Artists in Italy, 1500–1800* (2007), for example, pairs with developed discussions of senescence's depiction on the Renaissance stage and particularly in Shakespeare—treated before only in sporadic and often superficial articles—in works like Anthony Ellis's *Old Age, Masculinity and Early Modern Drama* (2009) and Maurice Charney's *Wrinkled Deep in Time: Aging in Shakespeare* (2010).[28] Although it restricts its focus to material from the seventeenth and eighteenth centuries, Lynn Botelho, Susannah R. Ottaway, and Ingrid H. Tague's eight-volume compendium of period sources on the topic, in process at the time I write as *The History of Old Age in England, 1600–1800,* should enable a continued stimulus to unabated further study of the topic.[29]

Most important to my present study's concerns, Nina Taunton's *Fictions of Old Age in Early Modern Literature and Culture* (2007) marked the first book-length analysis by a single author devoted exclusively to aging in the period to see publication. In that work, Taunton deftly elucidates the societal perimeters circumscribing aged comportment in the era, stressing the central role that decorum plays in early modern conceptions of and writing about old age. Despite its conspicuous strengths, the monograph's foundation nonetheless cracks beneath the weight of the presumption that aged subjects acquiesced to these restrictions. Taunton rightly poses the issue "Given that old age alone of all the ages of man was a disease from which one never recovered, how could one carry through into old age the conduct of life that was, until its onset, graceful and apt?" as the principal "quandary facing writers on old age" at the time. By reducing this to a rhetorical question, however, and proposing that "Their only option is to deal with it by recommending a retreat into the religious life, passive and contemplative, which seeks to distance itself from the ways of the world," she impedes her own investigation and ends up leaving insufficiently tested the orthodoxies that she catalogues.[30] In what follows, I radically part company with her position, summarized in a representative passage, that "According to the literature of the day, the only way in which one can grow old in a seemly fashion is to adopt attitudes embodied in an amalgam of biblical precept and stoicism. An old person's only recourse is to accept old age as a misfortune that cannot be avoided, since it cannot be overcome by human agency."[31]

My argument disputes such assertions, demonstrating instead how the aged figures in question struggle precisely to reclaim this agency, which is grounded in the private but equally authoritative self-awareness of one's own constitution. Delineating this conflict with externally constituted decorum as a central drive in surviving literary portraits of old age—from Elizabeth I's defiance of protocol and the temperamental recusancy of the character Thenot in Spenser's *Shepheardes Calender,* to the tragic self-immolations of Shakespeare's *King Lear*—I propose by extension that the experience and construction of senescence undergoes an elemental change that would subtly but irrevocably imprint modern attitudes. The very resignation that Taunton finds in the period record becomes, in my overarching argument, a point of departure and an impetus for literary creativity. The art of dying well surely remained an important concern for many of those who, imaginatively or actually, faced the mortality that old age in time inevitably brings; but attention to this line of thought has, it seems, blinkered us to an art of living well—of doing full justice to a bodily constitution regulating personal agency and the dignity that accompanies this—that also finds a new voice in early modernity, taking to task the gerontophobia that so pervasively threatens. I hope this contention, set within the confines of my narrower field of inquiry, will help to broaden our understanding of the way old age's subtle reconceptualization at this moment resonates with the very subjectivity that itself emerged to "constitute" a new ethos.

Critical attention devoted to old age in recent decades has consistently recognized the way in which questions of agency and identity stand at the center of our efforts to address the subject from antiquity down to contemporary assessments, molding the way we think and talk about senescence. When, for instance, in his digest of common misconceptions about human physiology, published in 1578 as *Erreurs populaires,* the French doctor Laurent Joubert vociferously affirms the aging male's ability to maintain sexual potency, the forty-nine-year-old author insists "it is the old man's constitution" (*c'est la disposicion du velhard*) that matters, "which can be hale and hearty, as is seen in some septuagenarians, and even in older ones, who do physical work with their arms and legs that another man of forty could not do. Why can he not be as vigorous in his genitals as in his other members?"[32] For Joubert, age defies boundaries set by mere social convention: "There is no exact limit one cannot go beyond, for years alone do not set the term, but the makeup of the body (*disposicion du cors*) and its use."[33] The doctor's contempt for efforts to reckon the life cycle from without resonates through to his conclusion, "a man's strength, both in matters of begetting and other actions, cannot be limited according to precise ages, which are nothing more than arbitrary numbers, but is rather a matter of constitution (*complexion*) and of one's state of health, which sometimes stay sound for a very long time."[34]

Although confined to the realm of masculine experience, Joubert's commentary ends up circumscribing the discursive field within which old age perennially finds itself situated. Behind his peremptory, somewhat defensive impulse to simplify the question of aged self-perception lingers the gnawing awareness of a broader and more enduring conflict. Physical potential alone, in Joubert's view, determines the stage of life with which one best identifies: beholden only to his own discrete biology or constitutional makeup, the aging subject defines himself in terms of his capacity to perform as an agent, sexual or otherwise. At the same time, however, the elder must contend with externally constituted social attitudes that presume to set limits upon his right to exercise such agency, even when he is physically capable of doing so. The respect with which a society is enjoined to treat the elder remains subtly or expressly contingent upon a self-deportment consistent with predetermined standards. Older generations are expected, as Leslie Fiedler has pointed out, to "withdraw from sexual competition and prepare for death, learn, in short, to be *properly old*."[35] To challenge such prescriptions is to court proscription, or at least contempt, more often than wonder or admiration. Whether they relinquish claims to certain types of agency or not, aged subjects find themselves posed, vulnerable to the bitter orthodoxy that Shakespeare pointedly distills in Regan's condescending rejoinder to King Lear: "I pray you, father, being weak, seem so" (2.4.201).[36] This perceptual disparity between whatever weaknesses old age threatens to bring and the demeanor the aged are expected to assume identifies a frontier of constitutional opposition that provides an integral subtext for the following chapters.

Modern theorists have come to examine in provocative and enlightening ways how, as Haim Hazan notes, a "socio-cultural construction of knowledge of ageing disguises an undercurrent of fear and anxiety," wherein "The term 'aged' not only describes individuals but also is used as a collective noun, and once individuals are identified as 'old' they are perceived exclusively as such."[37] In her provocative and important study, Margaret Morganroth Gullette builds upon this foundation to advocate an even more radical "age studies perspective" that regards chronological aging as "one of the most interesting inventions of civilization."[38] At the same time, Pat Thane has cautioned that "Old age cannot simply be a social construct, an artifice of perception, or fashioned through discourse—unquestionably bodies age, change, decay—but the images, expectations, and experiences of older men and women have been constructed in different ways at different times and for different people at any one time."[39]

This corrective to more totalizing oppositions between individual and society finds eloquent support in the work of Jenny Hockey and Allison James. Grounding their own explorations of age in Richard Jenkins's already seminal work on "social identity," Hockey and James argue that, since "Social identities only come into being through their embodiment or animation by *individuals*," then "there is an ongoing tri-partite relationship between social environment, human agency and the body" that directs one's self-image late into the life course.[40] Aware simultaneously of how time's effect on the body can qualify (if it does not altogether annul) one's capacity to implement agency in a meaningful fashion, and the external, societal prejudice and pressure that collect around this spectacle, the subject is left to formulate and present a more fully integrated self-perception upon which identity itself is to a large degree founded.

As recent scholarship has gone far to confirm, changing views of the body—the result of an increasingly sophisticated understanding of human physiology—would impact significantly the notions of "inwardness" that characterize the era. Michael Schoenfeldt's especially fruitful investigation of the topic delineates the way in which bodily regimen afforded early modern subjects a means of self-regulation.[41] Up to a point, Schoenfeldt's theory corresponds perfectly with a pervasive outlook toward senescence, reaching back to antiquity, that regarded the condition of elder subjects as largely self-determined. This was certainly the position militantly adopted by Cato, Cicero's spokesman for old age in his foundational *De senectute*, for whom "the blame & fault of al this mutteringe & compleyning is in the overthwartenes of mens wayward maners and not in age. For discrete, sober, and temperate olde men, being neither ill to please, froward nor churlishe, do live in their old age tolerably and quietly ynough, both to them selves and al others. But unbridled insolencie, and blunt uncurtesie, is to al age unpleasaunt, tedius, & yrksome."[42] From such a standpoint, the experience of age was, at root, an idiosyncratic affair. Within such cultural constructions, as Karen Cokayne suggests, the burden of responsibility shifts to the individual: "It was therefore thought that a man had a choice. If he lived virtuously, preferably from youth, in accordance with the Laws of Nature or the Laws of God, he would benefit from his lifelong studies and in old age gain wisdom. Old age, therefore, was what you made of it."[43]

On the other hand, as Shulamith Shahar observes more generally about medieval perspectives of age that linger into modernity, those "who were less inclined than Cicero to idealize old age, were not so emphatic about the overwhelming effect of the personality. Even those among them who noted individual differences and, like Cicero, stressed that a man's old age was the product of his character and entire life, referred to what they regarded as the unavoidable changes of old age as a whole, and especially of extreme old age."[44] The anxieties attending upon what has been called the "somatization of the self," moreover, can in age also prompt less of a self-realization than a radical self-alienation, as Kathleen Woodward describes: "as we age, we increasingly separate what we take to be our real selves from our bodies. . . . Our *bodies* are old, we are not. Old age is thus understood as a state in which the body is in opposition to the self."[45] When compounded with the evaluative gaze of public prejudice, even under the best conditions the reaction to old age would remain a fraught and wiry one. The authors I survey in this study all realized the high stakes of "making something" of old age, and the peculiar challenge facing the endeavor; their perspectives share enough to enable a more coordinated insight into this vital topic amid the novel brand of self-awareness ascendant in the period.

On the psychological register alone, an interesting complexity has, since antiquity, problematized the concept of a human being's constitution and its relationship to the aging process. In his Epistle 121, for instance, Seneca discusses the term as both a generic and a specific attribute. *Constitutio* designates, on the one hand, something like a set of instincts shared by all members of a particular species, or (in Thomas Lodge's 1614 translation) that "part of the soule, that in some sort hath some power over the bodie."[46] When Seneca comes to consider how "mans constitution is to bee a reasonable soule," however, he refines things further by elaborating that "Every age hath his constitution" or distinctive characteristics: "an infant hath one; a stripling another, an old man another, for all of them are accomodated to the constitution wherein they remaine." Despite this progressive adaptation, he asserts, a more uniquely constituted identity goes uncompromised: "So although each ones constitution be different, yet the accord thereof is alwayes one. For Nature commendeth unto me not a boy, not a yong man, or an old man, but my selfe" (p. 483). He recognizes, as Cokayne has remarked, "a change in behaviour through a physical, emotional and mental development, but he was also conscious of a continuity and a sense of agelessness."[47] More than this, the philosopher's desire to "accomodate" here betrays an intuition that the very *constitution* in which he roots a distinctive sense of "selfe" also enables a more anonymous diagnostic categorization from without. The aging physique, constituted both discretely and ideologically, stands in tension, in ways that his essay's taxonomy cannot altogether comfortably gloss. As he will bring to light elsewhere in the *Epistulae morales,* perceptions of one's own body and conceptions of one's corresponding status in the life cycle can starkly contrast with the judgments of a public gaze prepared to evaluate old age in terms of its own prescriptive measure of years passed or manifest bodily signifiers.

In his Epistle 12, Seneca reflects more dramatically on what it means to grow old by candidly recounting how he had returned to his "countrey-farme," only to find the property in serious decline (p. 179). When he lashes out at his chief servant's irresponsibility, he is told that the decay everywhere evident is the irreparable work of time. Incredulous that the villa and arbors he had himself built and planted had simply grown "over-olde and ruinous," the author ultimately turns his attention to the decrepit "carkasse of a strange man" sitting at the threshold, only to learn that the slave is his coeval, his *deliciolum* or "pet," Felicio, from childhood days (p. 180). The visit forces an unsettling confrontation, Seneca confesses, with the old age that "appeareth unto me which way soever I turne my selfe." Moreover, the shrill querulousness to which he admits in his self-presentation—angrily refusing to accept the fact of his own years and mocking his servant's aged decrepitude even after he discovers his identity—further exposes the bad temper, denial, and lack of self-awareness to which he had succumbed—traits projected stereotypically onto the elderly. The self-discovery prompts a sudden awareness of the need to "embrace and love" old age, since "it is wholly replenished with agreeable delights, if a man know how to make use of it." Yet he fails to articulate precisely what these "delights" are, and he does take care to qualify his definition of the period of life in question: "The age that declineth is also most agreeable, when as yet it is not wholly decrepit and spent." We are left to wonder if his encounter with his childhood companion, whose toothless mouth had suggested to his master an absurd second childhood, has adequately humbled Seneca, or if his coarse laughter at the servant's physical decrepitude rings on, however nervously, to reassure the robust self-image he otherwise takes to task.

If the countryside experience alerts Seneca to the reality of his advancing years, in other words, it also reconfirms the sturdiness of his own constitution, a physical and moral integrity that in fact has enabled him to overlook the passing of time. More exactly, his instinctual adaptation to the various phases of the life course has evened his experience to an easy sense of continuity. Only the witness of objects and people extrinsic to himself, such as the estate or the servant, can shock him into a sense of temporal difference. While old age was "constituted" by specific and distinct attributes, these varied across the sharply distinguished "constitutions" of different individuals. This elemental sense of physical or biological makeup would indisputably set him apart from the Felicios of the world, diminished by their station and weakness to a pathetic and forgotten state, already in the throes of "abrupt decline" even as Seneca records and assesses this last phase of life.

When we arrive at Senecan *constitutio*'s English resuscitation in mid-Tudor discourse, the word immediately finds itself immersed in this edgy ambiguity. It first appears, significantly, in Thomas Wilson's *Arte of Rhetorique* (1553) amid a discussion of age and the physiology of memory. "For where humours excede or want," Wilson explains, "there must nedes ensue muche weakenesse of remembraunce. Children therefore beyng over moyst, and olde menne over drie, have never good memories." He goes on to explain, "Therefore it availeth greatly, what bodies we have, and of what constitucion thei bee compacte together."[48] From this point on, the term remains particularly embedded in conversations about age. Levinus Lemnius's treatise on humoral physiology, Englished by Thomas Newton in 1576, best captures contemporary understanding of the processual mutation of individual constitution over the life course, where we read "For age is no other thing but the race or course of life, or the time that wee have to runne from oure Infancie till wee come to old age, in which time, the state and constitution of mans Bodye is altered, and steppeth from one temperamente to an other, and at lengthe (native heate beinge extincte) by death is divorced and broughte to finall dissolution."[49]

By century's end, as we have already seen in Fortescue and Harrison, the relationship between age and constitution has become a curiously self-conscious commonplace, often ill at ease with its own implications. When he comes to translate Andreas Laurentius's *Discourse on Old Age* into English in 1599, Richard Surphlet again has recourse to the term as the true indication of an individual's stage of life. After setting forth the temporal boundaries subdividing the life cycle—"Infancie," which lasts to thirteen years; "Adolescencie," which "holdeth on to twenty foure or tweny five yeeres"; "Youth," which "hath his course till fortie yeeres"; "man's age," which extends another ten years; followed by "Olde age which containeth all the rest of our life"—he concludes with an important qualifier:

> But I would not that from hence any man should so tye himselfe to the number of yeares, as that he should make youth and old age necessarily to depend thereupon: but that he would rather judge thereof by the rule of the

temperature and constitution of the bodie: for every man that is cold and
drie, is he whom I may call old. There are very many which become old men
at fortie, and again there are an infinit sort, which are young men at sixtie:
there are some constitutions that grow old very speedily, and others very
slowly. They which are of a sanguine complexion grow old very slowly, because they have great store of heate and moysture: melancholike men which
are cold and drie, become old in shorter time.[50]

Privileging the subjective over the strictly objective, the advisory blurs (if it
does not erase) the perimeters initially set in place by the physician.

Laurentius's waffling, like Fortescue's and Joubert's, divulges a troubled
awareness of old age as an evaluative as much as a descriptive concept. This
ambiguity stems from a deeply divided social regard for the elderly that
informed early modernity much as it continues to disturb contemporary
outlooks. However far it had graduated beyond the *contemptus mundi* that
characterized the Middle Ages—which found its most virulent expression
in a work like Pope Innocent III's *De miseria condicionis humane*—humanist culture showed lasting signs of a wary apprehension over the "discomforts of old age" (*de incommodis senectutis*) featured in that work.[51] Georges
Minois links the surviving ambivalence about old age he finds in the period with that typifying the ancient Roman ethos so obsessively revered
by Renaissance intellectuals. Less reliant upon oral traditions that tend
to promote elders "as links between the generations and as the collective
memory," these "legalist civilizations had less need of their old people's cus-
tomary experience," something that helped relegate them "to the category
of antiquated and useless things."[52]

While overstated, Minois's position alerts us to a dark strain that clouds
even the most benign period disquisitions regarding old age. For instance,
Petrarch, who in his correspondence vigorously champions senescence as
"a disease of the body, but the health of the soul" and whose impassioned
endorsement of "dear old age, venerable above all else, . . . in no way to
be feared by mortals, and, once known, a happy time of life" exceeds Cicero's own advocacy in the *De senectute,* must gloss over objections that he
has "still not reached the real discomforts of old age" as he writes, "that
I speak bravely because I have yet to grow weak with the years."[53] In the
De remediis, moreover, Petrarch casts senescence as a sinister, "stealthy"
nemesis who "follows step by step in darkness and silence," and goes on to
deconstruct physical vanity expressly in terms of a grim catalogue of time's
ravages on the body.[54] "Everybody wants to live to a ripe old age, but no
one wants to be old," the author confesses in exasperation. The very force
with which he feels obliged to inveigh against those who "consider old age

miserable, being called an old man an insult, as if it were shameful" argues for the prevalence of such attitudes.[55]

Published over a century after Petrarch's death, Gabriele Zerbi's *Gerontocomia*—the first modern treatise on care for the elderly—more frankly if sympathetically confronts time's potentially crippling impact on both the mind and body. For all the compassion he objectively summons, Zerbi himself regards the wrinkles and gray hair that inevitably come with age as a "disgraceful disfigurement." The frisson he evidently experiences before the decrepitude that "palpitates rather than lives" enjoins his mission to educate younger caregivers out of the repulsion that he takes for granted they will feel.[56] Even in the Venetian republic's political gerontocracy, where the privileging of age was legislated rather than merely preached, the point that "one of the anticipated advantages of electing elderly men was that one would not have to put up with them for long" (as Robert Finlay has observed) takes the strictly "reverential" edge off of the gerontocratic ideal.[57] Amid the most entrenched exemplum of constitutionally "authorized" old age a more dubious critical standard looms.

The extent to which these Italian instances might have entered the northern European ken of Tudor England remains unclear; but there is no question that the nation came in full contact with the early modern glorification of youth at the expense of age that we encounter in that most representative of period texts, Baldassare Castiglione's *Il Cortegiano*.[58] Sir Thomas Hoby, who would give the work an elegant English cast in his translation of 1561, recognized and amplified the gerontophobic disposition of the courtly society the book so immeasurably influenced, advertising the publication on its title page as "very necessary and profitable for yonge gentilmen and gentilwomen abiding in court, palaice, or place."[59] While it pervades the dialogue, Castiglione takes on the matter of old age most directly in his second book's opening commentary, where he defends the present against a grumpy nostalgia he identifies as age's "peculier vyce," a pathology that for him undercuts its reputed superior judgment amid a blighted picture of advanced years:

> yeares wearing away, cary also with them many commodities, and emonge other take awaye from the bloud a great part of the lyvely spirites that altereth the complection, and the instrumentes wexe feeble, whereby the soule worketh her effectes. Therefore the sweete flowers of delite vade away in that season out of oure heartes, as the leaves fall from the trees after harvest, and in steade of open and cleere thoughtes there entreth cloudy and troublous heavinesse accompanied with a thousand heart grieffes: so that not onely the bloude, but the mind is also feble, neither of the former pleasures receyveth

it anye thynge elles but a fast memorye and the print of the beloved time of
tender age. (pp. 103–4)

Subject to prejudicial distortion and breakdown, the memory that should
promote the experienced elderly in a society in fact renders them agents of
discord who end up blaming "the time present for yll, not perceyvinge that
this chaunge proceadeth of themselves and not of the tyme" (p. 105).[60] The
writer seeks "to followe the custome of our times" freed from the "controul-
ment of these olde men," whom he leaves to their self-praise (p. 108).

The vital exchange regarding the place of the old at court later emerges
in book 2's discussion of music, when Frederico Fergoso declares how it
is unfitting for an old man to play an instrument in public. The courtier
needs to "knowe his age," he brusquely asserts, since it stands as "but an
yll sight to see a man of eny estimation being olde, horeheaded and tooth-
lesse, full of wrinckles, with a lute in his armes playing upon it and singing
in the middes of a company of women, although he coulde doe it reason-
ablye well. And that, because suche songes conteine in them woordes of
love, and in olde men love is a thing to bee jested at" (p. 119). In response
to a protest that many elderly men demonstrate greater capacity and en-
joyment of this art than young ones, Frederico can only suggest that "in
case olde men wil sing to the lute, let them doe it secretly," a sentiment
that provokes Signore Morello da Ortona, an aged advocate of the elderly's
continued claim to courtly position, to protest Frederigo's implicit design
"to excepte all olde men and to saie that only yong men are to be called
Courtiers" (pp. 119–20). Faulting the risibility of old men who "study to
appere yonge, and . . . dye their hear and make their beard grow twise a
weeke," Frederico can only reiterate his condescending outlook that, in
order to spare himself and his audience embarrassment, the aged courtier
must strive to accept a pose of docility and passivity dictated by his failing
body, and work to "have a grace in utteringe that they knowe, applying it
aptlye to the purpose, accompanying with the grace of yeeres a certaine
temperate and meery plesauntnesse" (pp. 120–21).[61]

When, in the final book's most celebrated passage, Pietro Bembo steps
in to reconcile the desirable fact that, as a counselor to the prince, the
courtier "must in maner of necessitie be aged, for knoweleage commeth
verye syldome times beefore yeeres" with the question of how "whan he
is well drawen in yeeres, how it wyll stande well wyth hym to be a lover,
considerynge (as it hath bine said the other night) Love frameth not with
olde men" (p. 340) with his great tribute to Neoplatonic love, Morello attacks Bembo's idealism with the pedestrian query "And in case there were
some olde man more freshe and lustye and of a better complexion then

manye yonge men, whie woulde you not have it lefull for him to love with the love that yonge men love?" (p. 346). If his offhand dismissal leaves Morello (in Stephen D. Kolsky's view) "a warning to other old men, including perhaps Castiglione himself, not to behave in the same manner," it never effectively discredits his protest.[62] Courtly society, for all its purported investment in the *consuetudine* that sets it apart, designs an ethic that assures its own obsolescence by perpetually excluding old age from its center of power on all but the most provisional terms. Basing its central tenets on an ideology of beauty and decorum, it legislates tacitly that the damage time works on the former joins with the latter to retire the elder from the dialogic stage.[63]

The dubieties about old age that Castiglione expresses resonated with early modern England's no less divided outlook. As Keith Thomas relates, at a time when "awareness of their numerical age came to form part of most men's basic self-consciousness," a conflicted regard for senescence became all the more pronounced.[64] While respect for the elder remained a frequently emphasized foundational ethic, finding practical application in the way "the prevailing ideal was gerontocratic: the young were to serve and the old were to rule," their prestige was conditioned by "irksome constraints" on their accepted social conduct and the bleaker stereotypes associated with late life.[65] Despite Lemnius's claim (in Newton's translation) that the English "be people very civill and wel affected to men well stryken in yeares . . . which thing they that halfe suspect and have not had the full tryall of the maners and fashions of this countrey [he revealingly adds] wil skarcely bee perswaded to beleeve" (pp. 47v–48), Thomas notes how "the picture of old age yielded by contemporary literature is frankly pessimistic. Most writings addressed to the aged took it for granted that their readers were persons to whom life had become a burden. No one doubted that old age was a wretched time of physical deterioration."[66]

By the time of Elizabeth's accession, Tudor literary culture had already digested and retailed these harsher perspectives uncritically. Sir Thomas Wyatt's rondeau "Ye old mule," which ridicules an aging lascivious woman who must now "purchase" her sexual satisfaction "by payment and by prayer," takes Horatian glee in its virulent denigration of lingering desire.[67] Published two years after Hoby's *Courtier* translation, Thomas Sackville's induction to his sequence of tragedies in *The Mirror for Magistrates*'s second edition looks back to a medieval *contemptus* tradition in its description of senescence, lasting a full seven stanzas of rime royal. The broken caricature that Sackville's narrator meets in the "maze of miserie" he tours paints a doleful picture of Old Age:

Crookebackt he was, toothshaken, and blere iyed,
Went on three feete, and sometime crept on fower,
With olde lame bones, that ratled by his syde,
His skalpe all pilde, & he with elde forlore:
His withered fist stil knocking at deathes dore,
Fumbling and driveling as he drawes his breth,
For briefe the shape and messenger of death.[68]

Despite the "withered plight, and wretched paine" that his superannuation has brought upon him, the figure clings tenaciously to existence, praying "He myght a while yet linger forth his lief" (312 and 315). Like Urbino's courtly young aristocrats, Sackville tacitly regards senescence as both an indisputable physical state *and* a state of mind, marked by the subject's terrified refusal to acknowledge or accept the condition to which time has reduced him.

Since Hoby's translation of *The Courtier* at the beginning of the 1560s imparts such an elegant (and therefore more damningly consequential) voice to this gerontophobic standard, we may find in Thomas Newton's fresh Elizabethan translation of Cicero's *De senectute,* released at the decade's close, an antidote of sorts. While not the first time the work had been "chaunged into Englyshe Liverayes"—as early as 1481, William Caxton had published a rough-hewn vernacular rendering (likely the work of William Worcester and Stephen Scrope), followed by Robert Whitinton's version of 1535—Newton's emerged as the native Elizabethan audience's principal recourse.[69] After dedicating his book to the nonagenarian Lord Treasurer William Paulet, "Whom God hath blessed with so prosperous a race of longe lyfe, to see the Children of your Childrens Children," Newton condemns the treatise's previous English translator with a vehemence that transcends competitive fastidiousness. He alleges that "that translation beareth but the countenaunce of one, being none in dede to any purpose, being taken of the learned for noone at all, sithen never a page almost is answerable to the latine texte, I wil not saye, scantly any sentence" (fol. ‡iii verso and vi). Newton's prefatory stance subtly but unmistakably suggests the importance of getting this classic encomium of old age precisely correct at this moment, against the backdrop of a political regime already begrudgingly perceived as increasingly gerontocratic in character. The point is borne out in Newton's further refinements to his subsequent version of the text, which adheres even more closely to the manner and cadences of Cicero's original.[70] Theoretically displaced from the outer circles of courtly power, and embattled within its inner confines, senescence badly wanted the kind of authoritative encouragement that only its most formidable Roman exponent could afford. Yet as careful scrutiny of Cicero's performance suggests, the *senex* of his own day faced the necessity for a similar retrenchment, and this awareness explains the prickly apprehension that ruffles his work's surface composure.

The dialogue's central figure, Cato—though often misunderstood and maligned as an unsympathetic mixture of shrillness and complacency—displays a characteristic defensive perceptiveness that rescues him from this straw-man status by endowing him with an enduring interest and power. Cultural historians and modern gerontologists alike recognize the *De senectute* as seminal to Western thinking about old age, a critical challenge to the grim characterization of "men who are past their prime" that survives most authoritatively in the second book of Aristotle's *Rhetoric.* The elderly, in Aristotle's view, having contended for many years with the "bad business" of life, mature into a mercenary cynicism that leaves them distrustful and small-minded, grasping, shamelessly self-involved yet contemptuous of public opinion, and generally querulous.[71] Cicero's sustained valorization of old age, itself inspired by Socrates' brief exchange with the elderly Cephalus at the beginning of Plato's *Republic,* eloquently contests such assessments.

Despite its authority and singularity—no other sustained philosophical commentary on the subject survives from antiquity—the dialogue has not fared well among contemporary readers. The response of those relative few who have directly addressed Cicero's text has ranged from the lukewarm to the hostile.[72] Even Thane, who sympathetically suggests that the work's importance "lies in its own long life which suggests that it expresses . . . widely held hopes and feelings about old age from the ancient world onwards," recognizes its contemporary opposition by the tide of Roman drama and literature that "tended generally though not universally to depict old age negatively."[73] Alienated by the purportedly glib self-righteousness of Cato's stoic rationalizations, we have grown deaf to the drama of agency that unfolds in the dialogue. To gain a better sense of just how extensively the ambivalence I have been discussing is at work here, we need to recover the treatise's tense inner dynamic.

In his prefatory letter to Atticus, Cicero openly identifies Cato as a spokesman for his own views, but this very alignment should alert us to the complexity of his Catonian persona. Jon Hendricks is correct when he points out how "it is possible to see in Cicero a defense of all that is marginal made by one who had become thoroughly marginalized himself," as is Tim Parkin when he observes that the philosopher "sought to provide real *consolatio* for his own old age, upset as he was at the time by personal worries and political uncertainties.[74] For this very reason, however, Cicero offers us, not a caricatured apologist who myopically denies the rigors of old age, but a figure keenly attuned to his own vulnerability. *De senectute* stands less as the compensatory wish fulfillment of the displaced and embittered author-statesman than as an exploration of what it costs to maintain one's dignity in the face of age's harsher prospects. The revered personality remembered as the Censor may strive to bluster his way through the many objections and fears he catalogues at such length, but his rhetoric remains driven by the agitated hunger for authority that he recognizes as urgent yet at all times threatened.

For Cato, any indictment of old age is an indictment of the self: "For doltishe sottes, and beetleheaded fooles do lay al their owne faults and blame upon old age" (fol. 9). It is not age that occasions senility, so far as he is concerned, but weakness of character: "so this folishnes that entangleth and captivateth the senses of old men (which is commonly called Dotage) is not in al old men, but in those only which are light witted, & kepe not them selves wythin the limittes of reason" (fol. 24v). In contrast, Cato holds himself up to his young interlocutors as his own best example—*sed redeo ad me,* "But nowe to retourne and saye somewhat of my selfe," punctuates his discourse repeatedly—and he justifies his self-referential loquacity as a privilege of old age, citing the model of Homer's Nestor (fol. 19r–v). His self-righteous judgments have drawn the fire of modern commentators like Dean Rodeheaver, who indicts the lasting negative influence such presumptions have exerted. "To the extent that Horatio Algeresque gerontology successfully implies that individuals have the ability to control their own aging," he remarks, "it also implies that their failure to do so should be met with . . . no sympathy at all."[75]

This "ethic" of self-reliance in the *De senectute,* however, is less a prescription than a symptom of the virtual siege mentality that Cato displays. Cicero's genius in the work is to replace the generic Aristotelian image of old age with a fiercely personality-driven portrait of Cato: in this way, he deliberately sets up the conflict between the traditional stereotype and the undaunted agent who dares to elevate his own constitution to the level of the "anti-norm." Opting for a historical over a mythic spokesman, Cicero freights his work with a remarkable dramatic strain that serves as important a function as the philosophical assertions it contextualizes. In the fully realized characterization of the historical Cato, by turns determined and defensive, Cicero will ground his own text's "authority": as he makes expressly clear in his prefatory letter to Atticus, "the preminence and superioritie of the disputacion is not geeven to olde Tithonus, as Aristo Chius did in his Booke, least in suche a fained fable the whole discourse should bee the lesse esteemed among the Readers: but I attribute the chyefe dignytie of it unto the Old grayheaded sage Marcus Cato, to thend the Treatise shoulde have moore estimation credite and authoritie" (fol. ‡viii r–v).

Cato himself announces the centrality of *auctoritas* to his own presentation, declaring unequivocally, "the higheste title of prayse that can be geven to olde age is Authorytie" (fol. 45v). As important, Cato affirms that such authority does not come automatically with years but is an earned privilege. The trappings of revered old age take on significance only in the context of individual accomplishment. Cato quotes himself to his young interlocutors to the effect that "that old age which had no noble deedes to defende it selfe withal, but leaned onely to vaine jangling words & prating vauntes, was wretched & miserable. It is not the hoare head and wrinkled face which by and by bringeth honour and purchaseth estimacion," he goes on to say, "but it is an honeste and godlye life that hath ever bene conversaunte and trayned in vertue which getteth dignity and high aucthority in the end" (fol. 46v–47). From the start, however, Cato—who prides himself on the way his past military experience legitimizes his present senatorial campaign against the Carthaginian threat[76]—wages this way of life as a kind of war on two fronts: against the physical decay that can compromise the elder's quality of life and the social neglect or ostracism age may also bring. He addresses the former by the need for a lifelong practice of *temperantia* that provides one with strength to endure into advanced years (elderly debility he lays chiefly at the door of youthful dissipation) and the cultivation of character that enables one to deal with physical decline should it set in. To stave off the latter he poses the militant need to reassert oneself in societal affairs, which activity alone secures the influence and "aucthoritye" that "is muche more to bee esteemed and is farre moore woorthe, then all the vaine pleasures of headye and rashe Adolescencye" (fol. 46v).

To substantiate his general position Cato chooses the opposing examples of the athlete Milo, who reputedly wept for his own distended muscles as he watched, in old age, younger men compete, and the patriarchal Appius, who single-handedly maintains his household into advanced years. Whereas he reserves particular contempt for the man who despises his seniority and laments the debilities that time brings, describing him as "vaine and light witted" (fol. 17), he holds Appius up as a supreme model of vigorous, responsible authority. Despite blindness, Appius holds sway over all his dependents:

He reserved & kept his authoritye over all theym, that were under hys charge, and his family was ready at his becke and commaundement: his servaunts feared him, his children honored and reverenced him, and al men entierly loved him. In his household the customes of his noble pedagrew and Aunces-tours, and the discyplyne of hys Countrie toke place effectuallye. For herein is Old age honest and honourable: in defendinge and mayntayninge it selfe, in retayninge and keepinge his authorytie, in saving it selfe free from bondage and servitude, and in exercisinge rule [*imperium*] and authorytie over them that are under his charge, even until the last houre of death. (fol. 24v–25)

Only by maintaining a strict *imperium* can the aged hope to triumph over both themselves and their social environment. Aggressive maintenance of one's constitution enables the ongoing self-assertion that for Cato stands as our only defense against the threats of disrespect and disenfranchisement from without.

Cato's celebration of Appius's paradigm is telling. While Cicero's protagonist predicates a dignified old age upon a well-spent youth, the process is an ongoing one that (if anything) intensifies once one has reached *senectus*. The strictness behind the assertion—Newton softens the more severe inflection of the Latin *tenebat non modo auctoritatem, sed etiam imperium in suos* (11.37)—discloses Cato's tacit conviction of the increased vulnerability one experiences in advanced age. In contrast to his loftier assurances that society will respect a worthy elder, an awareness of a far more predatory reality undergirds his pragmatic self-image. Early on, he had invoked the traditional metaphor of the ship of state, wherein the elder acts as a pilot: though he sits stationary as the junior members of the crew move frenetically about the craft, his role remains of far greater significance to the well-being of all. But as he remarks a few passages on, "you shall finde that noble and flourisshinge common wealthes have bene broughte to ruyne and servitude by the unripe administracion of unskilful yong men, and the same by old & sage fathers to have bene maintayned, corroborated, and re-covered" (fol. 12v). Taken together, the statements signal an unspoken fear unsettling his original metaphor: the elder pilot faces a constant threat of mutiny, resident in the violent aggressiveness of a younger generation that too often does not respect the *ratio et consilium* integral to and necessary for *civitas* itself (19.67).

No less consequential is the conspicuous ambiguity of the incident Cato later conjures ostensibly to illustrate the respect that age universally commands:

a certain elderly man came on a time into the Theatre at Athens wher solemne Playes and pageauntes where exhibited to the people, where ther was not one man in the whole assemblye being his natural countrye men and fellow Citesins that shewed to him anye courtesie neither gave to him anye roume to sitte in . . . but when hee came amonge *Lacedemonians* . . . they al aroose & [gave] place to him. . . . At which curteous urbanitie of the *Lacedemonians,* when al the people in token of praise clapped their hands with many acclamations gratulatory, one of the Ambassadours brake out in these words & sayd, that the Athenians knew wel what was honest & vertuous, but to do it they would not. (fol. 47v–48)

The tale ends up betraying that an awareness of how one should regard old age need not compel a culture, even one so archetypally "civilized" as Athens, to practice this ideal. The only assurances, as Cato had asserted in his comment on Appius, rest in a vigorous self-protective aggression. A rigorous display of authority alone (*ita*) insures "honor."

Appius's example betokens the harshness of the campaign that Cato feels the elder needs to conduct ruthlessly and relentlessly. It stands behind the apprehension he expresses to Laelius and Scipio when he counsels that "We must . . . resist old age, and the inconveniences and faultes therof, must by diligence be recompenced and amended. And even as we muste arme our selves to fighte againste infirmities and sicknesse, so also muste wee strive againste old age" (fol. 23r–v). Age becomes a disease we need to combat through physical regimen, which is the only way to protect ourselves against the defeat of (consequent) marginalization. Cato's voice, in the end, is not that of a smug politician but of the wary soldier who regards old age with the same anxiety as he does Carthage. While the extent to which ancient or early modern readers were inclined to view Cicero's spokesman against his historical model remains unclear, Plutarch—who decidedly had the orator's injunctions in mind when he crafted his own broader meditation on age and authority in his *Moralia,* "Whether an Aged Man Ought to Manage Publicke Affaires"—elsewhere records how Cato, "being accused when he was fourescore yeeres olde and upward, in pleading of his own cause, thus answered for himselfe: It is an harder matter my masters (quoth he) for a man to render an account of his life, and to justifie the same before other men, than those with whom he hath lived."[77] The almost inevitable sense of alienation from his juniors that even such a respected and aggressively assertive member of the older generation seems to experience marks an uneasy footnote to both the Roman and the Greek writers' presentations.

Cicero's Cato structures the extended discourse that comprises the *De senectute* around a series of responses to what he defines as the four principal *causae* behind a prevailing disdain for old age. First, there is the general belief that in senescence "a man is impeached and hindered from taking in hand any function or charge in the common wealth," *quod avocet a rebus gerendis*—a significant fear, given the civic-minded ethos of republican Rome, where one's very identity was so intimately tied to public function. Next, advancing age "enfeebleth & weakeneth the body," *corpus faciat infirmius,* wasting the muscles required to distinguish oneself as soldier or athlete and the voice by which the orator can stir the Senate. Related to this, physical attrition specifically "doth almost take away al pleasure and lascivious voluptee," *privet fere omnibus voluptatibus,* by which he refers most precisely to sexual pleasure. Finally, the presumption that one "is not far of from death" in old age—*haud procul absit a morte*—unnerves the subject (fol. 9v–10; 5.15).

In the face of these formative classical and contemporary precedents, Elizabethan England reshaped its own cultural responses to the senescence it more immediately beheld. I have adapted the philosopher's sequence of objections as a way of compartmentalizing the following chapters' selective approach to the "constitution" of old age in late Elizabethan England. If Cato's rebuttals do not definitively controvert the fears Cicero had set out to allay, his anatomy effectively mapped the field of discussion for the humanist culture over which he exerted such a profound influence. Its progress affords a ground plan for exploring the strategies of aged self-reinforcement that contour some of the period's chief artistic and political expressions.

However consequential the specter of an aging monarch may have proven for her subjects' imaginations, Elizabeth I's sense of her own vulnerable yet hardy constitution would significantly determine her evolving self-image. I therefore turn first to a survey of the ways in which she at once defied and capitalized on public apprehensions about her advancing years to formulate what I term a "politics of longevity." From Elizabeth's early reluctance either to pronounce an heir or to marry and so continue the line of Tudor dynastic succession emerges a willingness to gamble national stability upon her physical capacity to survive. Beginning with the Alençon courtship she undertook in her late forties, I examine the queen's private poems and letters alongside the often violent responses to public discourse about the match with a Catholic foreigner twenty-two years her junior. Her lyric "When I was fair and young"—whose curious intertextual bonds with Sir Thomas Wyatt's poetry further complicate its superficial transparency—coordinates my reading of her unique negotiation with the matter of age. Far from the exercise of denial by which many biographers have characterized her later reign, the queen's conduct affirmed her age even as it challenged the perceptions of a new generation of courtiers who questioned her energies. I trace the way this emphasis on the mortality and decay she appears to have withstood drove her parliamentary speeches of 1586, her translation of Boethius (1593), her odd physical display to the French ambassador de Maisse four years later, and her handling of the Essex debacle of 1601. By turning away from traditional mythologies of the "king's two bodies" that have dominated discussion of Elizabeth's self-presentation, I try to open a new window on our understanding of this pivotal female figure's efforts to contend with prevailing cultural attitudes toward senescence, which become in their way as relevant as her more widely discussed contention with the gender politics of her day.

Coinciding with the national trauma of Elizabeth's Alençon adventure, the pastoral literature that inaugurated the great literary flowering of her reign's final two decades conspicuously and uniquely foregrounds the topic of old age. Traditionally displaced to the outer reaches of the form's already marginalized company, the pastoral elder steps forward to assert himself anew in the work of the 1580s' two premier poets, Edmund Spenser and Sir Philip Sidney, and (by extension) in the immediate followers they inspired. In his *Shepheardes Calender,* just after the introduction of his prematurely aged protagonist, Colin Clout, Spenser turns to a literal confrontation between youth and old age in the "Februarie" eclogue. Contesting Harry Berger Jr.'s provocative reading of the clash between the nonagenarian Thenot and his antagonist Cuddie, I redefine the old shepherd's surly aggression as a function of the self-reclamation he preemptively undertakes against the specter of his own presumed weakness and obsolescence. The reflexes conditioning his inversion of the classic fable he tells Cuddie, substantiated by his young antagonist's contemptuous disregard for the old man's physical and temporal "bent," speak directly to the "new poet's" reflection upon generational rage amid his own apprehensive relation to a literary tradition he both revises and honors. Likely drafted around the time of the *Calender*'s release in 1579, the original version of Sidney's *Arcadia*—whose fiction is itself deeply concerned (as I have argued elsewhere) with an older generation's anxiety over the transfer of authority to younger hands—shares this curious attention to the *senex.* Against a backdrop of aged courtly folly, the minor character Geron enacts a defensiveness tempered by an elasticity that sets apart his multivalent, ultimately sympathetic disposition. Nourished in the submerged classical tradition of relations between pastoral youth and their aged counterparts, where seniority honors its juniors with a gracious subservience, Spenser's and Sidney's elder shepherds claim in unprecedented fashion less deferential roles, declining to meet the presumptions of a dominant youth culture. In so doing, they subvert the harsh caricature of aged rigidity expounded in Aristotle's *Rhetoric* in favor of a distinctive capacity to grow and learn. They are not complex characters who happen to be aged, but characters whose complexity is rooted in their combative self-awareness of an aged status that, for better or worse, defines them for their societies.

Elizabethan love poetry participates in the ancient tradition stressing a youthful lover's need to keep sight of the inevitable physical attrition that time promises. My succeeding chapter explores how this gerontophobia itself comes under scrutiny in the period's celebrated lyric expression, through a survey of the peculiar frequency with which these poets turn their attention to the subject of aging and eros. Navigating between the scurrilous indictment of aged sexuality that informs the prevalent *senex amans* convention, the pathos summoned by the Latin poet Maximianus—whose largely overlooked elegies lamenting the erotic debility experienced in old age were still available to early modern readers—and the more benign compatibilities of lesser Anacreontic models, English lyricists of the period reassessed in their verse the psychological ramifications of sexual desire in senescence. After a survey of the aged lover motif that Ralegh reformulates in his poetic appeals for the queen's favor, analysis of Shakespeare's self-consciously aging speaker in the *Sonnets* provides an appropriate centerpiece to my discussion. By shifting focus from the conventional, threatening reminders that the beloved's beauty cannot last to the sonneteer's deeper anxiety over his own impending senescence, Shakespeare anatomizes the fears powering his speaker's conflicted allegiance to larger societal expectations that would deny his very right to the "voluptee" he longs to indulge. The chapter culminates in a close reading of Donne's early elegy "The Autumnall," which divides its lyric energies between a novel tribute to aging beauty and a bitter invective on the physical deformities brought about by time. I cast the poem as Donne's canny, summary diagnosis of the contradictions that threaten to deconstruct from within the very compassion for old age after which the lyric persona strives.

The book finds its logical conclusion in a sustained treatment of the period's great tragedy of senescence. *King Lear,* crafted originally in the years immediately following Elizabeth I's death in 1603, stands as both a grim antitype and an essential coda to the queen's legacy, bringing the playwright's own mature talents fully to bear upon this subject, which had seen only superficial representation on the English stage throughout its flowering over the previous decade's course. While almost everything written about the play in one way or another must address the matter of age, surprisingly few commentators have devoted their energies principally to this salient feature. In my reading, Lear's fateful resignation of power marks neither the old king's self-destructive vanity nor his senile dotage, but a radical (though abortive) effort to synthesize constitutional self-perception with the generationally conditioned designs of youth. I unfold the desperate plights of both the king and the Earl of Gloucester to demonstrate how the society they inhabit seeks simultaneously to displace the old and to recenter them as public displays. In light of this, Gloucester's lament that Lear has been "Confin'd to exhibition" marks one of the play's most significant insights. Beyond the duke's more elementary outrage that his king should be reduced to a pensioner lies an intuited awareness that Lear's royal body is thereby appropriated and converted into a controlled spectacle to reinforce the power and to assuage the conscience of an ascending generation. The play thereby comes to offer a radically fragmented image of late life: crippled yet frenetically mobile, sequestered yet unable to locate a physical or mental "space" where it can find respite from time's attrition.

Originally composed in 1604–5, *King Lear* steps beyond the otherwise strict Elizabethan boundaries I have set for this investigation. For those subscribing to the "dual text" theory that regards the play's Folio version as a substantial revision undertaken by Shakespeare around 1610, the tragedy extends even further into Jacobean territory. What mitigates for me this slight temporal anomaly and justifies inclusion is the work's status as a direct outgrowth of the later reign in whose immediate wake it was created. Issuing from a moment of tense political and cultural transition, *King Lear* stations itself Janus-like on a threshold from which it gazes retrospectively upon a now bygone era of executive senescence (even drawing upon Sidney's hallmark romance for inspiration) as it looks ahead to the more consistent and explicit attention that old age would come to command in Stuart literature.

As I hope is implicitly obvious throughout, Elizabeth survives as a moving force well beyond the chapter devoted to her; the prepositional clause in my title intends, not simply a set of termini, but a trajectory that arcs through the queen's own career to touch down in all the artistic representations of old age that I treat here, including the greatest instance of this play that Shakespeare conceived just after her death at almost seventy. While I propose nothing so reductive or simplistic as the notion that she supplied the playwright with a model for his aged monarch—whose plight was of course so radically different from her own—I do see Elizabeth's sustained successful negotiation with old age on the public stage of political power as a catalyst for creative efforts she did not herself directly sponsor. In the aftermath of her outstanding self-direction into late life, the surviving culture could never again regard senescence quite so casually or dismissively.

Helen Small has observed how very few of the scholars who have taken up literary works "explicitly about being or growing old . . . have read these works *for* what they have to say about old age." "Old age in literature is rarely if ever only about itself," she correctly asserts, "but as far as criticism has been concerned, it has oddly rarely been much about itself at all."[78] Partially in response to this pointed critique, the extended close readings of works chiefly by canonical authors that predominate in what follows aim to keep a rigorous focus trained precisely upon these influential figures' nuanced attention to the subject, especially within the context of the hostile, publicly constituted visions of senescence with which they wrestled. I hope my sustained indulgence in this approach never obstructs the broader argument I intend them to support: namely, that by the end of the sixteenth century in England a renewed awareness of the relationship between aging and subjectivity had begun to collide with such externally constructed stereotypes as what Keith Thomas has labeled "stratification by age" and "the redundancy of the elderly," and that this in turn excited some of the period's most creative literary talents to a vigorous rethinking of the way we as individuals experience and regard our own aging bodies. The subtle subversiveness that their personae and characters manage demands the kind of minute engagement with their actions and words I pursue throughout. Attentive likewise to the "neglect of the aesthetic dimension" lamented by Kiernan Ryan in his survey of recent scholarship on *King Lear,* "a failure to engage in detail with the poetic language and dramatic form that are indivisible from [the work's] identity as a source of pleasure and an object of study," I have seen fit to maintain an approach that risks seeming "old-fashioned" in its orientation—one perhaps especially suited to my topic, for all I can say.[79] Without losing sight of Thane's important call for us to deal ever more "explicitly with the relationship between cultural and material factors" in graphing old age's social history, I nonetheless think we must, especially in this case, begin with a closer reckoning with how these texts speak most directly "about" senescence itself.[80]

Finally, I am aware that my analysis never ventures very far into the related question of "late writing" explored so fruitfully by such critics as Kathleen Woodward and (more specifically in the early modern period) William Kerrigan and Gordon McMullan.[81] None of the principal figures

I treat, with the (eventual) exception of the queen herself, was "old" even by sixteenth-century standards at the time they crafted the works under discussion. The poetry and fiction of Spenser, Sidney, Ralegh, Shakespeare, and Donne were written by young men indeed, in their late twenties and early thirties; and even if *King Lear* continued to evolve as late as 1610, its author would still have been only in his mid-forties, far from "elderly." I look instead to the ways in which these artists, despite their youthful vantage points, exhibit an impressive capacity and willingness to reimagine the experience of an old age that has not yet reached them. These are not "autobiographical" impulses conditioning their own encounters with gerontophobia, and their very stretch beyond the time of life in which they were working renders their achievements all the more impressive. If the imaginations we most revere are those best equipped to take the long view, these writers' provocative efforts to reconceive that single most long-range vista of senescence, as I trust my chapters' individual arguments will affirm, stand especially worthy of our admiration.

In the passage from Aristotle's *Rhetoric* I cite as my epigraph, we see how the philosopher explicates metaphor's reliance upon proper decorum by reference to the sartorial propriety that discriminates youth from age in his day. The societal appropriateness he regards as natural sets age and youth in a "conspicuous" opposition that the elder would dare to violate only at his peril. The sobriety this world expects of him, reflected in the garments assigned to him, cloaks a flatter image of senescence as a time of inconspicuous demeanor, whose toned-down appearance implicitly defers to the more garish boldness of youth's crimson adornment. It is against such prescriptive expectation that the figures to whom I now turn find themselves aligned, however confidently or reluctantly. The case studies that follow assess the extent and effect to which Elizabethan subjects grappled with the competing interior and exterior states that collectively constituted their experience of selfhood in age. The need to square a pronouncedly individuated sense of agency with the proprieties set by external convention would prove simultaneously a source of grave anxiety and a vital opportunity for critical self-assertion. The failures, victories, and stalemates they record project a revealing image of emergent subjectivity against the vibrant backdrop of Tudor England's twilight years.

CHAPTER TWO

Elizabeth I's Politics of Longevity

R OBERT DEVEREUX'S EXECUTION for high treason in February 1601
marked the culmination—for better or for worse—of a grand generational conflict that had taken shape over the 1590s. However question-
able Essex's capabilities or designs may appear in historical hindsight, the
thirty-three-year-old earl embodied the restlessness of a social stratum im-
patient for promotion before the attenuated but lingering gerontocracy
concentrated in the person of the aging queen herself.[1] In the view of this
youthful constituency, the English court—bemoaned by the Spanish envoy Feria at the time of Elizabeth's accession over four decades earlier as
"entirely in the hands of young folks"—had by century's end atrophied
into a state of "sclerotic" retrenchment.[2] Elizabeth survived her fallen favorite and his co-conspirators by just over two years, into what William
Camden observes was "her Climatericall yeere, *to wit,* the seventyeth," an
age "Unto which no King of *England* ever attayned before."[3] Her capacity
to endure inspired the wonder of friends and foes alike.[4] Such longevity proved a mixed blessing, however, as recent assessments of the attrition that her popularity suffered amid the harsher military, political, and
economic realities of the 1590s have confirmed.[5] Camden himself most
poignantly diagnoses the queen's twilight, depicting her as a self-professed
"miserable forlorne woman," abandoned by her lords "whilest she altered
not from her selfe, but they from their opinion of her, either for that they
saw her now in her extreame age, or were weary of her long government,
(for things of long continuance, though good, are tedious)."[6]

While the elaborated rhetoric of the king's "two bodies" went far to
ameliorate the ideological stress that Elizabeth's femininity posed to her
patriarchal contexts, it remained frankly easier to think upon the queen's
"body natural" during her reign.[7] Susan Frye, who has so fruitfully explored the monarch's skill at "engendering" herself as the situation de-

manded, suggests that, in the 1590s, all of her tactics "could not entirely counteract the queen's greatest liability, her own *aging* female body" (my emphasis).[8] Elizabeth's instinctual response, in Frye's view, "was to shield herself physically and psychologically from the escalating threats while representing herself as the youthful figure at the summit of her society's social, religious, and political hierarchies."[9] However intuitively reasonable, Frye's reading presents a less dynamic picture of Elizabeth's regard for her own age than the evidence merits. Especially over the last movement of her long regime, Elizabeth evolved a more pragmatic and consequential sense of her aging body, in what we might term the "politics of longevity" on which she gambled. Taking as a point of departure Leah Marcus's suggestion that throughout the final phase of her long reign the queen conducted herself "as though she actually believed on some level that she could live out the immortality of her 'body politic,'" I want to explore the way in which Elizabeth's experience of age informed her expression, public and private, verbal and visual, and what this discloses about how age could be negotiated in the period by a woman of her unique station and temperament.[10]

Four separate episodes help chart these sensibilities. Since the Alençon marriage debate of the late 1570s and early 1580s first dramatically foregrounds the matter of the queen's age, I turn initially to the heated public debate that surrounded the controversy and the epistolary and poetic responses it provoked from her. The original verses she composed at this time look ahead to the curious translation exercises she undertook during the post-Armada years, which I treat in the following section, when the loss of lifelong confidants and ministers brought home even more starkly the exigencies of time's passing. Next, the peculiar performance that Elizabeth enacted before the French ambassador de Maisse in the winter of 1597–98 offers a telling glimpse of her construction and virtual deployment of her aged physique. Finally, I revisit the matter of the Essex rebellion and Elizabeth's last days, chronicled in the tense and often divided accounts of her intimate courtiers. In so doing, I establish how, up to the time of her death, Elizabeth maintained a complicated sense of struggle with—if not mastery over—the means whereby she could prompt others to regard her constitution, something ultimately as significant as the thorny matter of her gender.

Given the traumatic close calls she had known from the time of her infancy down through the Edwardian and Marian years, the new queen may well have regarded herself as living on borrowed time. The premature decline of her siblings had generated a larger apprehension about the "sickly Tudor line" that coalesced in early prophecies of her own death at a young age.[11] As the reign drew on, fears over the queen's fragility intensified proportionately. No later than 1575, a young Philip Sidney could speak of Elizabeth as "somewhat advanced in years, yet hitherto vigorous in her health, which (as it is God's will that our safety should hang on so frail a thread), is with good reason earnestly commended to the care of Almighty God in the prayers of our people."[12] But while Elizabeth's purported frailty unnerved the court, the evident hardiness with which she soldiered through so many crises—rendered legendary by Foxe's account in the *Actes and Monuments*—both elevated her image as God's chosen and left the queen with a heightened appreciation for her own resilience. Only twenty-five at the time of her accession in 1558, Elizabeth was not aged by any standards in 1562–63 when, in the wake of her near-death experience from smallpox, she dismissed the shaken lords' petitions that she appoint a successor or marry and beget an heir with a sardonic reassurance "that the marks they saw on her face were not wrinkles, but pits of smallpox, and that although she might be old God could send her children as He did to Saint Elizabeth."[13] In a Latin prayer published in 1563 she proclaims herself a prince "constituted" by divine appointment (*qui me tui populi principem constituisti*) though "slight of age" (*sum exigui temporis*), before expressing gratitude for her recovery of health, and in the eighth prayer of that volume celebrates herself as "unimpaired in body, with a good form."[14] Hereafter, the "constituted" monarch punctuates her speeches with affirmations of a physical vulnerability to which she stands acutely sensitized: "I know now as well as I did before that I am mortal," she proclaims before Parliament in 1563, sounding a note that will echo throughout her later rhetoric (*CW*, 71).[15] Her godson, Sir John Harington, preserved a letter that best summarizes the queen's self-image: "If my guest were not worse than the lodging, the rest were not worse than the travail. . . . The constitution of my minde's vessel is not so evil framed, as whereupon grevous diseases or perilous maladise have taken holde. I fynde not the mixture so evil made, as that any one of the foure elements of all overruleth so his fellow, as that the rest may envye his happ."[16]

However secure Elizabeth's conviction regarding her God-given constitution, and however much her privileged status as an unmarried queen distinguished her, women of all classes at the time experienced if anything a compounded version of the conflicted attitudes toward old age characterized in my opening chapter. As we saw there, by William Harrison's contemporary reckoning women were seen to graduate into later life around age forty—a good twenty years before their male counterparts—when "through bearing of children" they "began to wrinkle apace."[17] And as Erin Campbell observes more generally, "the early onset of widowhood for many women meant that women tended to enter sooner than men into the final socially significant phase of their lives," and so "were perceived to age faster than men and to progress through the stages of life more quickly."[18] Even though single women of the day, free from the substantial physical hazards of parturition and often from the dependencies and demands of earlier life stages, were, as Amy M. Froide has argued, perhaps "best positioned to enjoy a positive old age," yet those who had avoided marriage altogether "faced derogatory epithets such as 'old maid' and 'superannuated virgin' that made direct reference to their advanced age."[19]

Exploring the social impact of menopause in sixteenth-century culture, Lynn Botelho likewise turns to the emphasis on physical appearance with which women in the era especially had to reckon: "the end of reproduction probably did not signal the beginning of old age to early modern society," she observes, "but *menopause* did coincide with a host of culturally significant visual changes that resulted in women being labelled old at this stage." Given the unquestionable centrality of "outwardly observable signifiers of status in early modern England," Botelho concludes that "A woman became old when she looked old."[20] This notion takes an expressly humiliating turn in the gerontophobic, misogynist bias informing contemporary pictorial traditions that rendered figures like Helen, Cleopatra, or even Lucretia as elderly grotesques who might never have exerted the power they did over men could they have been envisioned in their decrepitude.[21] Keenly sensitive to such contexts, Elizabeth as head of state appreciated how the need to manage constructions of her appearance was a matter of political order. From early in her reign, she aimed to exert as much control over this domain as possible, an impulse that took on ever greater urgency amid the growing generational animosities that came to mark her regime's later decades.

Educated in the multiform terms of Elizabeth's public iconography, we have yet to investigate adequately the queen's complex sense of her own physical body as it aged. As a result, darker evaluations of the "Mask of Youth" convention so prominent toward the end of the reign have come to overdetermine modern judgments.[22] Our readiness to read her later self-representations as governed by vanity rather than strategy in many respects invests too literally in Ben Jonson's famous sneer that "Queen Elizabeth never saw her self after she became old in a true Glass."[23] Aware as we are of the cool circumspection that Elizabeth brought to all her political endeavors—the formulation of a public image not least among these—we need to resist presumptions that the elder queen was so casually seduced by her own propaganda and be willing to recognize her discreet capacity to embrace the advanced age that her body registered less as a physical liability than as an index of the experience that empowered her reign. Always protective of the way others saw fit to represent her for supportive or derogatory purposes, she knew what her subjects expected, and within reason was willing to honor their demands. Beyond this, answerable only to her own authority, she knew how to project her embodied sense of self with disarming authenticity.

In age as in youth, Elizabeth had the common sense to discern that, however much control a public figure exercised over her own representation, she could never fully govern her audience's response.[24] Over the course of her long career, she grew adept at parrying the "narrative of decline" with which she increasingly had to contend.[25] Perhaps the pivotal irony of Elizabeth's reign involved the way in which Parliament's adamant petitioning of the queen to marry from the time of her accession experienced so radical an about-face once she belatedly appeared to entertain the notion of the duc d'Alençon as a serious political match in 1579. Cowed by her programmatic opposition for over two decades, the militant Protestant faction within her court was ill prepared to process her abrupt assent to their wishes by pressing for a union with this Catholic foreign prince over twenty years her junior. However sincerely and to whatever end Elizabeth pursued the engagement, the experience would precipitate one indisputable, possibly unanticipated crisis for the queen: for the first time, she inescapably had to confront national as well as personal perceptions of her agedness. If we take stock in the French ambassador Mauvissière's contemporary report that Elizabeth experienced an uncanny rejuvenation as the negotiations took shape in earnest, it remains a genuine possibility that the "radiance" she displayed was as much a matter of maintaining a strong demeanor in the face of a rather devastating (if ham-fistedly well-intentioned) attack on her self-image that the ritual flattery of court politics could not altogether ameliorate.

In the salad days of 1560, Elizabeth had flirted playfully with the seventy-six-year-old Amyas Paulet, and did "bemoan him to be old," swearing that, if younger, she could "find in her heart to have him to her husband before any man in England."[26] Before reaching the age of fifty, she found herself disqualified in similar measure. As early as 1570, Alençon's older brother, who would go on to take the throne as Henry III, had rejected any suggestion of courtship with such "an old creature" as the thirty-seven-year-old queen.[27] A decade later, English subjects proved no less tactless in their own violent enmity to the subsequent venture. Even such encouraging counsels as those summoned by Elizabeth's ever politic Lord Treasurer Burghley could not avoid references to her age. While she might better have married "when she was younger in years," Burghley remarked, the judgment of those "most acquainted with her Majesty's body in such things as properly appertain" affirm that "all other things, saving the numbering of her years, do manifestly prove her Majesty to be very apt for procreation of children."[28] Similarly, so respectful a minister as Ralph Sadler delivered a speech in which he boldly recalled how "The inequalyte of yeres" between the parties was such that "her majestie might be his mother."[29] More bluntly, Francis Walsingham confronted Elizabeth in a 1581 letter touching her willingness to drag out the courtship he so opposed: "If you mean it," he prods, "remember that by the delay your Highness useth therein, you lose the benefit of time, which (if years considered) is not the least thing to be weighed."[30]

Among the many condemnations the match excited, none so obnoxiously concentrated on the matter of the queen's age as John Stubbs's *The Discoverie of a Gaping Gulf whereunto England is like to be Swallowed by another French marriage* of 1579. Early in the treatise, Stubbs proclaims "that it is a great disparagement for health to be joined in marriage with any foul disease, for beauty with deformity, youth with decrepit age, or to tender a townsman's daughter to a gentleman of birth."[31] His backward invocation of "decrepit age" leads revealingly into an indictment of Alençon's suspect motives, since "among us of the meaner sort not one in a thousand of those younger men that seek their elder matches but doth it in side respects." He also warns how the pope would without compunction annul a marriage, much to the queen's potential disgrace, on so slight a pretext as "because Monsieur could have no children by our Queen" (*Gulf*, 72–73)—a point he expressly takes for granted, challenging "wise physicians" to swear "how exceedingly dangerous they find it by their learning for Her Majesty at these years to have her first child" (*Gulf*, 51).[32] Lord Henry Howard was swift to rebut this effrontery, but the vociferous harshness of Stubbs's attack proved the last straw and led to his public mutilation in November of that year. It seems one of the crueler ironies that Stubbs's publisher Hugh Singleton, though originally sentenced to share the author's fate of having his hand chopped off, was pardoned at the last moment "on account of his age."[33]

For all her public fury over such presumptuous commentary, we have sufficient evidence that Elizabeth harbored no vain illusions about her perpetual youth. Her correspondence acknowledges the age discrepancy freely. When the French king and queen mother proposed the marriage in the summer of 1572, Elizabeth was the first to remark repeatedly on "the youngness of the years of the duke of Alençon being compared to ours"—an issue she will return no fewer than six times throughout the lengthy missive—insisting on a personal conference before anything can proceed since "nothing can make so full a satisfaction to us for our opinion nor percase in him of us in respect of the opinion he may conceive of the excess of our years above his" (*CW,* 206 and 210). Her direct correspondence with Alençon betrays an equally unmistakable apprehension to which the heated public debate about the match had sensitized her. In a letter of December 19, 1579, shortly after the Stubbs mutilation, she expresses frustration over the protracted negotiations with her suitor, insisting "I see that time runs on, and I with it, which renders me unfit to please as I would wish. And I am almost in agreement with the opinion of those who do not quit reminding you of my faults" (*CW,* 238). One month later, she continues in this abashed vein expressing mock-relief that, profound as her "defects" will be found to be, she cannot appear worse than her slanderers at the French court have made her out, and remarks "But at this hour I muse as do those [old women = *vieilles*] dreaming, not having slept well" (*CW,* 245).[34] Such remarks fit with those she makes to Simier in a letter of 1580 qualifying her writing to Alençon "so roundly," noting "the fact that young folk owe some reverence for the old, which will plead my cause."[35] After affirming "God is my witness that I never use subtleties or stratagems to do myself good at your expense," she indulges Alençon in her epistle of June 1581 with the wry self-caricature of a "poor old woman who honors you as much (I dare say) as any young wench whom you ever will find" (*CW,* 250, 251).[36]

Given the allegations of Elizabeth's actual relief when the negotiations finally grew moribund in 1584—including the joyous dance she reportedly did in her privy chamber upon Alençon's return to France in February 1582—it is unlikely we will ever know for certain what precise stake she held in this match.[37] The public indignity to which the episode subjected her, however, appears to have elicited some of the queen's most inspired lyric expression.

Elizabeth had long been accustomed to turning adversity into verse, from the epigrammatic graffiti of her imprisonment under her sister to the response to Mary Stuart's early threat, "The doubt of future foes," published and admired fulsomely by Puttenham in his *Art of English Poesy.* As a poet, she left her uniquely sophisticated stamp on the most conventional exercises, such as the best-known piece associated with the courtship, "On Monsieur's Departure."[38] More distinctive in its expressly age-bound focus, "When I was fair and young," also dated to the 1580s, identifies the topic of age as particularly evocative for her imagination. Together with the contemporary "Now leave and let me rest," the poem's seemingly transparent gestures in fact betray the writer's keen insight into the impact of passing time upon sexual desire, and her successful drive to write outside the received attitudes she had so thoroughly digested, while displaying her capacity as an expert parodist in dialogue with several of the century's finest earlier performances.

We can perhaps grasp the editorial reluctance, until very recently, to ascribe the lyric definitively to Elizabeth: its chastened and confessional demeanor bears little resemblance to the often defiant, unapologetic character otherwise evident even in her religious verse.[39]

> When I was fair and young, and favor graced me,
> Of many was I sought their mistress for to be.
> But I did scorn them all, and answered them therefore,
>   "Go, go, go seek some otherwhere,
>   Importune me no more."
> How many weeping eyes I made to pine with woe;
> How many sighing hearts I have no skill to show.
> Yet I the prouder grew, and answered them therefore,
>   "Go, go, go seek some otherwhere,
>   Importune me no more."
> Then spake fair Venus' son, that proud victorious boy,
> And said: "Fine dame, since that you be so coy,
> I will so pluck your plumes that you shall say no more
>   'Go, go, go seek some otherwhere,
>   Importune me no more.'"
> When he had spake these words, such change grew in my breast
> That neither night nor day since that, I could take any rest.
> Then lo, I did repent that I had said before,
>   "Go, go, go seek some otherwhere,
>   Importune me no more."   (*CW*, 304–5)

Defeated at last by the "boy" whose immunity to age ensures his eternal "fairness," the aging lover candidly acknowledges her ironic discovery that she has gotten exactly what she asked for. The "many" who sought her now busily seek "otherwhere," abandoning their futile solicitation for her favor. The "no more" that terminates each clipped stanza retrospectively carries a double inflection of both quantity (no *others* will importune her) and temporality (she will be pursued no *longer*). Time indeed marks the

performance's central paradox: having squandered the endless opportunities she had enjoyed while in "favor's" graces by indiscriminately rejecting
the importunities of those who sought her favor, its speaker finds herself
in time, out of time.

The poet locates her reflection's key pun within this curious relationship between "opportunity" and "importunity," newly available at the
time of composition. Although the verb "importune," meaning to burden,
trouble, pester, worry, or annoy, had been current at least since 1530, its
noun form emerged only in the 1580s, in specific contrast to the notion
of more timely occasion. In his *Gaping Gulf* (no less) Stubbs warns Elizabeth against Mary Stuart's predatory design "to snatch the crown from
her head by opportunity or importunity, whichsoever come first" (*Gulf,*
79). Ten years later, Puttenham observes that "Everything hath his season,
which is called opportunity, and the unfitness or indecency of the time is
called importunity."[40] "Importunity" had crystallized as an entity, a figure
of untimeliness. Given such a specifically defined context, we recognize
in the lament of "When I was fair and young" an even heavier cargo of
self-indictment. Elizabeth's coy mistress repents the essential *un*fairness of
her youth, when she forewent every opportunity, indifferently regarding
all as "importune." Now, she is left only with the indignity of the kind of
situation Stubbs had so tactlessly described in his argument that Alençon
was not to be trusted: young men who pursue older matches must be assumed to do so for ulterior motives, since their "young appetites . . . will
otherwise have their desire" (*Gulf,* 72). In other words, the lyric persona
longs for the resumption of an attentiveness that she intuits can only mock
her at this turn.

The poetic sensibilities that Elizabeth exhibited in her surviving verses
were, as her "replies" to Mary Stewart, Thomas Heneage, Paul Melissus,
and Sir Walter Ralegh confirm, deeply *re*active.[41] Remarkable in its own
right, "When I was fair and young" stands out even more dramatically
when read alongside the poems with which it displays subtle intertextual
bonds, Sir Thomas Wyatt's "They flee from me" and "My lute awake." Wyatt, whose breaking posthumous celebrity in Richard Tottel's influential
Songes and Sonettes coincided with Elizabeth's own political emergence,
offered a fitting point of lyric departure for her reflection on age in love.
He had of course been her mother's suitor, perhaps her lover, before Henry
stepped forward to monopolize her. Even more traumatically, Elizabeth
may have first encountered his poetry in the Tower, when she found herself
implicated in Wyatt's son's failed insurrection against Mary in 1554. Imprisoned with (among others) the elder John Harington, who had already be-

gun to assemble the verse collection that would supply Tottel several years on, she could have had manuscript access to this verse well before its publication.[42] If so, the author and his work would loom as largely in her private imagination as any of the talents who sought her favor and patronage in coming decades. Still among Wyatt's most widely anthologized lyrics, the poems that Tottel titles "The lover sheweth how he is forsaken of such as he sometime enjoyed" and "The lover complayneth the unkindnes of his love" together supplied Elizabeth an armature around which she might, in age, fashion her own imaginative expression of erotic loss.

"They flee from me" stands out as perhaps our best rendition of the lover past his prime who suffers the "continuall change" he had himself indulged in younger days. Abandoned by those who now "do not once remember / That sometyme they have put them selves in danger, / To take bread at my hand," he feeds his own resentment even as he salves his ego with reveries of the "especiall" time when his mistress had surrendered herself, catching him "in her armes long and small."[43] Despite the petulant dismay and self-pity that infuse his final contempt for the woman's "newfanglenesse," readers have noted how the anecdote of erotic conquest barely conceals the speaker's own enthrallment. The resulting dramatic tension transforms the central complaint into an unwitting yet poignant self-indictment, and defensiveness as much as disillusionment funds the published version's closing rhetorical demand, "How like you this, what hath she now deserved?" The coy mistress of "My lute awake," in contrast, excites the rancor of a lover vengefully prepared to imagine precisely what she now deserves before resigning his pursuit: "May chance thee lie with-erd and olde, / In winter nightes that are so colde," he projects,

> And then may chance thee to repent
> The time that thou hast lost and spent
> To cause thy lovers sigh and swowne.
> Then shalt thou know beauty but lent,
> And wish and want as I have done.   (26–27, 30–35)[44]

Pride, not chastity, he alleges, motivates the woman who gathers self-esteem at the expense of her adoring suitors, failing to grasp her actual reliance on them for enduring fame.

In reaction, Elizabeth's verbal mimicry in "When I was fair and young" synthesizes the first poem's aging anxiousness with the withered vanity of the second poem's addressee. Like the speaker in "They flee from me," her aged persona nostalgically recollects the lovers she had formerly collected with such ease to prop a now deeply compromised egotism. The admission

"How many sighing hearts I have no skill to show" likewise appears crafted
to provoke the resolution Wyatt voices in "My lute awake": "Should we
then sigh? or singe, or mone?/No, no, my lute for I have done" (8–9).
The stark denial of his refrain's "no" mocks the vacuous reiteration of "go"
that had measured the limits of her former power. She realizes the burden of Wyatt's speaker's curse with startling precision, as if the invocation of a time when she "was fair and young" pointed up the "witherd
and olde" condition he had wished upon his mistress. Also like Wyatt's
indicted lover, "Proude of the spoile . . ./Of simple hartes," she professed-
edly "prouder grew" with the successive conquest of innumerable "sighing hearts." Where Wyatt forecasts the woman's inevitable realization that
"beauty [is] but lent," Elizabeth learns this expressly at the hands of "that
proud victorious boy" who plucks her "plumes." As warned, moreover,
she has come to know that Cupid "hath [not] his bow forgot," but will
intensify her "regret" by never allowing her to forget her fleeting youth that
wastes before his own enduring boyishness. Consequently, she is left (again
as presaged) in the eternal, literal restlessness of one "In winter nightes that
are so colde,/Playning in vaine unto the mone": as she casts it, "neither
night nor day since that, I could take any rest." The "no more" that terminates each stanza echoes the "have done" of her model, as if she finds
herself condemned to a repentance that can never "have done."

As parody, Elizabeth's poem pays homage to Wyatt's work by imaginatively revamping and fulfilling its erotic complexities. While on one level
the performance appears to substantiate the vindictive masculine orthodoxy powering the tradition, however, the persona she develops emerges
as more than a defeated, humiliated figure. Unlike the disgruntled lover of
"They flee from me," Elizabeth's speaker manages a franker self-confronta-
tion. The solemnity, composure, and unflinching self-awareness that age
alone has enabled make her sympathetic and dignify her in the role she assumes. Shifting our gaze from the physical attrition she suffers—discreetly
reduced here to lost "plumage"—which had become the obsessive focus
of the convention's gloating misogyny, the speaker trains attention on her
implicit discovery of sexual passion outside the exclusive province of a
youth vainly encased in its own narcissistic self-preoccupation. The indictment of her own former ignorance fills out her confession and repentance,
but it also boldly proclaims the endurance or enhancement of desire in
maturity's increased erotic restlessness. The poem is therefore less about
sexual desperation than about the powerful stimulus we experience when
age sensitizes us to our own vulnerability to time's passage. And despite her
disclaimer, she in fact takes the opportunity in this very lament to display

an expanded rhetorical range and newfound poetic skill, whose modest eloquence offsets the passivity of her inarticulate youth, when arrogant dismissal took the place of more substantive expression. No longer lost in a fog of mere denial, she forcefully shapes the reawakened sexuality that age presents into a poetic account that holds its nostalgia and self-validating insight in fruitful tension.

In "When I was fair and young," Elizabeth redirects the doubt of future foes she had contemplated in her poetic response to Mary Stuart of 1571, wherein she defiantly proclaims, "Our realm brooks no seditious sects—/Let them elsewhere resort" (*CW,* 134), toward a painful awareness of past lovers, whom her persona had likewise commanded to resort "some otherwhere." But we find a more immediate companion piece to the poem in "Now leave and let me rest," also dated to the 1580s (*CW,* 305–6). Yet another reflective assessment of the experience of age and loss, this palinode—whose opening line echoes the dismissal to the suitors of "When I was fair and young"—flirts with a more conventional decline narrative in its pious farewell to youth's "doting days." Coming to terms with a Nature that "bids me learn to die" (6), the speaker reflects upon how "youth that yields men joys that wanton lust desires/In age repents the toys that reckless youth requires" (9–10). The perspective she now advocates emerges as the exclusive product of time:

> For words or wise reports ne yet examples gone
> 'Gan bridle youthful sports, till age came stealing on.
> The pleasant courtly games that I do pleasure in,
> My elder years now shames such folly to begin.   (15–18)

But amid the self-abnegation and traditional belaboring of youthful folly in a world where "all fair earthly things, soon ripe, will soon be rot" (7), we note several verbal signals that temper the performance's melancholy righteousness. First, the odd present tense of the verb featured in line 17 suggests an ongoing investment in the very folly the speaker rejects. Although both the Hartly and Arundel variants correct "do pleasure" to the past tense "delighted" and "did pleasure," they do not alter the following stanza's proclamation that "all the fancies strange that fond delight brought forth/I do intend to change, and count them nothing worth" (19–20). As a result, the speaker also withholds (in true Petrarchan fashion) a crucial final commitment to the new life she proclaims as best. In short, there lingers some doubt that the tide of convention, however substantial, has altogether dislodged her from the allegedly "vain pleasures" renounced here.

Swearing finally to "fleet from will to wit again" (23), the speaker leaves open precisely how she shall bring her "wit" to bear. It is altogether possible that she bequeaths the "pains" of age, and the lessons these supposedly teach, to those so inclined or disposed to regard maturation in this fashion. Resignation to the painful margins of old age with its hermit-like promise of banishing worldly pleasure, even when detached from the very courtly and worldly drives of the queen herself, reserves an equally ironic power to "choose among the best" as she "learns to die" on her own terms. Intimating that she still possesses the capability to partake of these pleasures if she wishes, the poem's speaker legitimizes rather than compromises her assertions, in the spirit that informs Montaigne's "Of Repenting": "A man cannot boast of contemning or combating sensuality if hee see her not, or know not her grace, her force, and most attractive beauties." With the French writer, Elizabeth might well agree that old age "sets more wrinckles in our minds then on our foreheads: nor are there any spirits, or very rare ones, which in growing old taste not sowrely and mustily."[45] However "aged by culture" she finds herself, the speaker betrays a drive to surmount this limitation through the poetic ironies she has mastered as an integral component of her survivor's "wit."

Elizabeth emerged from the Alençon courtship sensitized to public discourse about her age but nonetheless secure in her capacity to sweep aside the apprehensions it registered—a confidence that would, as it turned out, endure well beyond her French suitor's early demise in 1584. From the time of the Alençon affair's dissipation to the close of her reign twenty years later, Elizabeth indisputably found herself a continuous witness to the specter of time's corrosive force. The stress of Mary Stuart's increasingly desperate plots and eventual execution in 1587 took a heavy toll, provoking Essex's prediction to James VI of Scotland "that hir Majeste cowld not lyve above a yere or ii by reson of sum imperfeccion."[46] In the years leading up to her death, Mary had by her very presence increasingly served as a reminder to Elizabeth of time's passage.[47]

As the anxiety surrounding the rival queen's political threat peaked, however, Elizabeth's developing circumspection about her own mortality found nuanced expression in the speech she delivered before Parliament on November 12, 1586, following the discovery of the regicidal Babington conspiracy. Well into her fifties, and under attack from without, and now within, the realm by agents of violent regime change, she tempers her professions of world-weariness with an emphasis upon the "miraculous" preservation enabled by the plot's timely disclosure. Once again, she surrenders to a decline narrative chiefly as a means of reiterating what gives substance to her age, namely "that after twenty-eight years' reign I do not perceive any diminution of my subjects' good love and affection towards me," something without which she "would not desire to live" (*CW*, 186). Her announced indifference to her own survival ("which for itself I do not regard, knowing that the less life the less sin"), assurance that "for mine own part I am so far from desiring to live as that I think that that person to be most happy which is already dead," and consideration "that I have lived many years . . . and have felt more grief and fewer joys than haply to the world I may seem to have done," is ballasted by a cool security in her divinely sponsored privilege: "And yet must I needs confess that the benefits of God to me have been and are so manifold, so folded and embroidered one upon another, so doubled and redoubled towards me, as that no creature living hath more cause to thank God for all things than I have" (*CW*, 187–88).[48] Her drive to endure remains most intimately "folded" with a solid incentive not to surrender to expected "diminution," as she ardently maintains to her ministers that the hardships to which time pointedly subjects her can only deepen her resolve.

Elizabeth, of course, weathered Mary's execution and the even grander trauma of the Armada that it helped precipitate the following year only to witness the deaths of such long-standing ministers as Leicester, Walsingham, Mildmay, and Hatton, which effectively ushered in what John Guy has termed the queen's "second reign."[49] Politically and personally, historians have most often regarded this attrition, compounded by the deaths of three more trusted members of her privy council (Puckering, Hunsdon, and Knollys) by 1596, as a demoralizing liability for the queen, whose adamant refusal to honor Burghley's anguished petitions to withdraw from public life is seen as her conservative denial and failure to confront practical exigencies.[50] Far from indicating a retrenched determination to live in the past, however, the queen's efforts to retain her established coterie insofar as she was able could just as well be understood as a pragmatic design to maintain continuity in the face of inevitable change.[51]

Elizabeth was forced to suffer another, more emphatic wave of commentary on her senescence as she achieved the "critical" climacteric of her sixty-third year, when an array of well-meant but exasperating sermons again taxed her patience. For instance, Bishop Anthony Rudd preached before her of the way Samuel "cast a right account of his yeares, who when he was become olde, made his sonnes Judges of Israell, because he was not able to beare the charge." After offering for meditation an extended catalogue of the effects of bodily decline, he startlingly presumes to ventriloquize the queen herself in reflection upon her "long temporall life": "Lord, I have now put foote within the doores of that age, in the which the Almond tree flourisheth: wherein men begin to cary a Calender in their bones, the senses begin to faile, the strength to diminish, yea al the powers of the body daily to decay."[52] Sir John Harington reported how Elizabeth, "perceaving wherto it tended, began to be troubled with" the discourse, and rebuked the preacher that "he should have kept his arithmetick for himselfe," but also notes that she later relented, professing annoyance "Only, to shew how the good bishop was deceaved in supposing she was so decayed in her limbs and senses, as himself, perhaps, and other of that age are want to be; she said, 'she thankt God that neither her stomache nor strength, nor her voyce for singing, nor fingering for instruments, nor lastly, her sight was any whit decayed'" (*Nugae,* 2:216–18). John Manningham's diary adds Elizabeth's sarcastic but composed remark to Rudd afterwards, "M[aste]r D[octo]r, you have made me a good funerall sermon; I may dye when I will."[53]

In line with the self-reinforcement that Elizabeth incorporated into her public conduct throughout this tumultuous period, her more private literary endeavors once again served to reconfirm—most significantly to the queen herself—that her memory and verbal facility had not suffered attrition. An arch-beneficiary of the rigorous humanist training she had enjoyed under such tutors as Roger Ascham, Elizabeth from an early age demonstrated impressive skill as a translator. While no evidence exists that she intended this translation work to circulate beyond a close circle of intimates at court (if at all), even her juvenilia, as Marc Shell has demonstrated, exhibit subtle temperamental preoccupations.[54] One concern frequently on display in the texts at which she tried her hand was the melancholy character of long life. The excerpt she adapts from Seneca's tragedy *Hercules Oetaeus,* for instance, concentrates on the miseries of kings, but more specifically alludes to the virtue of an early demise by recalling the common disjunction between happiness and age:

> That might may equal harm, they power achieve.
> Whose living's thread, drawn out, is of such length,
> Whom hap not takes, ere Nature calls away?
> The horned, newed moon them blessed call,
> Whose wane them misers judge, when day doth fall;
> A man full rarely happy is, and old.　　(60–65)[55]

The seasoned weariness expressed here concurs with the frustrations she would endure in the post-Armada years, a time to which recent scholarship has dated the translation.[56] More significantly, the evocations of senescence's darker promises integrate tellingly with and set the stage for the queen's most formidable literary undertaking of the 1590s, her rendering of Boethius's *De consolatione philosophiae* into English, in its entirety: a supremely fitting gesture amid the age reflection that she was undergoing at the time.

We are uniquely aware of the specific circumstances in which Elizabeth undertook the Boethius. When Henry IV of France converted to Catholicism in the summer of 1593 to consolidate his claims to the throne, the queen dispatched an outraged letter to her former ally and according to Camden "sought comfort out of the holy Scriptures, the writings of the holy Fathers, and frequent conferences with the Archbishop," even as "shee daily turned over *Boetius* his bookes, *De Consolatione,* and translated them handsomely into the *English* tongue."[57] As with the Seneca, she surely found therein reflections on the miseries of royal power in such passages as 3.Prose.5, which opens with the observation that "kingdoms and kings' familiarities" can bring happiness only "if their felicity ever last[.] But full be old examples, and of present age, that kings have changed with misery their lot" and concludes with an even more pointed question: "Shall thy friends be helpers, whom not virtue but Fortune got thee? . . . What plague is there, more of strength to harm, than a familiar enemy?"

Given the unusually precise account of the composition preserved with the manuscript, however, Elizabeth evidently had more at stake in the exercise than the *Consolatio*'s therapeutic directives. By taking on a text as lengthy and complex as Boethius's, with its alternating verse and prose units, she would indisputably confirm for herself, and anyone who might otherwise suspect it had, that her intellectual acumen had not declined in age. She no doubt sanctioned the "Computation of the dayes and houres" it took her to complete the work, which survives in three different versions. Purportedly, she, "being at Windsor in the xxxvth yeere of her Raigne, upon the xth of October, 1593, began her translation of *Boethius de consolatione Philosophiae,* and ended it upon the eight [or, alternately, 'fift'] of November then next following, which were xxxty dayes." With all the deductions for sleep, Sundays, exercise, and business, her amanuensis determines that she completed the work in anywhere from twenty-four to twenty-seven hours total.[58] Not only could she manage the intricacies of Boethian philosophical rhetoric, she could do so with superhuman speed, and while incorporating it into the tightly ordered regimen of her daily routine. The exaggerated account affords an appropriate signature to the project's larger personal and public ambitions.[59]

Far more than the "holy Fathers" whom Camden claims she consulted in the wake of Henry's apostasy—authors she could just as "handsomely" have translated—Boethius carried for an English audience distinct political and literary associations: as Elizabeth well knew, both her medieval predecessor Alfred the Great and the first celebrated national poet Chaucer had translated the *Consolatio*.[60] Forging her own modern English version of the text, she implicitly joined their company and (in so doing) positioned herself as a philosopher queen of sorts. On a more intimate level, the *Consolatio*'s drama also provided the sixty-year-old monarch with another opportunity to wrestle with the matter of age itself. The work's familiar opening lines introduce us immediately to the broken, prematurely aged author, who laments his condition in grim retrospect: "Rhymes, that my growing study once performed; / In tears, alas, compelled, woeful staves begin," he mourns in Elizabeth's English,

> The glory once of happy greeny youth,
> Now Fates of grunting age, my comfort all.
> Unlooked-for Age, hied by mishaps, is come,
> And Sorrow bids his time to add withal;
> Unseasoned, hoary hairs upon my head are poured,
> And loosed skin in feeble body shakes.
> Blessed Death, that in sweetest years refrains,
> But, oft called, comes to the woeful wights.
>   (1.Meter.1: 1–2, 7–14)

Although herself closer both in age and status to Theodoric, Boethius's tyrant persecutor, capable of turning upon those faithful servants who dared question her judgments or hegemony—a sobering irony that perhaps conditioned and chastened her response to the philosopher's plight—the queen could readily align herself with the beleaguered protagonist whose words she inhabited, herself being besieged within "the old fashion" she militantly upheld against Henry's newfangled religious posture.[61]

The object of Boethius's dialogue, of course, was to free himself from this limited perspective, and he did so through the revitalizing ministrations of Lady Philosophia. If Elizabeth shared a space with both persecutor and victim in the text, she could take more hopeful refuge in the figure of the great wisdom divinity who dominates the exchange. The agelessly rejuvenated and rejuvenating character of Philosophia projects a perfect image of the queen's coveted stamina. She appears as a woman "Of stately face, with flaming eyes of insight above the common worth of men; of fresh color and unwon strength, though yet so old she were that of our age she seemed not be one. Her stature such as scarce could be discerned"

(1.Prose.1). She reminds her depressed interlocutor indirectly of the "dignities [he] received in youth, denied to older folks" (2.Prose.3), and builds by the work's end to arguments redirecting his attention from "that changing and transitory moment" to "Eternity," that "unending, whole and perfect possession of life." Whatever doubts she harbored regarding the time-bound disappointments that threatened to increase as she passed into late life, echoed in the distress of the *De consolatio*'s author, were more than offset by what Ernst Robert Curtius has called Boethius's "youthfully vital old woman," who "impresses us as a redemptress seen in a vision."[62] The goddess embodies a promise Elizabeth may well have striven to emulate at this tense political moment.

The queen continued her translation efforts sporadically throughout the decade, and though she never again produced anything so substantial as the Boethius, she clearly sought to challenge her skills. In what still strikes most commentators as bizarre, for instance, she turned Plutarch's prose essay from the *Moralia,* "On Curiosity," into English verse. Of greater interest to our purposes here, however, is her rendering of the first 178 lines of Horace's celebrated *Ars poetica* in 1598. Once more, her chief incentive to select this particular item for translation was perhaps the Latin poet's notorious difficulty. As Thomas Drant had declared in the introduction to his 1567 translation of Horace's *Ars* and selected works, "Certainelye Horace hymself is hard, and very hard," and goes on to emphasize "I can soner translate twelve verses out of the greeke Homer, then six oute of Horace."[63] Regarded as a philosophical treatise as much as a literary manifesto at the time, the *Ars* stood as one of the most intimidating pieces a professional translator could take on—the very kind of provocation to which Elizabeth's sensibilities seemed most to respond.

However enticing Elizabeth found the task she set for herself, she saw fit to proceed through only a little more than one-third of Horace's text. The point at which she deliberately terminated her version tellingly points, yet again, to her preoccupation with the subject of age.[64] About 150 lines into his poem, Horace argues in good rhetorical fashion for the necessity of observing decorum when matching "the manners of each age" to a corresponding discourse. After characterizing the boy, the youth, and the adult, he turns his attention to the "aged" man's disposition, in the passage with which Elizabeth closes:

> Cumbers, many a one, besiege the aged man:
> Or that he seeks, though found, as wretch he forbears,
>   And dares not venture th' use thereof;
> Or that in fear, or icy sort, all things he undertakes.

> Slothful; a vain hoper; idle; and greedy of change;
> Crabbed; whining; the praiser of past time
>   When boy he was; a judge, and beater of his younger.
> Growing years great avails do bring;
>   And, passed, gone, as many do deprive.
> Lest, therefore, aged part be giv'n unto the young,
>   And man's estate bequeathed to the boy,
> Let us abide in such as best agree, and in their time.   (183–94)

As if marking this moment as the culmination of her own investment in the endeavor, the aging translator holds up the mirror of senescence crafted by the arch-poet himself. Far from blinkering herself to the gerontophobic prejudices sanctioned by the most revered of classical artists and authorities, she confronts these directly, wielding her own enduring intelligence and sharpened wit to disprove the "idle" attributes of late life even as she transcribes them. In this respect, the performance signals a dismissal more than a denial of temporal pressure. The translation throughout does a respectable job of turning the Latin, and Leicester Bradner attributes the few mistranslations to haste and (interestingly) "possibly failing eyesight."[65] Fully aware of the limitations one exposes in any effort to test the self—"I, wanting to prove my strength—/ It made proof of my weakness [Voulant esprouver mes forses / fust esprou Ve ma faiblesse]" (29–30), as she reflects in one of her original French compositions (*CW,* 414; *AC,* 86)—she took pleasure nonetheless in the sport of making the wisdom, both assuring and adverse, her own. In so doing, she redefines for herself what discourse best fits "the manners of each age" (168).

As Louis Montrose has observed, "The discourse of contempt and the discourse of adulation were equally symptomatic of the Queen's last decade."[66] Since much of the complimentary rhetoric had to do with Elizabeth's immunity to old age, it becomes easy to disregard it as a mere function of mercenary or enforced flattery. At least part of the fulsomeness, however, represents a political establishment's anxious self-reinforcement as it ponders the consequences of the monarch's inevitable demise. Elizabeth's participation in this network was, as I have proposed, far more shrewd and subtle than simplistic dismissals of her vanity and imperiousness can acknowledge. One of the oddest moments in the surviving history of her "naked" subterfuge survives in the account of André Hurault, Sieur de Maisse, the French ambassador who visited the queen in the winter of 1597–98. Though often invoked, the episode has yet to find contextualization amid the monarch's larger refusal to surrender to preconceptualization about her person or capacities. It is here, in the peculiar exchange within the public–private intimacies of her privy chamber, that we get to see the queen in her most perplexing and revealing engagement with her own aged body.

In his journal entry for December 24, 1597, de Maisse records an idle exchange with the sixty-four-year-old queen. Genuinely impressed with her command of classical texts, to the point that "one can say nothing to her on which she will not make some apt comment," the politic envoy expresses his admiration: "Having told her at some point that she was well advertised of everything that happened in the world, she replied that her hands were very long by nature and might, *an nescis longas Regibus esse manus;* whereupon she drew off her glove and showed me her hand, which is very long and more than mine by more than three broad fingers. It was formerly very beautiful, but it is now very thin, although the skin is still most fair."[67]

Elizabeth's literally offhand emblematizing of her own body is at once elementary and artful. The Latin tag she uses to explicate her gesture— *Don't you know that kings' hands are far-reaching?*—quotes Ovid's *Heroides* 17, Helen's cautionary line to her would-be seducer Paris. Deftly substantiating de Maisse's observation of her quick-wittedness, she sets herself up simultaneously as the line's speaker (the subject but cunning Helen) and its referent (the dominant yet beguiled Menelaus). An interesting example of the queen's incisive cleverness, the passage also signals her ironic sensitivity to royal contingencies, even as it illustrates the ambassador's mixed critical reading of her aging body. The hand in question remains imposing and impressive, despite the attrition it also registers. In itself inconsequential, the anecdote helps to orient us toward the more provocative and notably unglossed self-display for which the journal is best remembered: Elizabeth's unsettling act of baring her breast and stomach to de Maisse during their Privy Chamber meetings. Working from the premise summarized by Carole Levin, that "Even in her most casual, seemingly spontaneous remarks, Elizabeth was playing a role,"[68] we can regard the spectacle that Henry IV's emissary describes as something more purposeful than we have so far credited. Elizabeth's self-disclosure within her court's most guarded enclosure functions not as an effort self-indulgently to deny her aged body, but rather to profess this very time-bound physicality. In her gestures, we in fact witness an evolution or refinement (if not a deliberate recollection) of her more celebrated moment of public rhetorical display, the "heart and stomach of a king" speech that she had delivered almost ten years earlier before her troops at Tilbury.

Cultivating the "wisdom" pose she had taken up at least since the mid-1580s, when she expressed confidently to James that "we old foxes can find shifts to save ourselves by others' malice" (*CW,* 262), Elizabeth had by 1597 become inured to her role as elder stateswoman. She proudly wore her "years," conjuring them as leverage over her junior subjects, as we find in her 1593 assurance to the members of Parliament that "having my head by years and experience better stayed (whatsoever any shall suppose to the contrary) than that you may easily believe I will enter into any idle expenses, now must I give you all as great thanks as ever prince gave to loving subjects" (*CW,* 332). In July 1597 she reprimanded Essex's impetuosity, reminding him how "Eyes of youth have sharp sights, but commonly not so deep as those of elder age" (*CW,* 386). Her famous rebuttal to the Polish ambassador that same month likewise sniped at his master's youth: "seeing your king is a young man and newly chosen," she answered the emissary's presumption in perfect Latin, "that he doth not so perfectly know the course of managing affairs of this nature with other princes as his elders have observed with us, so perhaps others will observe which shall succeed him in his place thereafter" (*CW,* 333). At the same time—and at another extreme altogether—she would remain the subject of fetish and fantasy, in spite of if not because of her age. She could not have known Simon Forman's notorious erotic dream of her in age, presented by A. L. Rowse as evidence of the "erotic stimulus that the menfolk derived from having a Virgin Queen upon the throne," but she could not have ignored the very public allegation of the executed Jesuit Thomas Portmort that his persecutor Richard Topcliffe had claimed intimate familiarity with the queen's naked features, claiming hers "the softest belly of any womankind."[69] She was aware, in other words, of the broadly various reactions that the sight of her body might have elicited from even so amicable and compliant a character as de Maisse.

Henry IV's ambassador—himself only five years Elizabeth's junior at the time and a seasoned veteran of foreign service—was charged with discovering Elizabeth's willingness to join his master in bringing their protracted and exhausting war with Spain to a close, something that England and France had agreed not to do independently the previous year. Elizabeth had learned the hard way about the French king's notoriously chameleonic character: the sting of betrayal at his conversion to Catholicism in order to secure the throne is evident in the depressed outrage of the letter she had sent him in 1593. Even after relations had normalized, Elizabeth still saw fit to stress the need for openness that focuses the polite self-denigration of a 1596 missive, where she suggests that a promised visit to her court "would remove all your trust in your ministers, who have abused you, I fear, by so much praise of that which, when you shall be the ocular judge, you will not find at all to answer to the half of what they make you believe, who disgrace me in thinking thus to advance my respect" (*CW*, 385).[70] "Full disclosure" not surprisingly sounds the keynote, therefore, in de Maisse's negotiations, as is evident in the formal directives the ambassador bears "to assure and draw closer than ever the union and good intelligence which ought to exist between their Majesties, their Kingdoms, and their subjects, for their preservation and greatness" (*Journal*, 126).

As in most such diplomatic exchanges, the pretense of openness was in essence a thin veil drawn over deeper suspicions with which both parties warily regarded one another, but it was one the queen was fully prepared to exploit. Elizabeth likely surmised that Henry indeed, with an altogether typical political duplicity she may well have admired, had already "resolved" to make peace in any case. Similarly distrustful of the queen's pragmatic willingness to keep her continental neighbors locked in combat with one another, the French entered the discussion "convinced that secret negotiations were going on between Elizabeth and the Spaniards."[71] Fully briefed on his royal host's imperious and idiosyncratic character, de Maisse was nonetheless ill prepared for what he encountered upon his first entry to the Privy Chamber, where he found the queen "strangely attired in a dress of . . . silver 'gauze,' as they call it. . . . She kept the front of her dress open, and one could see the whole of her bosom, and passing low, and often she would open the front of this robe with her hands as if she was too hot. . . . Her bosom is somewhat wrinkled as well as [one can see for] the collar that she wears round her neck, but lower down her flesh is exceeding white and delicate, so far as one could see" (*Journal*, 25).[72]

In coming weeks, Elizabeth continued this display. His record of their second conversation a week later recounts her self-exposure even more emphatically. Now beneath her "dress of black taffeta," she wears "a petticoat of white damask, girdled, and open in front, as was also her chemise, in such a manner that she often opened this dress and one could see all her belly, and even to her navel. . . . When she raises her head she has a trick of putting both hands on her gown and opening it insomuch that all her belly can be seen. She greeted me with very good cheer and embraced me, and then, having been some three feet from the window, she went and sat down on her chair of state and caused another to be brought to me, taking care to make me cover, which I did" (*Journal*, 36–37).[73] Progressively less startled, he describes her at the December 24 conference as "clad in a white robe of cloth of silver, cut very low and her bosom uncovered [echancrée fort bas et le sein descouvert]" (*Journal*, 55; Prevost-Paradol, 168). By their final interview, she appears simply "attired after her accustomed manner" (*Journal*, 108).

For de Maisse, the affectation that lay behind such exhibitionistic conduct was ostensibly as transparent as the aging queen's garments. Almost immediately as he and his entourage were ushered into the Privy Chamber, Elizabeth, he relates, feigned embarrassment and "began to rebuke those of her Council who were present, saying, 'What will these gentlemen say'—speaking of those who accompanied me—'to see me so attired? I am much disturbed that they should see me in this state'" (*Journal*. 24), as if she were unaware of precisely who would be admitted to her presence. The ambassador privately ascribes this disingenuousness to the vanity he had been led to expect. "She often called herself foolish and old [sotte et vieille]," he later explicitly remarks, "so that she may give occasion to commend her [afin de donner occasion de la louer]," and adds dryly, "When anyone speaks of her beauty she says that she was never beautiful, although she had that reputation thirty years ago. Nevertheless she speaks of her beauty as often as she can [Toutes fois elle ne laisse de la faire tant qu'elle peut]." At the same time, however, even the cynicism of the career diplomat cannot check his qualified admiration. He follows his detached observation by pointing out that "As for her natural form and proportion, she is very beautiful" (*Journal*, 37–38; Prevost-Paradol 156–57), just as he had recorded after their first meeting how "Her figure is fair and tall and graceful in whatever she does; so far as may be she keeps her dignity, yet humbly and graciously withal" (*Journal*, 26). And although he gives the seventy-seven-year-old Burghley's age as eighty-two, he thinks Elizabeth is no more than sixty, something that well might have amused his host.

Deeply sensitized to the notion of the queen's body as a unique matrix of political and cultural representation, recent scholarship nonetheless seems to share de Maisse's discomfort with the spectacle of Elizabeth's aged torso. Well-known to students of the period since G. B. Harrison and R. A. Jones's 1931 English translation, the journal's peculiar account has excited rather brusque responses from even the most sympathetic biographers.[74] Such abrasive judgments deny Elizabeth the sophistication these same readers attribute to her elsewhere, even as they betray an implicit repugnance for the aged physique so startlingly exposed. As a corrective, we need to retreat from the charges of false modesty and false vanity, and think instead about the performative value of the royal skin, and Elizabeth's more direct inclination to emblazon her body before de Maisse, as an index of both endurance and weakness. Lisa Jardine is correct in emphasizing that the journal tells us as much about its author's anxiety over the whorish illegitimacy of a female head of state as it does about his subject; but Elizabeth, anything but ingenuous, would hardly have been surprised to learn of the prejudicial cargo he carried to their meetings.[75] Partially in brazen response to this, she kept her aged body visible and readable, and her self-exposure served to affirm rather than suppress her physical age. The French ambassador would be allowed to witness, for the larger benefit of his younger sovereign, how her ability to maintain executive vitality co-operated with her physical subjection to time. That is, she opened herself fully to his constructions, to challenge (with whatever success she might) any preconceptions he imported.

Recent work on conceptions of the body as social boundary and the relationship between physicality and interiority available to early modern culture can help us better comprehend the self-exposure at issue in the journal.[76] We know that from her youth Elizabeth had thought in terms of the body's median position between inner and outer self. In a letter accompanying the portrait she had sent to her brother, the fifteen-year-old princess enjoined Edward "that when you shall look on my picture you will witsafe to think that as you have but the outward shadow of the body afore you, so my inward mind wisheth that the body itself were oftener in your presence" (*CW,* 35). As she grew, she would remap the terrain of such conventions for a variety of purposes. In an urgent letter to her sister of August 2, 1556, for example, Elizabeth entreats an audience with the suspicious and hostile queen, pleading how "among earthly things I chiefly wish this one: that there were as good surgeons for making anatomies of hearts that might show my thoughts to your majesty as there are expert physicians of the bodies, able to express the inward griefs of their maladies to their patient" (*CW,* 44). As queen, she would flavor her parliamentary discourse with similar invocations of a more candid, fictional alter ego, as she does in her profession to the assembly in 1576 that "for your behoof there is no way so difficile that may touch my private, which I could not well content myself to take, and in this case as willingly to spoil myself quite of myself as if I should put off my upper garment when it wearies me, if the present state might not thereby be encumbered" (*CW,* 170). Discussing this instance, Stephen Cohen points out how, particularly in her recourse to clothing analogies, Elizabeth repeatedly reconfigures the artificiality of outward show as the realm of the "private" persona that obscures the more essential, public sphere of unadorned inwardness. Her rhetoric "exploits the distrust of clothing as signifier not to privilege but to exteriorize and devalue the private."[77]

By the time she confronted de Maisse, Elizabeth had collapsed the registers of the Edward letter in the name of a lucid truthfulness. Lamenting the grim sensationalism of foreign rumors that she had clothed Catholics in bearskins and set dogs upon them for popular entertainment, she tells de Maisse that "She wished they could see the inside of her heart [le dedans de son cœur] in a picture and that it was at Rome, so that all could see it as it was" (*Journal,* 58; Prevost-Paradol, 170). While she cannot display her heart quite so literally or symbolically as she would her hand later in that same conversation, she will nonetheless permit the ambassador an unmediated glimpse of her flesh, showing forth her breast and abdomen "as it was."

The ambiguous spectacle of the hand Elizabeth unveils when she removes her glove provides a synecdoche of sorts for the general ambiguity of her torso, its skin slack yet "exceeding white and delicate." As if to call further attention to the disorienting incongruity of her form, Elizabeth conspicuously abstains from the cosmetics reputedly so much a part of her public persona, something de Maisse would surely have remarked given his eye for detail. As he retails the queen's startling nakedness, along with her bejeweled garments (computing even the relative worth of the gems she sports) and her "great reddish-coloured wig," her face alone remains surprisingly unenhanced, a glaring antitype to the "Mask of Youth" so carefully policed in the official iconography. "As for her face," he writes down, "it is and appears to be very aged" (*Journal,* 25). An even more stark and unmaskable sign of encroaching debility, Elizabeth's poor dental condition compromises her very capacity to express herself adequately: "her teeth are very yellow and unequal, compared with what they were formerly, so they say. . . . Many of them are missing so that one cannot understand her easily when she speaks quickly" (*Journal,* 25–26).[78] Elizabeth is self-consciously frank about the impact of this on her routine, as we see from a later entry that "She was on point of giving me audience . . . but taking a look into her mirror said that she appeared too ill and that she was unwilling for anyone to see her in that state; and so countermanded me" (*Journal,* 36). Despite such obvious signals of decline, however, de Maisse cannot suppress his own wonder: "It is a strange thing to see how lively she is in body and mind and nimble in everything she does" (*Journal,* 61). Elizabeth baffles him, presenting a composite visage of one unmistakably worn by time and the strain of executive responsibility yet remarkably well preserved.

The queen's resilience amid the illness to which her age renders her susceptible contrasts her with a figure like Burghley, whose decrepitude obliges him to be carried to meetings in his chair. But the most ominous specter of mortality haunting the journal's narrative is the dying seventy-year-old Spanish monarch, Philip II. The other implicated party in the present ambassadorial mission, he is rumored barely to be kept alive "by force" (*Journal*, 56), "fed with liquor blown into his throat by the Infanta," according to a dispatch received during de Maisse's stay.[79] The only reference to erotic passion in the journal in fact connects ironically with the political violence that it has allegedly inspired in Elizabeth's Spanish counterpart. Recalling to the ambassador the many "attempts that had been made as much against her life as against her state" sponsored by Philip II, the queen sardonically "related that one of her treasurers of finance had told her that it was the force of love which made the King of Spain behave so, and that it was a dangerous kind of love" (*Journal*, 38).[80] Though she is proud of her capacity to survive these plots, the fear of such physical threats lingers, as the common ritual that de Maisse observes of attendants sampling the food to ensure against poison before the queen is served recalls. Though the exposed body de Maisse beholds confirms for all that she has not reached Philip's mortal pass, the memento mori of his troubling counterpresence, in context, nonetheless intimates the inescapable limits faced even by the bodies of kings, as it draws the two aged figures into a physical parity.

The thought of Philip's impending demise on the eve of a possible peace no doubt took Elizabeth back almost ten years earlier to the most dramatic confrontation in their long-standing enmity, when she had realized one of her grandest moments of public self-display. In the face of the Armada's threat, she had ventured to the fortress at Tilbury to review and encourage the army stationed there under Leicester's command. In 1588, Elizabeth was already approaching her fifty-fifth year and the thirtieth of her reign. The speech she supposedly delivered that August day earned its notoriety mainly for the ringing configuration of the gendered yet empowered body at its core, her proclamation that "I know I have the body but of a weak and feeble woman, but I have the heart and stomach of a king and of a king of England too" (*CW*, 326). She entreats her army to look through her evident feminine exterior to the inner core of her being, where her determinate monarchical and national identity resides. Before arriving at this central assertion, however, she exploits a larger notion of her vulnerability amid the "armed multitudes" addressed. "I have been persuaded by some that are careful of my safety to take heed how I committed myself to armed multitudes, for fear of treachery," she begins, only to insist, "Let tyrants fear: I have so behaved myself that under God I have placed my chiefest strength and safeguard in the loyal hearts and goodwill of my subjects" (*CW*, 325–26).

Although the precise rhetoric of her delivery remains contested, the gesture of public self-exposure and its attendant risk obtains in other accounts, as does her strategy of projecting her own ennobling interiority onto the loyal interiors of the faithful subjects she has nurtured.[81] While Elizabeth does not invoke her kingly heart and stomach in Thomas Deloney's ballads on the event for instance, she does enjoin her army, "never let your stomackes faile you, / For in the midst of all your troupe, / we our selves will be in place" (166–68), and desires them "true English harts to beare: / To God, and her, and to the land, / wherein you nursed were" (190–92).[82] She remains beholden to the goodwill of those who behold her. Confirming for the troops that she indeed has (as we now say) guts, Elizabeth's brazen display achieves her important effect on morale through physical presence itself, her very public exposure a register of her fortitude in the face of her vulnerability.

Now, a decade on, the monarch found herself almost as exhausted with the protracted Spanish conflict as was her French neighbor. Unable to provide Henry with the economic and military reinforcements he would need to sustain the war, she was equally reluctant to make a peace that "would mean abandoning the Dutch, who were as determined as ever not to be ruled by a King of Spain." Nor had the immediate threat to English soil altogether lapsed: less than two months before de Maisse's arrival, news of a second Armada had taken the court unprepared, sending the nation into a sudden panic. While bad weather would once again reduce this enemy enterprise to an abrupt anticlimax, the surprise with which the hazard had broken upon the realm and the "very near miss" it presented rattled confidences.[83] As grateful as she was that circumstances did not call for a reprise of her earlier public performance, Elizabeth, on reflex if not by design, returned to the (now private) spectacle of her body, measuring against its glorious past an undeniably aged present that nonetheless shows her as yet unwilling to capitulate. Incidentally a sign of her virginal status, her exposed breast at once boasts the independence she had maintained from both Spanish and French matches, while affirming the attrition consequent upon this very survival.[84] When she laments that "she had no longer the Council that she had formerly, for she had lost twenty or two and twenty of her Councillors," and de Maisse observes that others had taken their places, the queen responds pointedly "that they were young, and had no experience in affairs of state" (*Journal*, 80). The physical fragility she owns, as precarious and enduring as the network of international relations they work to sustain, requires the seasoned wisdom also stamped upon her frame, more significant in this twilight of hostilities than ever before.

The roles Elizabeth adopted seldom remained static, as John King also recalls, developing, rather, in response both to "political events" and her own "life history."[85] In the figurative "naked" intimacy of her final exchange with de Maisse we also encounter a fascinating disavowal of the trust she had articulated at Tilbury. Whatever faith she put in her people, famously proclaimed before her army and beyond, Elizabeth had militantly announced to the ambassador "that she would not have either her body or her soul entrusted to any living creature" (*Journal*, 58). When asked by de Maisse prior to his departure if she had anything private to convey to the French king, Elizabeth tells the ambassador to "come nearer to her because all her Councillors were in the Chamber," and tells him to beg Henry "to consider the position in which she was placed; that she was a woman, old and capable of nothing by herself; she had to deal with nobles of divers humours, and peoples, who, although they made great demonstration of love towards her, nevertheless were fickle and inconstant, and she had to fear everything."[86] If a touch of self-pity inflects her confession (whether itself yet another instance of diplomatic posturing or something more "natural"), she is earnest in her conviction to maintain her duty. She closes by reminding him "*Quidquid delirant Reges plectuntur Achivi* [a tag from Horace that translates as 'Whatever wrongs kings commit, their subjects must suffer for them'], as if she was not without great sorrow" (*Journal*, 110). She will uphold the best interests of subjects whom she evidently hasn't been able to inspire over the long run, as she had hoped to do at Tilbury. In her last meeting with de Maisse, we no longer observe the earlier dichotomy between a woman's body and a king's interior, now effectively collapsed. She compels him not to look through her flesh to some iconic core but to linger on the substantial and substantiating surface. What de Maisse beholds is incontestably the breast and belly of a queen: nothing more, though absolutely nothing less.

Elizabeth sends Henry's representative back to his own duplicitous master with these "private" thoughts, along with a more detailed account of her curious sartorial "openness," for his consideration and construction. As observed earlier, her letter of 1596 confirming the alliance at issue for the present embassy had dismissed the misreportage of her beauty by Henry's previous emissaries, which would not hold up before *l'oculaire iuge;* so now her self-display corrects even as it feeds the imagination of the French king and all those privy to de Maisse's revelations. At the same time, we can accept at face value the counterassertion she had made earlier to the envoy, qualifying her self-denigrating utterances. No sooner does she remark to him "that she was on the edge of the grave and ought to bethink herself of death," than "suddenly she checked herself, saying, 'I think not to die so soon, Master Ambassador, and am not so old as they think.'" When her interlocutor responds "that she did wrong to call herself old so often as she did, and by God's grace her disposition was such that she had no occasion to call herself so," she agrees, and de Maisse must concede (again privately) that, "save for her face, which looks old, and her teeth, it is not possible to see a woman of so fine and vigorous disposition in both mind and in body" (*Journal*, 82).[87] Elizabeth seeks to occupy the unacknowledged space between the flatterers' reconstructions and the slanderers' misconstructions. The impression she makes on the ambassador will help relay her capacity for self-preservation as well as her vulnerability, which she will also manage to brave.

In her nakedness, Elizabeth provided de Maisse with as close a view as one can perhaps gain of another. With age, she had come to know the soundness of her own physical makeup, and now regarded the outward signs of the years as more of a badge than a liability. She was not above turning this display to rhetorical purpose—to intimidate, unsettle, or elicit sympathy from her captive audience—though she was too aware of the unreliable efficacy of such gestures for this to be her primary aim: as de Maisse's confused reactions suggest, the forces of prejudice and presumption—about age no less than about gender—were too substantial for even the most shocking challenges to dislodge. Rather, Elizabeth's image served her more particularly during the negotiations to convey to Henry's representative her composure in the face of historical currents that she had helped to shape but that ultimately lay beyond what the monarchs themselves could direct. Just as her fortitude before impending threats of military disaster had inspired her subjects at Tilbury in 1588, so the relaxed self-confidence she now displayed no less boldly might reassure her cagey ally that she would rise to meet whatever new challenges or successes their dealings might bring. The multivalent image of her physique might remain impossible to read with certainty, but at sixty-four she no less purposefully left it exposed to and inviting of her audience's politic construction. Sensitized to her body's capacity to deteriorate, to endure, and to impress others in its very complex of weakness and strength, Elizabeth embraced her age, departing upon the same question with which she had opened before de Maisse's embassy: "What will they say?"

The ambivalence of Elizabeth's canny self-characterization to de Maisse as at once "on the edge of the grave" and "not so old as they think" in large part defines the strategy she adopted in negotiating public attitudes toward her senescence throughout the twilight of her reign, as we gather from the conflicting impressions of her carriage that survive from the years following the embassy.[88] Rowland White's correspondence with Sir Robert Sidney provides perhaps the best continuous thread of commentary. In a letter of August 29, 1599, for instance, White confides that "Her Majesty, God be thanked, is in good health, and likes well of *Nonsuch* Ayre. Here hath many Rumors bene bruted of her, very strange, without any Reason, which troubled her Majestie a litle; for she wold say, *Mortua sed non sepulta*." White himself nervously vacillates between assurances of the queen's vitality and fears for her "whose Health, Safety, and Contentment, I heartely pray to God may be eternall."[89] The queen's "troubled" self-characterization as one "dead but not yet buried" betrays her own frustration over national anxieties that advanced age had relegated her to a physical and political fragility that little corresponded to the stamina she evidently felt.[90]

Elizabeth publicly belied such suspicions with a regimen of brisk physical activity chronicled in White's subsequent missives. By the end of 1599, we hear how she "is in very good Health, and comes much abroad these Holidayes"; and late the following summer still "goes Abroad every Day to ride and hunt," a season during which she also resolved "to goe on her long Progress to *Tottenham,* the Earle of *Harfords,*" in sardonic defiance of ministerial counsel. "The Lords are sorry for it," White reports, "butt her Majestie bids the old stay behind, and the young and able to goe with her" (Collins, 2:155, 208, and 210). By that September, he informs Sidney how, "God be thancked, she is very mery and well," remarking later that the queen continues "excellently disposed to hunting, for every second Day she is on Horsbacke, and continues the Sport long" (Collins, 2:213 and 214).[91]

Less negotiable for Elizabeth were the twin events that most heavily burdened her final years: Burghley's death in 1598 followed by Essex's disgrace and fall in 1599 and 1601. John Harington's account of how on the eve of her Lord Treasurer's demise the queen "did intreat heav'n daily for his longer life:—else would her people, nay herself, stand in need of cordials too," confirms the queen's awareness of what a practical blow the elder statesman's loss would be to her (*Nugae,* 1:237). Although as early as 1591 Burghley had earned the nickname of "olde *Saturnus*," the "melancholy and Weyward Planet" (Collins, 1:331), the anonymous biography composed not long afterwards asserts that the minister's even temper was compromised only "within 3 or 4 years before his death when age, the mother of morosity, and continuance of sickness altered even the course of his nature, with pains in his body, griefs and cares in his mind, crosses in Council, and oppression with multitude of business for his country."[92] As traumatic as the deaths of Leicester, Hatton, and Walsingham had been a decade earlier, the demise of this last remaining figure from the start of her reign no doubt subjected Elizabeth to the psychological stress experienced by any lone survivor.[93] As the recovery recounted in White's letters suggests, however, her hold on full executive authority went undiminished even under so profound a strain as this.

That summer would prove similarly fateful for Essex, who during the infamous council meeting the month before Burghley's death had in the midst of a heated exchange reached for his sword when the queen struck him. The failing relationship was brought to a head in late September 1599 when the earl abandoned his post in Ireland and returned unannounced to Elizabeth's bedchamber at Nonsuch, where he confronted her "newly up," in White's description, "the Hare about her Face" (Collins, 2:127). The queen's unretouched appearance would likely have made little impression on Essex, as the "rash youth" and his adherents had taken small trouble to conceal their contempt for what they expressly regarded as the court's dotage. In a letter to his sister Penelope Rich, the earl makes reference to "the tyme wherein wee live" as "more unconstant then womens thoughtes" and "more miserable then old age itself."[94] When Elizabeth refused to renew his patent on sweet wines the following year, in essence facing him with the prospect of bankruptcy, the former favorite exclaimed, according to Sir Walter Ralegh, "that the Queen was cankered, and that her mind had become as crooked as her carcass."[95] In the months before the abortive insurrection, the man whom Essex later indicted as "one of the chiefest instigators of me in all these my disloyal courses into which I have fallen," namely his secretary Henry Cuffe, authored a work published seven years later as *The Differences of the Ages of Mans Life: Together with the Originall causes, Progresse, and End thereof* (Devereux, 2:169). Although a reader would be hard pressed to detect conspicuous subversion in the treatise's rambling philosophical discourse, we cannot help but hear topical irony in his summary comment that "Decrepit *crooked age,* from the angrie aspect of drie *Saturne,* sucketh the poisonous infirmities of crasie sicknesse and waiward pettishnesse."[96] If Cuffe had intended any facetiousness, it must have haunted him as, two weeks after Essex's beheading, he followed his master to the gallows.

Again, speculation about "the indignity of being caught in a condition which so cruelly shattered the fable that time had left her unscathed" fails to respect the queen's more pragmatic fury at the presumption of Essex's untimely intrusion into her chambers, just as charges that she had emotionally suffered "utter shipwreck in the infatuation of her old age" sells her composure short.[97] Elizabeth not only acknowledged freely the disparity in their ages, but insisted upon the earl's focusing his attention on this fact. Two years earlier, his ill-starred expedition against Spanish shipping had prompted her to emphasize her own seniority: "Eyes of youth have sharp sights, but commonly not so deep as those of elder age," she writes, "which makes me marvel less at rash attempts and headstrong counsels which give not leisure to judgment's warning, nor heeds advice, but makes a laughter of the one and despises with scorn the last" (*CW,* 386). Her regard for Essex was neither besotted nor abject: she saw in him a prospect for a future generation that could embody the best of what had so self-consciously collected itself and flourished over the course of her protracted reign. His failure provoked a disappointment in her that transcended any stereotypical spinsterish infatuation, and her disillusionment had less to do with slighted vanity than with failed political vision.[98]

Elizabeth was prepared to embrace her role as royal elder well before the de Maisse episode and continued to exert a charismatic influence over those who remarked upon her appearance at this late turn. One German visitor in 1598 commented on the "majestic" cast of her "fair, but wrinkled" visage, while another, miscalculating the queen's age as seventy-four in 1599, nonetheless deemed her "very youthful still in appearance, seeming no more than twenty years of age. . . . God has preserved her wonderfully at all times."[99] Only days before his own death, the elderly William Lambarde, given charge of documents at the Tower of London in early 1601, presented to her his *Pandecta,* or bibliography, of the collection there on August 4 of that year. The queen "chearfullie" received the book in her Privy Chamber, we are told, remarking to Lambarde that "she would be a scholar in her age, and thought it no scorn to learn during her life, being of the mind of that philosopher, who in his last years began with the Greek alphabet" (Nichols, 3:552–53).

Casting herself fittingly in the mold of Cato, the spokesperson for age in Cicero's *De senectute,* Elizabeth remained contemptuous of those who would write her off prematurely: a letter of August 21, 1600, to James proclaims, "though a King I be, yet hath my funeral been prepared (as I hear) long or I suppose their labour shall be needful . . . whereat I smile, supposing that such facts may make them readier for it than I."[100] Just as she had dissolved her 1593 parliament invoking her "years and experience," so one account of 1601's "golden" speech caps her address to the Lords with the claim that God's aid and "our long-lived experience (though in a mean wit), shall make us able to discern and embrace that which shall tend to the prosperity of our people" (*CW*, 354). The queen, who outlasted even the recorder of ages in her own archives, relished to the end the longevity that distinguished her from predecessors who had not shared her strong constitution. It was no doubt in exasperation that James reportedly conjectured she would "endure as long as the sun and moon."[101]

Testimony suggests that the queen's physical health remained sound to the very last. As late as September 23, 1602, Fulke Greville assured the countess of Shrewsbury that Elizabeth's "healthe and disposition of body . . . is excellent good; and I have not seen her every way better disposed thes many years" (Nichols, 3:597). Closer to the end, Harington wrote to his wife that Elizabeth "dothe now bear shew of human infirmitie," citing her irritability and forgetfulness, above her own profession that "my bodilie meate dothe not suite me well."[102] John Chamberlain likewise diagnosed the queen's late malady "to be nothing but a settled and unremoveable melancholy, insomuch that she could not be won or persuaded, neither by the Council, divines, physicians, nor the women about her, once to taste or touch any physic."[103] Sir Robert Carey's account of his last meeting with Elizabeth confirms the rumor, and in his diary entry for March 23–24, 1603, Manningham speculates that Elizabeth "might have lived yf she would have used meanes; but shee would not be persuaded, and princes must not be forced. Hir physicians said shee had a body of a firme and perfect constitucion, likely to have lived many yeares."[104] Having made a career of outliving foes and friends alike, Elizabeth claimed a right to meet death largely on her own terms.

To whatever extent the queen herself had upheld the "Mask of Youth" convention late into the reign, her final gesture regarding the preservation of her image appears to mark a candid and enduring acknowledgment of the advanced age which she proudly attained. Although Elizabeth's funeral effigy has not survived, historians now speculate "that naturalistic principles were rehabilitated" for the commission, crafted by John Colte, and "that a death mask was used" in its execution.[105] Should this have been the case, the postmortem impression would have required the monarch's deathbed permission—a deliberate replacement of convenient political fictions at the last moment by a more genuine, realistic representation. The one description of the effigy that does come down to us from the English antiquarian George Vertue, who in 1725 beheld it in Westminster Abbey, offers a worthy retrospect: "not tall, midling her head cutt in wood. antient a little wrinkley her face. tho the truest countenance of her face."[106]

In the wake of Elizabeth's death, Harington recorded, from his retreat at Kelston, "Here now wyll I reste my troublede mynde, and tende my sheepe like an Arcadian swayne, that hath loste his faire mistresse; for in soothe, I have loste the beste and faireste love that ever shepherde knew, even my gracious Queene" (*Nugae,* 1:180). The courtier's fantasy of retiring to a pastoral haven where noisome public ambitions were exchanged for integration within a simpler community was a conventional enough gesture. Yet within this bucolic setting, refurbished by the writers who inaugurated the flowering of Elizabethan letters in the 1580s, aged figures face an even greater marginalization. As we turn from the queen herself to the poets who distinguished her late reign, we witness a novel impulse to rethink pastoral senescence. In the adversity uniquely presented by age, the bucolic elders portrayed by Spenser, Sidney, and their followers realize a peculiar complexity precisely as they struggle to break free from the dispositional fold within which society would seek to pen them.

CHAPTER THREE

Out to Pasture: The Bucolic Elder in Spenser, Sidney, and Their Heirs

WHEN HE COMES TO PRESCRIBE a regimen of care for the elderly in the second book of his *De vita,* Marsilio Ficino prefaces his instructions with an advisory. "Those who have already completed their forty-ninth year and are nearing their fiftieth," he suggests, "should reflect that young people are signified by Venus, while old people are signified by Saturn, and that according to astronomers these stars are the most hostile of all to each other." Several chapters later, his remarks about optimal environments for the aged betray an odd mingling of consideration and condescension that figures their innate plight: "In winter, let old people like sheep seek places exposed to the sun; in summer let them like birds revisit the pleasant places and rivers. Let them dwell continually among green and sweet-smelling plants; for these living and breathing things conspire to augment the human spirit."[1] Protected as a potentially valuable resource, the elder faces a more dubious prospect of sequestration to the fold, reliant upon the very younger generation whose restrained enmity is nonetheless presaged in the heavens.

Ficino's counsel is of course both well-intentioned and (to a point) appropriate. Given its traditional association with the relinquishing of burdensome responsibilities in favor of a more personal, recreative withdrawal, the pastoral landscape seems a haven ideally suited to old age. The exiled Duke Senior of Shakespeare's *As You Like It* memorably adopts such a perspective when he inquires, "Hath not old custom made this life more sweet / Than that of painted pomp?" (2.1.2–3). Nonetheless, the philosopher's analogy—which distantly anticipates our own vulgar expression about putting those who survive beyond an expected level of productivity "out to pasture"—carries a more suspect valence. Despite its promise of retreat and regeneration, pastoral's literary domain often proves a deeply unaccommodating space for its aged inhabitants. So marginal seems their presence within its boundaries that, in his classic study, Thomas G. Rosenmeyer disputes their significance to the genre altogether. "Youth, rather than maturity or old age, is in control," he asserts, "vigor, not wisdom, is the norm"; as a result, the old man in the Theocritan model "is best suited to the role of . . . a listener, or a former pastoral hero, or an umpire, but not a central figure."[2] And while Steven Marx proposes to recover this centrality in his claim that "Old age is a version of pastoral, complementary and yet opposed to the pastoral of youth," even he must acknowledge the elder's beleaguered station within the generational "dichotomy" he finds integral to the form.[3] Beneath an amiable veneer, the aged shepherd's relations with his younger counterparts remain throughout the tradition a contingent and tenuous affair, harboring a terrific potential for apprehension, defensiveness, and rage—sentiments that, as I argue in this chapter, reach a flashpoint in the groundbreaking work of Edmund Spenser and Sir Philip Sidney, who together explore in an unprecedented fashion the anxious self-awareness conditioning the elder's reflexes within the bucolic realm he inhabits.

As surely as pastoral inaugurates one of the most prolific eras in English literary history, its practitioners exhibit in their fictions a novel regard for senescence's plight. Published in 1579, Spenser's *Shepheardes Calender* presents in its initial dialogue the superannuated figure of Thenot, whose open assault on youth breaks dramatically with tradition. The rancor so vigorously on display emanates from a deeply "enfolded" sense of impatience and outrage with determinate generic attitudes toward old age. Likely in draft around the time of the *Calender*'s release, the original version of Sidney's *Arcadia* likewise attends curiously to the *senex*. Contrasting the aged courtly folly Sidney elsewhere mocks in his romance, the minor character Geron focuses an alternative vision of temperate and pliant senescence. Like Thenot, he betrays an essential circumspection that belies his bristly defensiveness and discovers the range of his rich, sympathetic disposition. Under the influence of these innovations available in Spenser's celebrated achievement and (at least) the revised, published version of Sidney's equally revered text, English pastoral verse of the 1590s sustains an engagement with old age, as a survey of works by Thomas Lodge, Francis Sabie, Michael Drayton, and Richard Barnfield confirms. Viewed through the mesh of subtle though elemental changes evident in the poetry, the elder shepherds of Elizabethan pastoral step forward to challenge the conventions that would tether them.

.   .   .

The eminent position that pastoral held in the literary hierarchy erected by early modern poets and theorists owed much to the form's reputed generic seniority, which spoke to the culture's deeply nostalgic preoccupation with origins. Even those who disputed pastoral's status as the oldest poetic mode honored what they saw as its discreet ethical authority and enduring didactic potential, a mature purposefulness that shaped its design (in Puttenham's words) "to contain and inform moral discipline, for the amendment of man's behavior."[4] Given this generic disposition, pastoral intuitively reserves a privileged station for the elder who, as an embodiment of wisdom gained through life experience, commands respect from the greener, youthful beneficiaries who dominate the idyllic foreground. One of the best modern images of the generational harmony this configuration can ideally sponsor arrives early in Sidney's revised *Arcadia* when Kalander, the aged minister to Duke Basilius, recounts for his young guest Palladius (actually the disguised prince Musidorus) his country's current political circumstance. At the close of his extended narrative, Kalander offers an apology: "if I have held you over long," he says,

> lay hardly the fault upon my old age, which in the very disposition of it is talkative—whether it be . . . that nature loves to exercise that part most which is least decayed—and that is our tongue; or that knowledge being the only thing whereof we poor old men can brag, we cannot make it known but by utterance; or that mankind, by all means seeking to eternize himself so much the more as he is near his end, doth it not only by the children that come of him, but by speeches and writings recommended to the memory of hearers and readers.

The old man's self-deprecation cues Palladius's amiable rejoinder, "Never may he be old . . . that doth not reverence that age whose heaviness, if it weigh down the frail and fleshly balance, it as much lifts up the noble and spiritual part." The youth goes so far as to advance "another reason" for aged loquacity: "that their wisdom makes them willing to profit others, and that have I received of you, never to be forgotten but with ungratefulness."[5] Mutual deference meets in perfect symbiosis: "enamoured with a fatherly love" for the young man to whom he instinctively becomes a "servant by the bonds such virtue laid upon him" (*NA*, 14), Kalander expresses good-natured regret for having burdened his listener; in kind, Palladius's respectfulness "lifts up" his host's esteem as much as the "heaviness" of the years simultaneously (he takes for granted) enfeebles the old man's body.

The gracious reciprocity distilled by Sidney here enjoys a long pedigree. Earlier in the century, Jacopo Sannazaro's *Arcadia* had featured the respected elder Opico who, called upon by the "extremely youthful" Carino to sing for the rustic gathering, declines, citing time's effect upon his once able voice:

> My son, all earthly things, yea and the spirit itself, although it be divine, do the years and devouring age bear along with them. And I can remember many times as a lad that I sang from the time that the sun came forth until it set again, without ever one whit tiring myself; and now all those verses are vanished out of my mind; even worse, my voice is completely wanting, because the wolves have caught sight of me before I was ware of them: but granting that the wolves had not deprived me of it, my hoary head and frozen blood give no command that I should undertake that which properly belongs to young men. It is a long time now that my pipe has been hung up to rural Faunus.[6]

While "Such courtesies freely dealt take the place of engraved law among the shepherds," as William J. Kennedy rightly points out, the liberality on display faithfully reproduces social customs already clearly formalized in the form's antique sources.[7] Sannazaro's passage itself conflates two representative loci, Virgil's ninth eclogue and the opening pastoral of his third-century follower Nemesianus, where invitations for the elder to perform consistently meet with polite refusal in the name of youth's superior qualifications.[8] Just as the *fortunatus senex* or "lucky old man" we meet at the very start of Virgil's *Eclogues* retains his happy *otium* at the behest of a "divine" political authority expressly invoked as a "youth" (*iuvenis*), the aged shepherd characteristically nourishes the goodwill of his younger peers through a benevolent affirmation of their more timely excellence—a celebration that comes at the price of his own self-abnegation.[9]

At the same time, closer reading may beg the question of just how "freely" these pleasantries are dealt. As even pastoral's more irenic scenarios intimate, the idealized cycle of nurture and veneration can prove as tenuous as it is paradigmatic. For all the reverence afforded him, the pastoral elder's history consistently remains one of a professed inadequacy that transcends routine modesty topoi. According to the aged figure's own profession, senescence—like the fabled wolf that silences any victim he sees first—ultimately denies him even a voice. Correspondingly, the old man's acquiescence to youth's capabilities comes to appear as much a precondition as an inspiration for whatever respect his juniors see fit to grant. So gentle a criticism of youth as we encounter in Mantuan's sixth eclogue or the "Ecloga prima" opening Barnabe Googe's *Eclogues, Epitaphs, and Sonnets* (1563) emerges only from the aged speaker's simultaneous self-critique.[10] More tellingly still, when an old shepherd presumes to covet the lyre that Daedalus had fashioned for a younger poet in Petrarch's *Bucolicum*

Carmen, he meets with a sharp reprimand: "Late to your heart come such longings. The flower of youth has faded—/ *That* would have been the right season. In truth it's a sorry lesson, / Learning a good thing too late to avail us."[11] Amid a landscape as pacific as Sannazaro's, moreover, an elder's jesting effort to bring out a morose young shepherd "by the use of cutting words" elicits from the youth a surly, contemptuous reply (p. 96). In other words, pastoral literature traditionally offers more a prescriptive than an encomiastic portrayal of old age, an artistic reminder of the obligations the old must meet if they are to hope for the enduring affection of the generations whose reverence they might be foolish to take for granted. The aged figure who fails to uphold his assigned role as "servant" to the needs of his younger peers faces a social fate that compounds the indignity of a physical diminution that he must also explicitly affirm.

In this way, the pattern of deferential behavior into which the pastoral elder finds himself generically locked offers a perfect example of what Helen Small has in another setting deftly termed "the coercive idealization of the old."[12] Honored as a repository of wisdom, itself construed as dispassionate and objective insight, the aged individual is simultaneously constrained by a decorous resignation to what "Time and Nature" purportedly legislate. Any impulse to resist this subjection accordingly provides cause for criticism and dismissal: if not serenely docile, he fades into a caricature of elderly cantankerousness. By extension, therefore, the wisdom attribute comes to reinforce, as Kathleen Woodward has suggested, a "cultural prohibition of anger in older people," a foreclosure of emotion that deprives the aged of a legitimate and substantiating critical outlet.[13] Capable of drafting pastoral figures who fully conform to generic behavioral norms, Spenser and Sidney also strike out to enrich the tradition by imagining characters who meet the prospect of enforced retirement to subservient "wisdom" roles with a resentful defiance nourished in an ardent self-respect for their own constitutional integrity, mental and physical. In their resistance against imposed delimitation, their rage proves not only cathartic but empowering, an occasion for self-validating, even creative, opposition.[14]

Intergenerational engagement, as readers have long recognized, is a topic well suited to the inaugural effort of "this our new Poete" to assume his place within a national literary dynasty extending back at least to "the olde famous Poete Chaucer."[15] In the best overall assessment of *The Shepheardes Calender,* Harry Berger Jr. identifies the "dialogue, or convergence, or collision, of old with young, ancient with modern, past with present" as a key organizing principle in what he calls "Spenser's drama of literary imitation."[16] More startling is the youthful innovator's conspicuous allegiance to a cultural past widely denigrated in his day.[17] At a well-known turn in his *Defence of Poetry,* Sidney can summon only lukewarm praise for the chief poet of "that misty time," whose "great wants" he backhandedly deems "fit to be forgiven in so reverent an antiquity" and in practically the same breath proceeds to qualify his admiration for Spenser himself, faulting the "framing of his style to an old rustic language."[18] In the *Calender's* own introductory epistle, E. K. defensively frets the tension between an impulse to "affect antiquitie, as coveting thereby credence and honor of elder yeeres," and the hazard of "olde and obsolete wordes" that, "as in old buildings," can "seme disorderly and ruinous" (pp. 4–5). But we have overlooked Spenser's canny awareness that obsolescence is more often socially determined than organic or natural—a sensibility that emboldens this poet, who takes the opportunity in his pastoral watershed to rethink seniority's relevance to a heritage he aims to sustain rather than supplant.

The broad generational perspective that Spenser brings to his project is most immediately evident in Colin Clout, the persona he creates for this work and fittingly retains to the end of his career. The "Shepeheards boye," whose solo performances in the "Januarye" and "December" eclogues provide a critical frame for the entire sequence, literally embodies a generational collapse as a *puer senex* or "aged youth," a plight he announces at the very outset. "Such rage as winters, reigneth in my heart, / My life bloud friesing with unkindly cold," he laments, "As if my yeare were wast, and woxen old. / And yet alas, but now my spring begonne, / And yet alas, yt is already donne" (25–26, 28–30). No less paradoxically, "December" finds him surveying the intervening year's attrition, which despite his designs to "proportioneth his life to the four seasons" only recapitulates in slightly more graphic fashion the early blight he had confronted at the start:

> The carefull cold hath nypt my rugged rynde,
> And in my face deepe furrowes eld hath pight:
> My head besprent with hoary frost I fynd,
> And by myne eie the Crow his clawe dooth wright.
> ("December," 133–36)

All out of season, the "new Poete" struggles with fears of retirement, his creativity "nypt." In the person of Colin—aged before his time, for better or for worse—Spenser effectively unsettles conventional somatic alignments of the seasons and life's stages, and through this disorientation prevents us from taking shelter in the familiar temporal allegories his persona at once delineates and violates.[19]

While a static self-containment endows Colin with a peculiar complexity, however, his unchanging "pale and wanne" demeanor markedly contrasts the kinetic dynamism of Thenot, who dominates the explosive exchange to which the introverted musings of "Januarye" abruptly yield. Ironically, the very range displayed by this nonagenarian shepherd, both within the "discourse of old age" that comprises "Februarie" and across the eclogues within which he appears, has become a source of critical disfavor. Variously a sympathizer (in traditional fashion) with youth's preoccupations and fresher talents and an acrimonious opponent of their pretensions, Thenot makes his debut as an intemperate advocate of stoic composure, a purveyor of the very decline narrative he aggressively contests, a circumspect moralist who retails only derivative, tendentious allegories and stock aphorisms: not an easy personality to fathom, much less embrace. The distaste he often inspires may say much about our enduring demands for the elder's normative behavior. His refusal to adhere consistently to custom evokes our dismissal much as it does that of his youthful "Februarie" antagonist, Cuddie.[20]

Yet Thenot merits closer reconsideration precisely for his anomalous conduct, since through him Spenser stakes a boldly novel claim for the elder within pastoral tradition. Despite E. K.'s typically ingenuous denial that "Februarie" is "bent to any secrete or particular purpose" (p. 18), we need to recover a character whose physical "crookednesse"—by which Thenot knows he is fundamentally judged—is offset by the oblique wit he deploys as an ironist and master storyteller, which in turn signals his generic obliquity. The old shepherd boasts a creative, antagonistic vitality in Spenser's design, challenging as he exposes the gerontophobia roiling just beneath the "wisdom" conventions that he sends up and positions himself beyond.

So dramatic seems Thenot's transformation over the course of the Calender's trajectory that Berger questions how we can take the character's "fictional autonomy" seriously.[21] By "Aprill," Thenot has already traded his initial combativeness for a more compassionate stance, evident in his softened reprimand of the lovelorn Colin's withdrawal: "Ys love such pinching payne to them, that prove?" he commiserates to Hobbinol, and concludes that "Great pittie is, he be in such taking" (18, 156). By the penultimate eclogue, whose notoriously misplaced zodiacal reference further points up its symmetrical connection to "Februarie," he has come to adopt the rec-

ognizably benign manner of a conventional pastoral elder. Modeled explicitly on "Marot his song, which he made upon the death of Loys the
frenche Queene" (p. 103), "November" at last presents Thenot as the sponsor of Colin himself. Not only does the old man express sympathy for his
junior's long suffering "through loves misgovernaunce" (4), but we learn of
his own reputation as a former composer of "light virelayes, / And looser
songs of love" (21–22). Rather than attributing his mercurial temper to
authorial inconsistency or, worse yet, the elder's hypocrisy, however, I propose that Thenot can own the intergenerational fellowship he progressively
displays only after he has militantly claimed his ground in "Februarie"'s
radical confrontation. Dispositionally an enemy of neither youth nor love
in themselves, he fiercely disputes social standards that privilege these to
old age's exclusion in terms of a bodily, sensual emphasis deployed against
those designated as beyond their prime, whose "crookednesse and unlustinesse" render them useless save as thralls to the "Lords of the yeare." Thenot takes the stage fully prepared to challenge these conventions, and to
reassert a more genuine authority in the process.

   The elder's plight to which Thenot shows himself so keenly sensitive is
in fact starkly codified in the original text whose "olde name" Spenser expressly appropriates for his "new worke" (p. 8). In a section of *The Kalender
of Shepherdes* that aligns life's stages with the months' progression, we read
that when a man reaches his allotted span of seventy-two years "than had
he lever have a warme fyre than a fayer lady and after this age he gothe
into decrepetus to wax a chylde agayne & can nat welde hymselfe and
than yonge folke be wery of theyr company and without they have moche
gode they be full lytell take hede of god wote, and the more pyte for age
sholde be worshyped in the honoure of the Fader of hevyn and for his sake
chyrysshed."[22] Having long since graduated with his "thrise threttie yeares"
into the scheduled "decrepetus," Thenot presents himself as all too aware
of the impotence and general physical debility assigned him, along with
the bitter indifference this entails. In response, he identifies himself with
an angry God, down to his motto's assertive "Iddio perche è vecchio, / Fa
suoi al suo essempio," which E. K. renders as "God, which is himselfe most
aged . . . maketh those, whom he loveth[,] like to himselfe" (pp. 26 and
28), though cognizant of how such a notion finds little enough credence
amid the drearier wisdom of experience. However much E. K. subscribes
to the belief that "we honour and reverence gray heares for a certein religious regard, which we have of old age" (p. 4), Thenot remains skeptical,
alive to all he has to prove—"the more pittie"—to a social prescriptiveness
all too ready to write him off.[23]

Even before he comes to display his talents as a storyteller, Thenot reveals himself a skilled interpreter of others' postures. His very sensitivity to prevailing constructions of senescence attunes him to the self-absorption informing the call for "pittie" with which the "unhappy Heardmans boye" Cuddie opens the eclogue:

> Ah for pittie, wil rancke Winters rage,
> These bitter blasts never ginne tasswage?
> The kene cold blowes through my beaten hyde,
> All as I were through the body gryde.   (1–4)

Beneath an innocuous complaint against the weather Thenot presciently discerns the youth's irritable impatience with all the "ranke" season's associations. At best, Cuddie's attention to his own "beaten hyde" signals a tactless indifference to the shared sufferings of one whose time of life he dismissively presumes to "accord full nie" with winter ("This chill, that cold, this crooked, that wrye" [26–28]); at worst, it sounds a disingenuous swipe at the aged physique he will soon ridicule more openly. More significantly, Thenot recognizes in Cuddie's outburst an implicit demand for edification—if not a literal edifice or shelter against the elements, then at least words of reassurance and comfort that (as he later professes more blatantly) will "ease" him (245), something he clearly regards as the elder's sole asset in this domain. Unwilling to gratify such expectations, Thenot from his earliest rejoinder instead determines to show the boy what "Winters rage" truly looks like.

As much as it departs from generic convention, we are given to understand that Thenot's reply also marks a critical turning point in the old man's temperament. "Lewdly complainest thou laesie ladde, / Of Winters wracke, for making thee sadde," he heatedly attacks, only to invoke his own stoic demeanor:

> Selfe have I worne out thrise threttie yeares,
> Some in much joy, many in many teares:
> Yet never complained of cold nor heate,
> Of Sommers flame, nor of Winters threat:
> Ne ever was to Fortune foeman,
> But gently tooke, that ungently came.   (9–10, 17–22)

We need to pay close attention to the past tense of the manner he here characterizes. Thenot *has* "gently" accepted the adversities of the way things are said to be, but he evidently will do so no longer. In this confrontation, he foregoes the pacific acquiescence expected of him, which (as his later fable will illustrate) he regards as demeaning, even potentially lethal, for one of his station. His surly answer reveals, not a sorry lack of self-awareness on his part, but a vital impulse toward self-recovery.

Critical disdain for the "bromidic" wisdom that Thenot conspicuously indulges throughout "Februarie" likewise stems from our reluctance to grant that the elder speaker stands fully aware of the discrepancies deliberately inflecting his sententiousness.[24] His endurance beyond whatever "bent" his body has come to register demonstrably ironizes his tireless rehearsal of the decline narrative that passes for fact in the world he inhabits. "Must not the world wend in his commun course," he asks, "From good to badd, and from badde to worse, / From worse unto that is worst of all?" (12–14); but the question he matches to Cuddie's initial inquiry about the prolongation of winter's "bitter blastes" proves less rhetorical than it at first appears. His "Satyricall bitternesse" (something by which E. K. distinguishes the "Moral" eclogues [p. 11]) against this very presumptuousness quickly breaks through: no sooner does he sardonically cater to such aphoristic sentiments than he challenges their efficacy with reference to his own violation of the pattern. At age ninety, Thenot voices the seasoned heartiness that leaves him disinclined to bemoan his "beaten hyde" in the manner of his younger counterpart. Boldly asserting a capacity to wear out the very temporal passage scheduled to wear *us* out—"Selfe have I worne out thrise threttie yeares"—he simultaneously grasps how Cuddie's hostility to winter betrays a corresponding disgust for life's later stages and strikes preemptively at this.

Thenot summons traditional attributions of lassitude and debility to old age with a muscular relentlessness that subtly discloses his outrage at the attitudes he mocks. His subsequent caricature of "breme winter," which E. K. emphasizes "may bee indifferently taken, eyther for old Age, or for Winter season" (p. 27), only serves to parody the blatantly pejorative analogies that his attack had elicited from Cuddie. To those whose myopic "surquedrie" or pride curtails a more broadly encompassing and continuous conception of the life course, such a fiction becomes self-fulfilling, as senescence promises nothing more than a predetermined reduction to the "chamfred browes" of a season "Full of wrinckles and frostie furrowes: / Drerily shooting his stormy darte, / Which cruddles the blood, and pricks the harte" (43–46). In turn, the "Youngth" Thenot takes to task as

> a bubble blown up with breath,
> Whose witt is weakenesse, whose wage is death,
> Whose way is wildernesse, whose ynne Penaunce,
> And stoopegallaunt Age the hoste of Greevaunce,   (87–90)

in the "verye moral and pitthy Allegorie" that E. K. admires, frames less a specific time of life than a perspective that pervasively erects and condemns itself to a "stoopegallaunt Age" it then refuses to honor (90). It is this limited disposition more than anything else that the elder pillories in the "laesie" temper he affiliates with Cuddie's detestation of winter.

From his own "stoopegallaunt" perspective, Thenot not only regards the feared old age of convention as one that harbors the grievances of mis-spent youth but reflects ironically on how the maligned elder is expected to play "hoste" or patron to youth's self-indulgent complaints. The peculiar term "stoopegallaunt" obviously conjures the physical "crookednesse"— suited in the standard formulation of E. K.'s "argument" to this "droup-ing" time of year when "in our bodies there is a dry and withering cold, which congealeth the crudled blood, and frieseth the wetherbeaten flesh, with stormes of Fortune, and hoare frosts of Care" (p. 19)—that Cuddie most viciously targets. If Thenot intends his provocatively confrontational stance to expose the actual disgust for the aged body lying just beneath pastoral convention's respectful veneer, he quickly realizes his design. Cud-die is readily goaded into the (none too consistent) allegations that the old man's decrepitude renders him at once ideally acclimated to winter's sever-ity and absurdly infirm before its "wrathfull cheare." "Ah foolish old man, I scorne thy skill," he taunts,

> I deeme, thy braine emperished bee
> Through rusty elde, that hath rotted thee:
> Or sicker thy head veray tottie is,
> So on thy corbe [crooked] shoulder it leanes amisse.   (51, 53–56)

Failing to meet with the consolations expected from his generic counter-part, the young man reflexively dispenses with protocol, impugning the elder's physical and counseling utility alike. Since he has seen through Cuddie's sensualist character from the outset, Thenot can hardly feel sur-prised at the more specific attack on aged impotence (in this month of Saint Valentine) that predictably ensues. The elder's charge of "lewdness" is readily met with a countercharge of "unlustinesse." Cuddie baits Thenot as one ripe for rejuvenation at the hands of his own mistress, Phyllis ("Such an one would make thee younge againe" [68]), and, unlike the virile bull-ock into which one of his formerly "ragged rontes" has conveniently trans-formed, a sorry avatar for the "lustlesse" flock he oversees:

> Thy flocks father his corage hath lost:
> Thy Ewes, that wont to have blowen bags,
> Like wailefull widdowes hangen their crags:

> The rather Lambes bene starved with cold,
> All for their Maister is lustlesse and old.   (80–84)

For Cuddie, Thenot's presence profanes the season in a fashion more unpleasant than the foul weather of which he had originally complained.

Thenot rebuffs Cuddie's indictment of his aged "unlustinesse" with an insistence that "All that is lent to love, wyll be lost" (70), which in context smacks less of a general, embittered antieroticism than a specific countermanding of his companion's inflated claims for love's power. As the *Calender's* audience has already seen in "Januarye," and as Thenot himself will lament in "Aprill," erotic infatuation is as likely to accelerate the aging process as it is to make one "younge againe." Yet both this terse riposte and the subsequent "pithy" caricature of youth as a "bubble" only set the stage for the extended "Icon or Hypotyposis of disdainfull younkers" (p. 27) that follows. The old man's expert capacity to discern and ironically play to his audience's expectations finds its best illustration in his strategic transition of lines 91–93, where he abruptly adopts the very accommodating manner he has so violently resisted up to this point. "But shall I tel thee a tale of truth," he gently offers, "Which I cond of *Tityrus* in my youth, / Keeping his sheepe on the hils of Kent?" an invitation that quickly pacifies Cuddie, eagerly disposed (his own mind now "bent," as he puts it) to "heare novells of his devise: / They bene so well thewed, and so wise, / What ever that good old man bespake" (94–97). The invocation of this figure from Thenot's own past is especially deft, since as we discover in the *Calender's* "June" eclogue, Tityrus enjoyed a supreme reputation in life as one who would "tell us mery tales, to keepe us wake, / The while our sheepe about us safely fedde" (87–88). Despite the back-handed jibe at Thenot's wasted physique that Cuddie possibly indulges in his praise for Tityrus's "well thewed" tales (suggesting not only "full of morall wisenesse," as E. K. insists [p. 27], but also sinewy or muscular), the youth clearly welcomes the conventional graciousness he associates with "*that* good old man" as a relief from Thenot's hostile—and, therefore, oddly "novell"—posture.

The narrative of the Oak and Briar will of course prove anything but the diverting tale of "youth," "love," or "chevalrie" that Thenot tantalizingly attributes to Tityrus (98–99), even though the vigor with which he delivers it, "so lively and so feelingly, as if the thing were set forth in some Picture before our eyes, more plainly could not appeare" (p. 19), openly belies the old speaker's "crookednesse and unlustinesse" in E. K.'s view. Instead, the fiction Thenot envisions for his young companion reveals his own revisionary disposition, as he drastically reorients the received fable to suit his discrete perspective. E. K.'s confusion over the story's provenance

is well placed: unable to locate a source in Chaucer (with whom he identifies Tityrus), he notes how "it is cleane in another kind, and rather like to
Æsopes fables" (p. 27); as readers have long recognized, however, Thenot's
allegory squares with none of his models.[25] More consequentially still, in
every prior instance—from the classical versions of Aesop, Plutarch, and
Avianus down to the contemporary retelling we find in Nicholas Breton's
Workes of a Yong Wyt (1577)—it is the tree that stands "full puffed up with
pride" and lords its supremacy over the lowly reed up to the time of its
tragic reversal of fortune.[26] Under Thenot's direction, the story's substance
and moral undergo a dramatic inversion, as the Oak must now suffer the
indignities of the "foolish Brere" who "cast him to scold, / And snebbe the
good Oake, for he was old" (125–26). Parrying Cuddie's youthful arrogance
by arrogating a narrative that itself becomes a study in appropriation, the
old man shifts focus away from pastoral's youthful orientation and challenges the cultural bias that sustains this disposition.

Just as he had earlier parodied decline narratives, Thenot in his fable
fictionalizes their effect in a myth of age's displacement. The Oak's plight
artfully mirrors and translates Cuddie's allegations from the eclogue's
opening movement. Thenot trains his attention first upon the physical
attrition this tree, formerly "King of the field," has experienced over time.
Although it retains its former dignity, "The bodie bigge, and mightely
pight, / Throughly rooted, and of wonderous hight," decay now compromises the tree's honor:

> But now the gray mosse marred his rine,
> His bared boughes were beaten with stormes,
> His toppe was bald, and wasted with wormes,
> His honor decayed, his braunches sere.   (106–7, 111–14)

So far has this decay demoted him that he must suffer the indignities of the
"foolish Brere" who "cast him to scold, / And snebbe the good Oake, for
he was old" (125–26). The Briar's charges, correspondingly, target the tree's
fruitlessness and incapacity to provide adequate shelter: "Nor for fruict,
nor for shadowe serves thy stocke" (128). While he valorizes and sympa-
thizes with aged seniority, however, the narrator simultaneously indicts
the Oak's tacit participation in its own victimization through its silent
passivity: "Little him answered," we are told, "But yielded, with shame and
greefe adawed, / That of a weede he was overcrawed" (140–42). The tree's
quiescence—markedly in contrast with Thenot's aggressive outspoken-
ness—only facilitates the ambition and anger of his nemesis, to the point
where later feeble attempts to "replie" to the Briar's slanders go unheard

by those in authority unwilling to entertain such self-affirmation at all. In a setting where younger figures actively seek pretexts for the clearing away of what they perceive as deadwood, demanding its shade yet discontented with the kind of shelter it has to offer, a stoic senescence stands little chance of dignified survival.

Thenot's appropriated fable is poignantly flavored by the teller's awareness of how all our cherished myths—like that of "holy eld"—are ironically prone to obsolescence when the time suits, evident in the peculiar tangent his story takes in its penultimate phase. Describing how the Husbandman's axe seemed to glance aside from the trunk, "halfe unwilling to cutte the graine" of this "auncient tree, / Sacred with many a mysteree," the narrator reflects, "But sike fancies weren foolerie, / And broughten this Oake to this miserye / For nought mought they quitten him from decay" (204, 207–8, 211–13). If sarcasm infuses these lines, as some have found, it is directed specifically against the bad faith of the genre's purported respect for its elder constituents, who in the name of convenience are just as readily cut off, in his reading, and left "pitied of none" (221).[27]

Although the elder shepherd regards the voice he struggles to assert as his last best hope against the obliteration that the Oak so ignobly suffers, he clearly comprehends that it cannot ensure his ability to maintain control on his own terms. Like Colin before and after him, Thenot fails to reach his target audience who, taking a closing opportunity to dissociate value from duration in his slur "Here is a long tale, and little worth" (240), points out how the story has failed in what he sees as its main function: "little ease of thy lewd tale I tasted" (245), he proclaims, before dismissively packing the old man off to his own shelter: "Hye thee home shepheard, the day is nigh wasted" (246). His premature reflex to "conningly cutte of[f]" the speaker comically fulfills Thenot's very point, of course; but Cuddie's refusal to "hearken the end" as Thenot had directed (101) also fittingly curtails the narrative's fuller implications. Beyond the overt moral that "younkers" should not disdain or patronize their elders, Thenot's fable crafts a subtle etiological myth explaining why young people so virulently detest the cold: after the Oak's fall, the Briar, nipped by the "byting frost" (231), ends where Cuddie had picked up at the eclogue's start. The old man's tale cleverly circles back around on its listener to trace the misery that the junior shepherd had selfishly bemoaned to a mythic exposure grounding the seasonal myopia of youth, unable to see or imagine beyond its "flowering" present.

Even more feelingly, however, the fable of the Oak and Briar intimates a subtle but surprisingly essential camaraderie between life's early and late stages. Ostensibly placed in dramatic opposition, the youth and senescence configured in Thenot's allegory both suffer indifferently at the hands of a common enemy, the Husbandman. For all its conceited hostility, the Briar can threaten the Oak with no actual harm beyond noisy disrespect, any more than Cuddie can injure Thenot. To do this, it must enlist the support of those in their Aristotelian prime—representatives (in the elder narrator's calculation) of a violent manhood that cares no more for the decorative underbrush whose "piteous plea" he zealously takes up only to leave it "trodde in the durt" afterwards (157, 235), than for the blasted, aged trees encumbering his estates. From the temporally central position he occupies, the Husbandman "cuts off" the Oak's self-defensive appeal long before he more literally cuts down the tree—"Anger nould let him speake to the tree," we are told, "Enaunter his rage mought cooled bee" (199–200)—only to subsequently ignore the young "Vassall" Briar, whose cause he had defended, upon the Oak's "disconsolate" fall. In other words, beneath the acrimony of Thenot's rage lies an awareness of a need for intergenerational empathy. While all this remains lost on Cuddie, who ironically concludes his own motto with the charge that Thenot himself lacks respect for divine seniority—"Niuno vecchio, / Spaventa Iddio," or "men of yeares have no feare of god at al" (p. 28)—the reader can see that whatever truth inheres in the parting insult is owing to the old man's awareness that he has substantially more to fear from fellow mortals far too eager to dismiss those outside their immediate preoccupations as self-styled "Lords of the yeare."

From the later vantage point of "November," we recognize the *Calender*'s Thenot as a figure traversing generational boundaries. Failing to elicit a love story from Colin, who (consistent with the melancholy disposition he owns from the outset) associates such matter with "youngth and sommer dayes" (20), Thenot commissions the beautiful "Melpomene" dirge for Dido, "The fayrest May . . . that ever went" (39). Her demise in the springtime of life, mourned by the prematurely aged poet, upon the encouragement of an elder who longs for "jovisaunce" or mirth, captures Spenser's sustained ambition to unsettle facile paradigms of the life course. As the year turns round to approach the start of a new cycle, Thenot defers to Colin with an allusion to his own earlier fable:

> Nay, better learne of hem, that learned bee,
> And han be watered at the Muses well:
> The kindlye dewe drops from the higher tree,
> And wets the little plants that lowly dwell.   (29–32)

Spenser's well-honed empathetic regard for his received pastoral heritage grants him the precocious circumspection to see his way free of the novice ambitions that can too easily lapse into self-caricature. He looks to the past not by way of an intimidating influence he must compete with or surmount, because he knows tradition—like his character Thenot—edifies only on his own terms, never aiming merely to accommodate. Fiercely jealous of his independence, the elder shepherd (as the "November" dusk suggests) stands capable of nurturing, though is never beholden to, the talents of succeeding generations.

Spenser's very reverence for the antique tradition he inherited paradoxically compels him to break ranks with his predecessors in *The Shepheardes Calender*'s sympathetic portrayal of an old age that grounds its dignity in a fiercely ironic, confrontational sense of self. That work's dedicatee, Sir Philip Sidney, on the other hand, knew a far more conflicted relationship with seniority, especially as the embodiment of forces that alternately spurred and frustrated the precocious ambitions shaping his abbreviated career. The conspicuous brilliance and charisma with which Sidney even as a young man dazzled the statesmen he encountered on his travels abroad appears to have ignited the apprehension of his queen, whom he regarded as elderly even in her forties, and the factionalism of court politics often put him at odds with her regime generally.[28] While the passionate sponsorship of Hubert Languet—thirty-six years his senior—from the time of their first meeting in 1572 afforded Sidney an endearing model of the genteel, nurturing elder, the French humanist's high expectations for the young protégé, so relentlessly asserted in their extended correspondence, only added to the exasperating pressure with which he persistently had to contend. As Katherine Duncan-Jones observes, Sidney "was at the receiving end of an exceptional amount of counsel and guidance from older men all eager to play the Polonius rôle. This abundance of advice may in turn have contributed to a build-up of rage and frustration in a child who was unusually passionate and sensitive."[29] Languet himself saw fit to caution Sidney against a too stringent opposition to authority, since "Old men generally make an unfair estimate of the character of the young, because they think it a disgrace to be outdone by them in counsel."[30]

This divided sensibility of course left its stamp on Sidney's own pastoral. Whatever direct influence Spenser's *Calender* exerted upon his *Arcadia*—professedly the product of a "young head not so well stayed as I would it were," and not intended "for severer eyes"—Sidney interestingly foregrounds senescence as a central critical concern in his narrative.[31] While the *Arcadia* in both its original and revised forms offers a Mantuanesque, blanket indictment of human folly across generations and classes, its comic

though ultimately sobering fiction presents a substantially darker image of
late life than had his Italian predecessor. The plotline is largely determined
by the aged infatuation of Duke Basilius, whose sexual self-indulgence en-
dangers his realm, his family, and (almost) his own life. Moreover, at one
key turn Sidney's own persona in the work, Philisides, offers a scathing
attack on elderly pretension from the perspective of righteous, indignant
youth. Yet the author also complicates both of these figures, betraying a
deeply inquisitive fascination with the old ruler's conduct and nervous res-
ervations about the "over bitter" claims that his own spokesperson dares to
advance. Most notably, Sidney concentrates his exploration of the pastoral
elder's plight in the suitably named shepherd Geron, whose status as caricature or emblem of old age opens unexpectedly into a fuller, multivalent,
and finally more sympathetic portrayal.

From the very start of the original version, now commonly referred to
as the *Old Arcadia,* Basilius steps forward—at first subtly, and soon more
overtly—as an embodiment of executive mediocrity and aged willfulness.
(Though his precise age is never specified here, the revised *New Arcadia*
places him close to eighty.)[32] It is his failure to "act his age" sexually, however, that most pronouncedly elicits the barely suppressed ridicule of Sidney's
narrator. Withdrawing to the pastoral countryside in the hope of thwarting an oracle that predicts he will within the year lose both his daughters
and his throne, the old duke succumbs to an erotic infatuation with the
Amazon princess Cleophila—in fact the cross-dressed foreign prince Pyrocles, who with his kinsman Musidorus has assumed a disguise in order
to gain access to Basilius's confined daughters: "so had this young siren
charmed his old ears," as we are told (*OA,* 36). Before long, "the poor old
Basilius," suffering "a sufficient eclogue in his own head betwixt honour,
with the long experience he had had of the world, on the one side, and
this new assault of Cleophila's beauty on the other side," surrenders to "the
longing desire to enjoy Cleophila, which finding an old broken vessel of
him, had the more power in him than, perchance, it would have had in a
younger man. And so, as all vice is foolish, it wrought in him the more absurd follies" (*OA,* 45). While he ultimately conducts himself no worse than
the equally obsessive younger characters, his self-indulgence nonetheless
looses a chain of events that will flirt with disaster for all, and so he stands
more culpable and deserving of contempt.

I have elsewhere argued for the pressing political anxieties that moti-
vated Basilius's sexual designs. Far from merely a besotted old man in the
throes of senile prurience, the sonless duke fears the transfer of authority to
younger, foreign forces that his daughters' marriageability now threatens;

his sudden lust for an Amazon princess marks an attempted reassertion of virility whereby he might secure a coveted male heir to maintain his dynasty.[33] While such psychic drives or political ambitions never exonerate him for the author, Sidney evidently aimed at something more than an opportunity to lampoon elderly misbehavior. A certain admiration for the animus that Basilius displays beyond the decorous restraint expected of his time of life tints the characterization. If the duke begins as a more elementary illustration of love's "unresistible force" (*OA*, 49), Sidney doesn't begrudge his creation an impressive physical, sexual vigor.

Evident throughout his courtship of Cleophila, the revitalization that Basilius undergoes is neatly spotlighted early in the second book. Beset at first by the courtly lover's typical malaise and "greatly despairing for his own unworthiness's sake" (*OA*, 54)—his doubts exacerbated by a shamed awareness of the senescence to which he is subject—the duke soon discovers himself "complaining likewise of love very freshly, . . . love having renewed both his invention and voice" (*OA*, 95). In evidence, the narrator records the sonnet he crafts in defense of age in love:

> Let not old age disgrace my high desire,
>   O heav'nly soul in human shape contained,
> Old wood inflamed doth yield the bravest fire,
>   When younger doth in smoke his virtue spend.
> Ne let white hairs (which on my face do grow)
>   Seem to your eyes of a disgraceful hue;
> Since whiteness doth present the sweetest show,
>   Which makes all eyes do honour unto you.
> Old age is wise and full of constant truth;
>   Old age well stayed from ranging humour lives;
> Old age hath known whatever was in youth;
>   Old age o'ercome, the greater honour gives.
>   And to old age since you yourself aspire,
>   Let not old age disgrace my high desire.   (*OA*, 95)

Instinctually anticipating the "disgrace" to which aged sexuality opens itself, Basilius marshals arguments that prove either logically spurious (because lovers find her milky complexion attractive, she should find his white beard so) or contextually dubious (his infatuation for her instantiates the very "ranging humour" that contradicts the constancy he professes). As is usually the case with seduction lyrics, however, the sonnet's virtue lies not in the efficacy of its rationale but in its fertility of wit; and as the narrator himself begrudgingly admits, the poem exemplifies how love has resuscitated Basilius's creative spirit. What reinforces and elevates the lines' otherwise slippery assertions into a worthy poetic performance is the strategic subtlety that the speaker markedly brings to bear. The second line's apostrophe to the mistress's "heav'nly soul in human shape contained" gracefully recalls her own physicality to her, preparing the way for the second-last line's symmetrical reminder that old age is something she herself hopes to reach. Moreover, the rich ambiguity of line 12 demonstrates the very ingenuity to which the elder lover's seasoned passion lays claim: if his addressee disregards senescence as a reproachful condition, she must grant him "greater honour" for having (through love's agency) "o'ercome" its reputed impotence; if she respects old age as a time of sage self-restraint, then she should be more flattered that her power to "o'ercome" age's natural defenses lends *her* the "greater honour."

The narrator invites us to dismiss the sonnet as an instance of the "pretty kind of dotage" to which Basilius had declined, yet he also observes how "thus did the duke, feeding his mind with these thoughts, pass great time in writing of verses, and making more of himself than he was wont to do" (*OA*, 97). Upon completing the rehearsal of his poem, the old man had "looked very curiously upon himself, sometimes fetching a little skip, as if he had said his strength had not yet forsaken him" (*OA*, 95). However ludicrous such impulses, they mark the reawakening of a "curious" self-regard that cannot altogether be laughed away. No sooner has Basilius "combed and tricked himself more curiously than any time forty winters before," than we witness how amid the second book's insurrection he, "having put on an armour long before untried, came to prove his authority among his subjects, or at least to adventure his life with his dear mistress" (*OA*, 113–14, 124). And even though Cleophila's initial rebuke of his advances so devastates the aged suitor "that his legs bowed under him, his eyes waxed staring dead, and (his old blood going to his heart) a general shaking all over his body possessed him" (*OA*, 115), his robust "manner of dealing" (in Sidney's comic circumlocution) when in the darkness he embraces his wife Gynecia, thinking her to be Cleophila, betrays one "fuller of livelier fancies than many years before he had been" (*OA*, 227). Without the aid of the aphrodisiac Gynecia brings to what she thought would be her own tryst with Pyrocles, Basilius proves himself capable of a "long disaccustomed" sexual consummation that—despite his humiliated wife's reprimands that his "grey hairs have been but the visor of a far unfitting youthfulness" and how "very untimely are these fires in you"—stirs him to begin "something to mark himself in his own doings" rather than surrendering blandly to the socially imposed strictures of age (*OA*, 276–77, 278).

The *Arcadia*'s author, in brief, appears both repelled by and somewhat in awe of the erotic vigor that Basilius continues to display. In his revision, Sidney compounds his account of the duke's potency, with Crecopia's above-mentioned recollection of the sixty-year-old ruler's marriage to Gynecia that produced the princesses whose marriage and succession he now, at nearly eighty, seeks to forestall. The mixture of disdain and wonder recalls a moment in Theocritus's Idyll 4, where the young shepherds Corydon and Battus allude to the sexual antics of an unnamed elder:

> *Battus*
> Tell me now, Corydon, is the old fellow still screwing that black-browed
> Sweetheart of his, the same beauty who formerly tickled his fancy?
>
> *Corydon*
> Up to the hilt, you poor silly. I happened upon him myself just
> The other day by the barn and surprised him while he was hard at it.
>
> *Battus*
> Splendid, the randy old lecher! His kind, you might say, are in constant
> Close competition with bandy-legged fauns and insatiable satyrs.[34]

As Judith Haber aptly remarks of this passage, "the old man is seen as capable of 'rivaling'—and perhaps ultimately displacing—figures from legends and myths; he is a hero of bestiality, to be sure, but he is a hero all the same."[35] In like manner, Sidney's Basilius finds himself "o'ercome" by passion, though his very lust signals the conquest of senescence's reputed exhaustion and desiccation.

The exasperation with senescence that inflects Sidney's portrayal of Basilius throughout finds a more concentrated articulation in the melancholic youth Philisides. His exchange with the elder shepherd Geron in the First Eclogues, loosely modeled on Sannazaro's Eclogue 8, translates the original's genteel harmonies into a dialogue spiked by the young man's sustained expression of gerontophobic rage. When Geron attempts to recall Philisides from the unrequited love that enervates him, resorting ultimately to misogynistic reflections on women's unworthiness of such obsessive and self-destructive affection in the style of Ovidian *remedia amoris,* the youth's barely suppressed impatience with his counsels gives way, not to an indignant defense of femininity, but to a withering assault against the "well authorized lie" of aged virtue (*OA,* 74). Old age's best quality, so far as Philisides is concerned, is its proximity to death, which will silence the tedious prattle to which time has attenuated the subject (if the boredom suffered by the audience doesn't prove fatal beforehand):

O gods, how long this old fool hath annoyed
My wearied ears! O gods, yet grant me this,
That soon the world of his false tongue be void.
O noble age who place their only bliss
In being heard until the hearer die,
Utt'ring a serpent's mind with a serpent's hiss!

He indicts the physical repulsiveness of senescence no less than the "false-hood" of its advisory pretensions, demeaning Geron as "This live-dead man in this old dungeon flung." Elderly obsolescence excites the thinly veiled violence of his observations that "Old houses are thrown down for new we see; / The oldest rams are culled from the flock," and (in a line that possibly glances back to the *Calender*'s "Februarie") "The ancient oak well makes a fired block." Age can offer nothing worthwhile that is not mined from youth itself: "And herein most their folly vain appears, / That since they still allege, *When they were young,* / It shows they fetch their wit from youthful years." Conversely, youth's folly manifests itself chiefly in the toleration and respect it bestows on the undeserving elders: "Old men themselves do love young wives to choose; / Only fond youth admires a rotten stock." Respectable seniority becomes a function of inward maturity in Philisides' calculation rather than a matter of years. "O when will men leave off to judge by [gray] hair," he asks rhetorically, "And think them old that have the oldest mind?"

Having reduced Geron to a mere "tongue," which he then refuses to attend—"Hath any man heard what this old man said?," he disdainfully concludes (*OA,* 75)—Philisides comes in this single verse passage to exemplify youth's resentful irritability. So stringent is his attack that we must call into serious question the contention of Neil Rudenstine (who himself notes the ad hominem character of this "extraordinarily naïve and youthfully impetuous" figure's arguments) that Philisides "is clearly the hero of the piece."[36] In the wake of his tirade, the young shepherd Histor offers a wry critique:

Thus may you see how youth esteemeth age,
And never hath thereof arightly deemed,
While hot desires do reign in fancy's rage,
Till age itself do make itself esteemed.   (*OA,* 76)

Histor's own fair-mindedness, of course, belies the universality of intergenerational enmity; and by the Third Eclogues, even Philisides' furor against old age has significantly abated. There, in one of the romance's most transparently autobiographical references, Philisides prefaces the political "Ister bank" fable with an homage to the "old Languet" who taught it to him. Possibly aiming to ameliorate the vehemence of his earlier attack on Geron, Philisides recalls how Languet had (in conventional fashion) helped him overcome his youthful limitations: "With his sweet skill my skill-less youth he drew," he fondly recollects, confessing how "He liked me, but pitied lustful youth. / His good strong staff my slipp'ry years upbore" (*OA*, 255). The affirmation does not so much contradict his earlier response as it completes it. Just as the initial invective had in its mean-spirited vehemence gone far to render sympathetic the very senescence it had aimed to ridicule and demote, the more tempered, subsequent acknowledgments of a reliance on elder guidance reinforce our sense of the limitations suffered by youth rather than age. Once more, Sidney mounts his most intensive interrogation of aged ineffectuality only to discover the hollowness of such presumption.

Although undeniably focal characters, Basilius and Philisides are, strictly speaking, interlopers in the pastoral landscape, amid but not of the shepherds' company they keep. For Sidney's key portrait of the indigenous pastoral *senex* we must turn to Geron, the figure whose very name identifies him as the *Arcadia*'s chief representative of old age. For Haber, the eclogues he inhabits stand "quite literally out of time," and "the 'real' shepherds who participate in them exist only in the 'golden world' of pure art"; as such, Geron might be seen to offer little more than a "simplified" reflection of the narrator's larger pressing concerns.[37] Far from an abstraction, however, Geron contends with the adversity that afflicts the elder in his all-too-hostile world in an integral and complex manner. The contrarian attitude he adopts tentatively rescues him from lapsing into the assigned conventional role (in the manner of Spenser's Thenot), though at the cost of the narrator's gerontophobic caricature. We first encounter him as a "grave" enemy of Cupid, "thereto the more inclined, as that age, having taken from him both the thoughts and fruits of that passion, wished all the world proportioned to himself" (*OA*, 64), and outspoken in his discontentment that "age should become an auditor" to youth (*OA*, 71). Yet his anxieties over displacement, resentment of ingratitude, and the lingering indignation he displays, no less than his striking capacity for self-reflection and reform, signal a peculiarly dynamic "lustiness" which is (once more) openly admired, even through the veil of glib mockery he endures.

Like Thenot, Geron has also suffered ample recrimination at the hands of modern critics eager to empathize with Philisides. Whereas Rudenstine expresses distaste for the old man's "self-congratulatory rigidity," Richard

McCoy finds what he calls Geron's "bullying" to compromise the elder's "moral authority," and reduces his efforts at counsel to "pompous banalities" by which Philisides is "pestered" in "stereotypical" fashion.[38] For Robert Stillman, "Geron is more than an angry man, he is a speaking picture of anger."[39] Such adverse commentary tends to overlook the fact that the elder's chief transgression is his failure to acquiesce when, despite his sincere attempt to lift the melancholic youth's spirits, he is put in his place by the surly addressee. The narrator recounts how Geron "strake him [Philisides] upon the shoulder with a right old man's grace that will seem livelier than his age will afford him," a gesture that sounds more benignly ingratiating than imperious or condescending (*OA,* 71–72). If anything, he shows exemplary restraint when the youth brushes aside his approach with "Who ever taught a skill-less man to teach?" and sarcastically anticipates "Time shall in one my life and sorrows end, / And me perchance your constant temper lend" (*OA,* 72). Even when Philisides insults him in the more aggressive vituperation cited above, Geron's harshest retort is that "fondlings fond know not your own desire, / Loath to die young, and then you must be old, / Fondly blame that to which yourselves aspire"; as he generously goes on to assert, "Thy words, though full of malapert offence, / I weigh them not, but still will thee advise" (*OA,* 75).

However much Geron genuinely seeks to undermine youth's idolization of eros and resorts to commonplace arguments to promote his point, his convictions never betray malice or presumption. Even the antifeminism to which he resorts emerges as contextual hyperbole rather than doctrine for him, as we discover in his later admonitions to Histor against celibacy: "God forbid women such cattle were / As you paint them," he cautions the disappointed young companion, "Who only sees the ill is worse than blind. / These fifty winters married I have been; / And yet find no such faults in womankind" (*OA,* 262). The firm yet gentle guidance he offers, either against cupidinous love's soul-deadening depressions or on behalf of marriage's companionate felicities, features little of the "shrillness" with which he is too often unfairly branded.

More significantly, Geron shows himself uncomfortable with the polarization that generational conflict entails. Left "out of countenance" by Philisides' harsh rebuke, and "ashamed to see his grey hairs despised," the elder shepherd repairs to the company of an "old acquaintance of his called Mastix" (*OA,* 76) to nurse his public wounds. Beholding his dogs "jarl" on the way, he takes the opportunity to moralize on their strife as a kind of animated beast emblem of the generational contention he has just tasted and reprimands both the older and the younger animals for harassing one another. When he laments to his friend, "Thou heardst e'en now a young man sneb me sore / Because I red him as I would my son," he reluctantly concludes, "Youth will have will, age must to age therefore" (*OA,* 77). The reply offered by Mastix—characterized as "one of the repiningest fellows in the world, and that beheld nobody but with a mind of mislike" (*OA,* 76)—nonetheless seems to take his companion off guard in its cynical dismissiveness of old and young alike. Mastix's notion that one should feel little wonder at the churlishness of youth, since "our saddest shepherds" never seem to outgrow a mean, unimaginative obsequiousness, and the bad example they provide merely feeds into the vicious cycle (*OA,* 77), only further alienates Geron. "Fie, man, fie, man; what words hath thy tongue lent," he breaks in, "Yet thou art mickle warse than ere was I, / Thy too much zeal I fear thy brain hath spent" (*OA,* 78). Shocked by the fervor of Mastix's aged misanthropy despite his own bruised ego, Geron is quick to divorce himself from such a perspective. "I pray thee what hath e'er the parrot got?" he asks,

> A cage (gilded perchance) is all his lot.
> Who off his tongue the liquor gladly pours
> A good fool called with pain perhaps may be,
> But e'ev for that shall suffer mighty lours.

Upon examination, the somewhat cryptic analogies suggest that what he finds most offensive in Mastix's jeremiad is not the larger indictment of shortsighted stupidity to which all can be prone (since he agrees by the close that our own errors compromise our right to judge others) but the insidious defeatism of aged self-contempt undergirding his cynicism, which feeds gerontophobic prejudice against the embitterment that age "naturally" brings. Like the metaphorical parrots and fools that Geron invokes, Mastix's outlook can only win further condemnation from the "great" youth to whom it panders. The point of Geron's allegory of the swan (who is deprived of its voice because of its tendency to find fault with all other birds) is the elder's constant need to resist the misanthropy to which the victimization that old age can suffer might lead, and the crude self-righteousness often accompanying this.

In short, Geron both defends the just indignation he feels before others' (particularly youth's) bigotry and maintains independence from ghettoization—"age must to age therefore"—while keeping himself in check with an announced understanding of his own limitations. He thereby arrives

at a remarkably comprehensive kind of circumspection that more firmly
substantiates the wisdom he had looked to impart, only to win "so little
reputation" at the hands of youth (*OA*, 76). Seeking without success to
edify a younger generation, he emerges with an even clearer understanding
of himself.

Geron's closing reflection not only articulates the self-critical awareness
he has attained but puts this into practice with his final exoneration of
Mastix:

> Let our unpartial eyes a little watch
> Our own demean, and soon we wonder shall
> That, hunting faults, ourselves we did not catch.
> Into our minds let us a little fall,
> And we shall find more spots than leopard's skin.
> Then who makes us such judges over all?   (*OA*, 79)

His gesture represents the only instance of genuine growth and self-discovery not compelled by severe external trauma or constraint in the entire narrative, among any age group. The achievement will not secure him
the company's full respect; he "straight" takes his leave, we are told, "as if
he would be sure to have the last word, all the assembly laughing at the
lustiness of the old fellow, who departed muttering to himself he had seen
more in his days than twenty of them" (79).

Geron is nonetheless able to face their laughter with a greater, more defiant composure as he leaves the stage a vindicated, regenerated figure. If his
responses do little more than afford the listeners, many of whom will go
on to fall victim to their own ridiculous impulses and "lustiness," with an
occasion for amusement at his expense, his dignity clearly no longer relies
upon their approval. He certainly will not forego his critical judgments, as
is evident in the "revenge" he later takes on Philisides, whom the narrator
acknowledges "had taken him up over-bitterly" in the earlier eclogues. He
there faults the youth's "Ister bank" fable for bringing in "a tale of he knew
not what beasts at such a banquet when rather some song of love, or matter for joyful melody, was to be brought forth," with the added barb that
"this is the right conceit of young men who think then they speak wiseli-
est when they cannot understand themselves" (*OA*, 259–60)—a critique
reasonable enough in context. In this regard, he stands, not in opposition
to the "old Languet" of Philisides' prelude, but in league with that elder's
dedication to a "jump concord between our wit and will" (*OA*, 255). His
subsequent advice to Histor, noted earlier, casts him clearly in the role of
one who skillfully draws "skill-less youth." It is no accident that "good old

Geron (who as he had longest tasted the benefits of Basilius's government so seemed to have a special feeling of the present loss)" opens the lamentations of the old duke's presumed death in the Forth Eclogues (*OA*, 327). He leaves an indelible mark on the romance, a powerful counter-image to the courtly folly enacted by the principals, young and old: an aged figure capable of learning and reforming himself by maintaining a responsible perspective on his own stage of life amid the storm of disrespect and misunderstanding he confronts as a matter of course.

The uniqueness of Geron's self-discovery obtains into the radical revision Sidney undertook in the years following the original draft's completion. The extensive editorial mediation involved in the fragmentary later version's transmission and publication in 1590 and 1593 prevents us from authoritatively knowing Sidney's final design: a portion of Geron's dialogue (along with much of the *Old Arcadia*'s eclogic material) is displaced from the first printed text, only to rejoin the narrative under Mary Sidney's direction in the "hybrid" 1593 issue.[40] Yet one of the new poems that joins the first eclogues in this latter edition confirms Sidney's casual recognition of the elder's vitality. The shepherd Lamon's account of a frenetic game of barley-break among the rustic company portrays Geron, "though olde yet gamesome," as an active participant, who shrewdly knows how to outwit his younger, physically stronger opponents:

> *Geron* strave hard, but aged were his feet,
>   And therefore finding force now faint to be,
>   He thought gray haires afforded subtletie.
> And so when *Pas* hand-reached him to take,
> The fox on knees and elbowes tombled downe:
> *Pas* could not stay, but over him did rake,
> And crown'd the earth with his first touching crowne:
> His heels grow'n proud did seme at heav'n to shake.   (254–61)[41]

Likewise, in the far more somber contest of Book 3's battlefield scenes, the author introduces "the old knight Æschylus, who though by years might well have been allowed to use rather the exercise of wisdom than of courage, yet having a lusty body and a merry heart, he ever took the summons of time in jest (or else it had so creepingly stolen upon him that he had heard scarcely the noise of his feet), and therefore was as fresh in apparel and as forward in enterprises as a far younger man" (*NA*, 341). While neither old man attains victory in his respective undertaking, both demonstrate a capability and willingness to compete that discredits whatever prejudices their youthful cohorts bring to the field.

Many of these older characters who proliferate in the revision will either steer closer to conventional pastoral characterization of the benign elder (such as Kalendar) or compound the portrayal of aged folly.[42] The most influential of these, the Paphlagonian king episode that provides the Gloucester subplot for Shakespeare's *King Lear* (to which I return in Chapter 5), revisits the subject chiefly to showcase the fidelity of virtuous youth. Despite this, and however Sidney's fictional rendition of old age may ultimately have taken shape, his enduring preoccupation with this peculiar topic remains conspicuously pronounced. The *Arcadia* plots a clear emphasis on the pastoral elder that explores cultural outlooks toward the authority that comes with age and on the capacity of the elder to manage these. However misguided or discerning in its dealings, the old age he envisions will refuse to be placed innocuously "out to pasture" or to surrender its accountable agency in which dignity and shame alone can reside.

The Shepheardes Calender and the *Arcadia* indisputably rank as two of the late Elizabethan era's most influential literary products. The publication history of Spenser's pastoral—which saw five editions by century's end—graphically affirms its enduring popularity throughout the period. Although Sidney's fiction, by contrast, would need to await a belated posthumous release before its full cultural impact could be realized, its manuscript circulation and reproduction during the author's own lifetime, as H. R. Woudhuysen has demonstrated, "was permitted on a generous scale" and therefore might well have proved accessible to a sufficiently privileged or tenacious reader.[43] Individually, each offered a compelling model of how the genre might be revitalized for a modern audience; together, they provided a potent stimulus for young poets to rethink the form's component features. Among these renovations, the dramatic repositioning of the elder that I have delineated in Spenser's and Sidney's performances left a demonstrable impression on their successors: never again could the aged figure so formulaically be relegated to pastoral's margins. As even a brief survey of selected works from the period attests, old age came to occupy a far more consistent and consequential narrative space among English practitioners of the 1590s than had previously been the case.

As we have seen, earlier pastoral tended to typecast and restrict the elder's role: old age must act in support of youth, if at all, or face the consequences. Whatever defensive critiques the senior shepherd may dare to advance must issue from the innocuous privacy of a segregated community to which he has been expected to "repair," in a kind of forced retirement from the withdrawn bucolic realm itself. In Spenser and Sidney, this "incidental" status gives way to an aged demeanor that demands (and realizes) more sustained, closer inspection, as elder characters step forward to claim an unprecedented proportion of poetic attention and development. Gaining more than merely a greater quantitative representation, these figures survey their own age-specific plights from a variety of complex perspectives. So integral and germane had senescence become to pastoral experience in the aftermath of these poets' provocative achievements that by 1603, in the funerary pastoral that closes the era, it seems not at all peculiar for Henry Chettle, in the persona of Spenser's now-aged "Collin," to review the time since "I was yong almost thirtie yeares agoe," and pay tribute to the deceased Eliza by celebrating (in reference to the "Poor Law" legislation of 1597 and 1601) how "there have beene more particular Almes-houses builded for the reliefe of the aged, then in anie sixe Princes Raignes before."[44]

In the dedication to his prose romance *Rosalynde* (1590), Thomas Lodge claims to have undertaken the work five years earlier, during his "voyage to the Ilands of *Terceras* & the *Canaries*."[45] Modern readers have nonetheless detected Sidney's influence on the work, most familiar as the story line that Shakespeare's *As You Like It* translated to the stage toward the decade's close.[46] Lodge himself had reshaped an earlier source text, the fourteenth-century verse romance *Gamelyn,* into a distinctly pastoral narrative in the manner of *Arcadia,* as political upheaval and intrafamilial rivalry displace various parties from court to countryside. From its opening passage forward, the author lingers over matters of old age that transcend the source's general descriptions. We meet Sir John of Bordeaux on the point of dividing his estate among his three sons, having grown aged and (in typical form) preparing for death. "[H]is haires were silver hued," Lodge elaborates, "and the map of age was figured on his forehead: Honour sat in the furrowes of his face, and many yeres were portraied in his wrinckled liniaments, that all men might perceive his glasse was runne, and that Nature of necessity chalenged her due" (1:9–10).

In opposition to this portrait of aged resignation, however, the author develops the elder steward, Adam, into a character who, though subservient to the young master, Rosader, boldly devises a ruse to free him from the unjust oppressions of his older brother, volunteering to take arms with him to "make havocke" among their enemies. "[F]or Adam Spenser," he later declares, "if he die not at your foote, say he is a dastard" (1:51 and 53). In more pacific fashion, Shakespeare's Adam in turn asserts, "Though I look old, yet I am strong and lusty," and begs his master Orlando "Let me go with you, / I'll do the service of a younger man" (2.3.47, 53–54). When he succumbs to weakness from exposure more swiftly than his young companion during their exile in the forest of Arden, Lodge's Adam offers to nourish Rosader literally with his own blood, since "I am olde, and overworne with age, you are young, and are the hope of many honours," spurring the youth to renewed courage (1:56). His own charitable, self-sacrificial courage is recast as a function of his willingness to defy destiny itself, "For there is no greater checke to the pride of fortune, than with a resolute courage to passe over her crosses without care," as he declares (1:55).

On the level of the actual shepherds in the tale—entirely of Lodge's invention—the aged Coridon likewise plays a supporting role that comes to disclose a more active, participatory vigor. When he attempts to draw his young friend Montanus out of his grief for the unreciprocated love of Phoebe, he educes the typical charge that "wythered age" stands "Uncapable of loves impression," although Montanus does grant that "crooked elde hath some experience left," and they maintain a companionate civility toward one another despite their pronounced differences (1:42). At the narrative's close, however, amid the familial reconciliations and lovers' pairing that round things out, the old shepherd significantly appears "in his holiday sute mervailous seemely," which the narrator describes in paragraph-long, minute detail (1:126). By the end, we learn, Coridon has elevated himself to a virtual master of ceremonies: "Thus attired, Coridon bestird himselfe as chiefe stickler in these actions, and had strowed the house with flowers, that it seemed rather some of Floraes choyce bowers, than anie Countrey cottage" (1:127).

In the wake of this, it seems especially fitting that the elder shepherd closes the festivities in a lyric "fit of mirth," a song of consummated love that, in the manner of Geron's later celebration of married bliss or Thenot's famed amorous songs, looks to bless the erotic unions with the grace of one who wanted "nothing that might make him amorous in his olde dayes" (1:135, 126). It is not surprising that Lodge has him and Adam partake of the general promotions awarded by the king at the close. Despite the conventional restrictions imposed by both their class and their age, Coridon and Adam remain agents vital to the story's development in a manner that transcends any mere counselor office. Lodge thereby chose the stricter supporting role of convention and translated it into a stance that further dignified the elder's stamina. The old men of *Rosalynde* act aggressively upon their allegiances as a test of their own substantial mettle rather than as obsequious expressers of devotion.

Lodge revisits the pastoral dialogue of age and youth several years later in his sonnet sequence *Phillis* (1593), whose "Ecloga Prima," interpolated among the shorter poems, sets the elder shepherd Demades once more to counsel the lovelorn youth Damon against his heady infatuation. In support of his encouragement to "cast off these discontented lookes, / For griefe doth waight on life, tho never sought," the old man by this turn even invokes Spenser's emblematic elder hero: "So *Thenot* wrote admire'd for Pipe and bookes" (2:27). The routine standoff obtains here much as it had in *Rosalynde*'s Coridon–Montanus exchange, with the youth objecting to his senior, "You scorne kind love, because you can no more," and embellishing the notion with the thought that "Where chillie age first left love, and first lost hir, / There youth found love, likt love, and love did foster" (2:29). Nevertheless, the argument stops well short of the contentiousness featured in Spenser's and Sidney's models, Damon observing a proper measure of respect for age as a check to more vehement replies: "Did not thine age yeeld warrantise (olde man) / Impatience would inforce me to offend thee" (2:32). It is as if the poet intended to reinforce or reinstate a more gracious respectfulness to atone for the explosive confrontations that marked the new paradigms recently set in place.

Two years later, Lodge published *A Fig for Momus,* drafted in "this my retired age and studie" (3:4)—though the author was not yet forty and survived for another three decades. All but one of the four eclogues dispersed among the satires and verse epistles that fill out the volume deal expressly with elder shepherds. In Eclogue 1, dedicated to Spenser as the "reverend Colin," Lodge appropriates the pastoral convention of youthful invitation and aged deference only to turn it into a celebration of senescence's superior talents. When the youth Ergasto calls upon the old shepherd Damian to sing, only to hear that "moderne and newfangled laies" simply prove how "olde men seeme but sorie singers," the young man persists by championing "what concentfull laies / Our Fathers chaunted in their daies":

> For often have I found this true,
> The sence is olde, the words be newe:
> What ere the yonger boast and brave,
> Their worth, & wit, from eld they have:
> Olde sence by upstarts newlie suted
> In words ill warpt, is not reputed
> The deede of him that formd the stile,
> But his that did the sence compile.   (3:15–16)

Inspired by Ergasto's impassioned defense, "Since thou canst argue so for age," Damian takes up the opportunity to perform the extended *cantus* that ensues, "a wittie lay" that meets with the youth's closing applause.

Adopting a different tack, Eclogue 2 fashions its praise of senescence in political rather than artistic terms. There, Philides solicits "old Eglon" to say why he "hath with-held / Thine honorable age from governing the state" (3:20), tacitly affirming both the eligibility and desirability of the elder to rule. The old man, in turn, justifies his Achillean withdrawal by citing the depressing gerontophobia he has come to suffer since "my youthfull yeares were cancel'd by mine age," prompting him to depart contemptuously from the "publique noyse, and brawles of judgement seate" which misconceive all his actions. He laments how his

> late-purchas'd age, (besides all other paines)
> Is subject to contempts, accus'd of avarice,
> And youth, with selfe conceit, hath so bewitcht his braines,
> As he esteemeth yeares, wits chiefest prejudice.

As before, the elder's protest excites his interlocutor's indignation over the way people "forget the reverence" that "They should in justice, yield to silver-suted haires," prompting him to ask "Is duetie so despis'd. (enjoyn'd by natures lawe) / That youth impugneth age, in mannaging affaires?" (3:21). In this regard, Philides argues, it is youth that has "degenerated." Unlike in the previous eclogue, however, the younger friend's sympathetic encouragement cannot shake the old man's resolution to leave behind the "hope of further fame" that proved the downfall of Cicero himself (no less); for Eglon, "great content is bought" on his own terms, and his aged self-possession proves such that it is Philides who determines to "leave the world" in his company (3:22).

Finally, Lodge's fourth eclogue moves the issue of old age into the realm of military affairs, as Delivorus conjures his elder companion, Felicius, in this time of "clattering armes" to, "Like aged *Nestor* guirt thee in thy steele," since "Thy courage, with thy yeares, thou hast not lost" (3:28). Felicius answers with a reasoned account of how "Eld is ordain'd to counsell, youth to fight," and how the work he does in planning behind the lines if anything exceeds the ardors of the battlefield "more a hundredth folde":

> I live not then obscurely, as I seeme,
> But as the master of the ship performes
> Far more then common yonkers in great stormes,
> So guiding of our states well may I deeme,
> I doe, and merite more, then most esteeme.   (3:28–29)

In contrast to the previous eclogues' interlocutors, Deliverous proves a more recalcitrant figure, refusing to grant the efficacy of claims made by anyone who dares not join in the physical fray, avowing that "Our stratagems now differ from the old," and that any retreat into bookish theory marks little more than cowardice (3:33). This round, Felicius resigns the youth to his own prejudice and "left him setled in his thought" (3:34). Enthusiastically affirming age's undiminished martial potential, youth still fails to grasp the additional, possibly superior, capabilities that advanced years alone afford. In context, the exchange serves to flesh out the attitude that had so exasperated Eglon in the previous poem.

Across these discrete performances, Lodge manages a coordinated reflection on the pastoral elder's participatory drive on multiple registers, faced (correspondingly) with reverent support, delimited (and therefore futile) encouragement, or hard-nosed and myopic appreciation from younger parties. Most significantly, the old man holds his own in all the exchanges, even when he fails to win his junior audience over to his way of thinking. The elder taken to task in Satyre 4 for the covetousness to which he has descended is culpable mainly in that he has allowed himself to become a stereotype; Lodge's senior shepherds clearly occupy a new landscape, one wherein they advocate and justify their own centrality or retirement.

Where Lodge's dialogues infuse fresh complexities into earlier convention, Michael Drayton's *The Shepheards Garland* of 1593 presses on with the variations introduced by the *Arcadia* and *The Shepheardes Calender,* to which it expressly looks for inspiration. As Sukanta Chaudhuri observes, "Drayton takes Spenser's sole example [of the debate between old age and youth] in 'Februarie' and extends it into a leading motif," something that "lends special point" to what he calls "Drayton's nostalgic ideal."[47] Chaudhuri misconstrues, however, the poet's featured elders as merely "old men turning a contemplative eye upon a world that has passed them by."[48] In line with Spenser, Sidney, and his own companion Lodge, Drayton develops both the old shepherds he fashions and the dialogic circumstances into which he places them. *The Shepheards Garland* devotes two of its nine eclogues to old age, pairing the second and seventh in almost chiastic fashion. In the "Second Eglog," the tables are reversed, as a benignly sympathetic youth, Motto, attempts to console the melancholy elder Wynken, who is absorbed in reflections of lost former vitality and the "simple truth" of "mans frayle wayning age."[49] Wynken's devastatingly embittered self-image as a mere "cumber-world" leaves him immune, however, to his companion's gracious lyric appeals, as the young man quickly diagnoses:

> Even so I weene, for thy olde ages fever,
>   Deemes sweetest potions bitter as the gall,
> And thy colde Pallat having lost her savour,
>   Receives no comfort in a cordiall.   (21, 33–36)

To illustrate love's incapacity to preserve life's delights, the old man catalogues at length time's corrosive effects on the body. But even as he advises
his young companion against "the follies of my wandring yeares" (28), he
in fact reveals himself as one whose obsession with youth constrains him to
aged self-loathing. "That Jewell gone wherein I joyed most," he laments,

> My dreadful thoughts been drawen upon my face,
>   In blotted lines with ages iron pen,
> The lothlie morpheu saffroned the place,
>   Where beuties damaske daz'd the eies of men.   (17–20)

Wynken idolizes youth's "gamesome" character more thoroughly than any
youthful lover might (Motto himself acquiesces conditionally to his dire
warnings in his parting lines, "If that there be such woes and paines in
love,/Woe be to him that list the same to prove" [138–39]), and so finds
himself trapped within the bleak self-assessment that for him makes old
age its own curse.

   By contrast, Drayton's "Seventh Eglog" discovers the "truth" Wynken
had peddled as anything but univocal or "simple." There Borrill, an aged
contemplative shepherd, is accosted by Batte, "a foolish wanton boy,/but
lately falne in love," who wishes to lure the elder from what he regards
as "thy loathsome cave" (17). Although the old man placidly defends his
withdrawal from the realm of "foolish worldlings" by celebrating the more
modest pleasures he knows (which include the reading of "antique Ro-
mants"), Batte petulantly sneers in Cuddie-like fashion at the elder's physique as suited to such tedious pleasures:

> Thy legges been crook'd, thy knees done bend for age,
>   and I am swift and nimble as the Roe,
> Thou art ycouped like a bird in cage,
>   and in the field I wander too and froe,
> Thou must doe penance for thy olde misdeedes,
> And make amends, with Avies and with creedes.   (85–90)

Where Borrill, countering "Thou art as deafe even as thy god is blinde"
(117), offers to sing of love's hazards, the young man furthermore transforms Cuddie's eagerness to hear the elder's narrative into another occasion
for mockery: "*Borrill,* sing on I pray thee let us heare,/that I may laugh to
see thee shake thy beard" (121–22). In response to the song, which incidentally indicts old age's own susceptibility to eros's charms as "dotards folly"
(141), Batte overgoes Philisides's harsh dismissals:

> Olde doting foole, for shame hold thou thy tongue,
>   I would thy clap were shut up in my purse.

It is thy life, if thou mayst scoulde and braule:
Yet in thy words there is no wit at all.   (153–56)

Despite the elder's calmly indignant response, Batte voices only contempt for the pity he expresses that his adversary will not have to wait for old age to realize the grief he anticipates, departing in sardonic mock-gratitude "for thy company, / for all thy jestes and all thy merrie Bourds" (199–200). Reading eclogues 2 and 7 together, we are left feeling that if Batte is destined for Wynken's regretful senescence, Motto will likely age into Borrill's measured composure. Once more, old age comes under careful reflective scrutiny in the pastoral exchange, which delineates senescence's virtues and miseries as largely self-determined, regardless of hostile or supportive gestures from without.

Although by no means a poet of Lodge's or Drayton's caliber, Francis Sabie displays a similar awareness of senescence's new prominence in pastoral in his *Pans Pipe,* released the same year as *A Fig for Momus.* Just the opposite of Lodge, Sabie advertises in his brief preface "To all youthfull Gentlemen" his own status as "a yong beginner."[50] Regardless, two of the three eclogues show him not immune to the refreshed attention to senescence shared by his late Elizabethan countrymen. His second eclogue casts the narrative of Faustus's virtuous love for and marriage to Alinda as a conversation between the woman's old father, Melibeus, and his fellow elder Damon, wherein "old age" and "crooked age" are regarded as "enemies unto worke, enemies unto profit," urging the young to learn a trade at an early age (C2). By the third eclogue, Faustus himself appears as "an aged man, master of harmony," who addresses his junior companions as one "much reverenc'd for his age of the rest" (C4v). Delighted at having lived into the present time of safety and prosperity (essentially reversing the nostalgic "Golden Age" motif conventionally aligned with old age), he encourages camaraderie among the young men when they fall into the flyting of one another's women—including an attack on "withered *Alice*" who "lookes like an olde witch scortch'd in a kilhouse" (D1). The singing contest he goes on to sponsor and judge features a song in honor of Eliza, who for "many yeares" has defended and nourished her people, which ends with a prayer that "long she may flourish" (D4r–v). Even in such novice work, the would-be pastoralist finds himself drawn to what by now seems a commonplace inclusion of the elder shepherd as a key player in the genre's dialogue.

Where erotic love serves as a chief point of contention in the pastoral debates that emerge in the period, Richard Barnfield's *The Affectionate Shepheard* of 1594 offers the spectacle of the "dotards folly" that Drayton's

Borrill had attacked, with a curious twist. In the complex web that Barnfield spins, Daphnis bemoans his unrequited love for Ganimede, who in
turn loves "the faire Queene *Guendolen,*" herself mourning a deceased lover and pursued by one "That in his age began to doate againe; / . . . / When
through old-age enfeebled was his Braine."[51] As the lamenting speaker
mythologizes, Death and Cupid had mistakenly exchanged arrows, a mishap that results in the demise of the young lover and the old man's reduction to a "doting foole" who courts the young mistress to suitably comic
effect:

> Now doth he stroke his Beard; and now (againe)
> He wipes the drivel from his filthy chin;
> Now offers he a kisse; but high Disdaine
> Will not permit her hart to pity him.   (p. 7)

The grotesque picture rendered by the speaker easily exceeds the *Arcadia*'s
mockery of Basilius; but after this initial scenario passes, Daphnis begs
Ganimede to re-direct his attention away from the mourning Guendolen
back to himself. Suggesting that the youth will one day be "deformed"
by time and so lose whatever sympathy she may harbor for his beauty, he
notes that "age puls downe the pride of every man" (pp. 11, 17). But after
listening to his protracted litany of counsels for an upright life, we come to
discover that the speaker is himself "Age-withered":

> Behold my gray head, full of silver haires,
> My wrinckled skin, deepe furrowes in my face:
> Cares bring Old-Age, Old-Age increaseth cares;
> My time is come, and I have run my Race:
>   Winter hath snow'd upon my hoarie head,
>   And with my Winter all my joyes are dead.   (p. 23)

Barnfield's uneven verses and the strange economy of his narrative carry
an intriguing perspective on aged amour: fully capable of suffering love's
pangs without the mythological back story he recounts at the start, the
aged speaker simultaneously voices his revulsion for the very picture of the
infatuated elder.

The rich psychological awareness discovered afresh in the pastoral characters these poets introduced points to the way this casual inclusion of
old age in the form's construction henceforth maintained a hold. The period in fact marks a point of origin for what Steven Marx identifies as the
"hardnosed, leatherskinned old countrymen" who "are no trespassers in
the rural landscape; their old age reflects their rugged settings and generates an essential bucolic vision of the good life."[52] At the same time, the in-

junctions against aged eroticism portrayed in figures like Sidney's Basilius and Barnfield's "affectionate" characters also become an abiding concern of the lyric poets who dominated the period. The kinds of self-assertion and insecurity empowering or afflicting the pastoral exponents of old age carried over to these writers' equally provocative enactments. I turn now to consider how they wrestled with expressions of an enduring sexuality that old age—in the face of society's decorous efforts to rationalize or shame it away—cannot bring itself to relinquish.

CHAPTER FOUR

Sexuality and Senescence in Late Elizabethan Poetry: "Old Strange Thinges"

W HEN CRAFTING HIS *Affectionate Shepheard,* Richard Barnfield drew upon no less popular a text than Geffrey Whitney's *Choice of Emblems* of 1586 as a source for his interpolated account of how, when Death and Cupid unwittingly take up one another's quivers, youth begins to die as old men "dote." Although Barnfield's application gives the myth a more vituperative turn, Whitney's poeticized tag to his emblem "De morte, & amore: Iocosum" (see fig. 1)—adapted in turn from Andrea Alciato's *Emblematum liber* (1531)—takes a sanguine, "joking" look at the theory that, amid this cosmic confusion, "aged men, whome deathe woulde bringe to grounde: / Beganne againe to love, with sighes, and grones."[1] Whitney's etiological account of Mors and Cupid's accidental exchange of arrows attempts a measure of mythic justification (if not vindication) of the amorous elder. Even after the mixup comes to the attention of the deities responsible, who perceive "how youthe was almoste cleane extinct: / And age did doate, with garlandes freshe, and gaye, / And heades all balde, weare newe in wedlocke linckt," the adjustment leaves several arrows in the wrong quivers: "Then, when wee see, untimelie deathe appeare," we are told, "Or wanton age: it was this chaunce you heare." If "natures lawes" are expressly "infringed" by the inversion, the spectacle of the elder's passionate desires was evidently as familiar or recognizable and prevalent as premature death—and was something that, in the popular imagination, divine rectification itself could not hope to preclude.

Age in love would of course find its lyric champions throughout the period, however compromised or compassionate their performances, from Sidney's Basilius to the speaker of Thomas Campion's "Though you are yoong and I am olde," who pointedly affirms, "Yet embers live, when flames doe die."[2] Yet such gestures remained the generous exceptions within a national lyric anthology that unapologetically gave voice to a more malign sensibility. For instance, in what the variorum editors speculate was his first surviving epigram—and therefore among his earliest surviving poems—John Donne targets the antiquarian proclivities of one Hamon: "If, in his study, Hamon hath such care, / To hang all old things, let his wife beware."[3] In subsequent versions of the text, the second line's "old things" expands into "old strange thinges," an amplification as deft as it is nasty. The original epigram had been content to redirect its satirical roguery from the antiquarian collector (already a butt of literary abuse in the 1590s)[4] to his spouse; the redaction enlarges, by means of this adjectival insert, into a poem about "estrangement" and the objectification that comes with age. As the erotic intimacies of youth fade, the couplet sardonically implies, familiar people inevitably devolve to the status of strange things. The antiquary's wife needs to beware the dusty knickknacks cluttering her husband's ridiculous displays less because of the penury such extravagant

Fig. 1. Geffrey Whitney, from *A Choice of Emblems* (Leyden, 1586). Reproduced by permission of The Huntington Library, San Marino, California.

152   *De morte, & amore : Iocosum.*

To EDWARD DYER *Esquier.*

WHILE furious Mors, from place, to place did flie,
And here, and there, her fatall dartes did throwe :

purchases typically threaten than for their human cost—specifically, the
emotional displacement configured by these gathered curiosities, among
which she now takes her unremarkable place. In old age, the lover comes
to look upon his previous object of affection as (at best) a grotesque artifact
worthy of inclusion in his museum, itself representative of a pathetic desire
to recover and reconstruct a now remote past.

This early epigram's concern for the disengagements threatened by time's
physical effects would itself mature to preoccupy much of Donne's verse.[5]
It is also symptomatic of a prevailing impulse to de-eroticize old age, and
the correspondingly scurrilous indictment of aged sexuality that extends
from antiquity to early modernity (and beyond). Nowhere were the social
or psychological consequences of late life more dramatically pronounced
than in matters of sexual conduct. Poetically, the presumed antipathy between sexuality and senescence finds characteristic expression in William
Jaggard's 1599 anthology of pirated lyrics, *The Passionate Pilgrime,* in a verse
excerpted from a longer piece published elsewhere as "A Maidens choice
twixt Age and Youth":

> Crabbed age and youth cannot live together,
> Youth is full of pleasance, Age is full of care,
> Youth like summer morne, Age like winter weather,
> Youth like summer brave, Age like winter bare.
> Youth is full of sport, Ages breath is short,
> Youth is nimble, Age is lame
> Youth is hot and bold, Age is weake and cold,
> Youth is wild, and Age is tame.
>   Age I doe abhor thee, Youth I doe adore thee,
>   O my love my love is young:
>   Age I doe defie thee. O sweet Shepheard hie thee:
>   For me thinks thou staies too long.[6]

Unable to sustain physically the amorous "sport" for which youth longs,
careful age for all its authority can hope to inspire no more than defiance
in a younger generation it still desires. Whatever indignities the old had to
tolerate, few were more unequivocally enforced than the strictures against
erotic desires that survived, if not beyond the subject's capability, at least
beyond the act's alleged propriety.[7]

Amid the love poetry that flourished in the final decades of Elizabeth I's
reign, old age encountered its greatest literary challenge, as my discussions
of the queen's own "When I was fair and young" and Elizabethan pastoral
have revealed. This chapter surveys how the presumptions informing this
tradition came under scrutiny as English writers of the period reassessed in

their verse the psychological ramifications of sexual desire in age. A closer look at Ralegh's tense appropriation of the "aging lover" topos in his poetry directed to Elizabeth, the self-conscious fear of senescence haunting Shakespeare's persona in the *Sonnets,* and the lyric split between a reverential celebration of aging beauty and a harsh indictment of the physical deformities that time threatens to bring in Donne's early elegy "The Autumnall" provide a sense of how these poets discovered in the topic a complexity integral to the emergent subjectivity characterizing late Tudor culture.

The object of disgust and derision, sexual desire among the elderly was reviled in the *senex amans* tradition reaching back to antiquity. The randy, aging male became a stock comic figure in the drama of Plautus and Terence, and the particularly devastating caricature of sexual dysfunction that Juvenal crafts in his Satire 10 contributed significantly to a veritable tradition of the *vituperatio senectute,* or invective against old age, that evolved over the course of the Middle Ages, one point in a much longer religious program of worldly renunciation and the attack on human vanity.[8] Horace's odes and epodes cultivated an equally fierce and widely emulated scorn for lustful old women.[9] The carpe diem pose endemic to lyric practice down to the Renaissance exploited, in Cathy Yandell's words, "an implicit terror concerning the future" by threatening "the young woman addressee with the literal or implied portrait of her withered old age, which is presented as the alternative to her loving the poet now, while she is still beautiful."[10] An index of all physical infirmity, the aging body atrophies into a bitter anaphrodisiac for subsequent poetic milieus.

More complex is the reaction provoked by the unnerving scrutiny to which the sixth-century elegist Maximianus exposes age and eros. His speaker's disarmingly frank attention to old age's physical debility and the contempt this excites in others scripts a litany of suffering that exceeds his most gerontophobic predecessors' invectives. Significantly, however, he laments the extreme miseries of senescence not from the viewpoint of a spectator but from within, and the poignant lament and self-criticism that fill out the six poems consequently end up making us sympathetic to his humiliation:

> iurgia, contemptus violentaque damna secuntur
>   nec quisquam ex tantis praebet amicus opem.
> ipse me pueri atque ipsae sine lite puellae
>   turpe putant dominum iam vocitare suum.
> irrident gressum, irrident iam denique vultum

    et tremulum, quondam quod timuere, caput.
      cumque nihil videam, tamen hoc spectare licebit
    ut gravior misero poena sit ista mihi.

    [Insults, contempt, sharp losses come in turn,
    No friends to help in their adversity.
    The very boys and girls now think it shameful
    To call me master, putting up objections.
    They mock my gait, they mock my countenance
    And shaking head, which once they feared. Although
    I may see nothing, yet I shall look on this.
    This pain is heavier for wretched me.]   (1:281–88)[11]

Karen Cokayne rightly observes of the long opening elegy that "Maximianus mocked the babbling old man, but at the same time drew attention
to the old man's desperation to be listened to, his need to assert his own
identity and still be someone of importance."[12]

   The sexual impotence he specifically bemoans in the second elegy unexpectedly rethinks the condemnation to which earlier Latin poets had
subjected aging women who cling to the lost beauty of youth. In this performance, the elderly male confronts a lover who, for all the signs of age
she betrays—such as graying hair and skin discoloration—has retained her
sexual appeal, to the point where she now experiences and expresses disgust for the poet's more conspicuous physical surrender to time. Refusing
to acknowledge "nec me quod potius reddidit ipsa senem [that it's she who
made me an old man]" (2:8), the mistress imperiously confines him to a
pained memory of all he has lost, even as she sustains her attractiveness:

    atque tamen—nivei circumdant tempora cani
      et iam caeruleis infecit hora notis—
    praestat adhuc nimiumque sibi pretiosa videtur
      atque annos mecum despicit illa suos.
    et, fateor, primae retinet monimenta figurae
      atque inter cineres condita flamma manet.
    ut video, pulcris etiam vos parcitis, anni,
      nec veteris formae gratia tota perit.

    [And yet, though snowy locks surround her brow
    And now time stains her with its darkish age-spots,
    She still looks stunning, thinks well of herself,
    And now disdains the years she spent with me.
    I will admit she keeps her youthful figure
    And hidden flames remain beneath the ash.
    Even you, the years, I see, spare something lovely,
    All grace of former beauty does not die.]   (2:25–32)

Whatever rage at her "ungratefulness" percolates beneath his complaint is muted by the sense of self-abnegation and shame over his own decay.

Besides the rare portrayal of loving relationships among aged married couples that we find in Ovid's tale of Baucis and Philemon in *Metamorphoses* 8 or Ausonius's Epigrams 34 and 40, where time's passage mellows the couple into a deeper appreciation for one another's company, classical lyrics praising the attractions of aging lovers do survive. While the *Greek Anthology*'s fifth book offers several instances of how "time cannot subdue nature" in this regard, however, the "handful of poems *in praise of* older women highlights the very atypicality of such an approach," as Tim Parkin has suggested: "this is the novel point of such exercises, attempting to persuade the reader of the possibility of finding such women sexually attractive."[13] Even the more concerted lyric formulation of the elderly sensualist we meet in the *Anacreontea* where, in an "attempt to create an uninterrupted space of symposiastic conviviality," the elder joins or even competes with a company of younger companions in dancing, drinking, and courting, aged capabilities find their limits. In Stella Achilleos's apt summation, the "gap between desire and actual fulfillment" renders the performance as a whole "a voyeuristic trip during which expectation for sexual satisfaction builds strongly but is hardly ever met."[14]

Some of this very frustration infuses the Anacreontic spirit that the fifteenth-century Italian poet Giovanni Gioviano Pontano adopted in his *Baiae*. At one point in the collection's second book, the aged male speaker—ready enough to sponsor the sexual escapades of the young men and women who gather in the hothouse resort ambience of the Neapolitan baths, and at turns prepared to mock his fellow elders who give way to their erotic yearnings for these youths—tells the woman named Focilla not to write him off teasingly as harmless on account of his years. "Be careful," he threatens, or risk harsh consequences: "senem perpetiere verpulentum, / et clames volo: "Reddo, reddo, reddo!" / pro quo sic ego: "Subdo, subdo, subdo!" (2.12:16–18; Suffer and receive an old man's tool. / I'll have you cry, "I'll give, I'll give, I'll give!" / And I'll reply, "Take that, take that, take that!").[15] The urge to seize the day takes an especially fraught turn in the alternate *carpe vesperum* that these writers formulate when they come to inhabit the figure of the aged poet, who discovers both the limits and the rewards of reflecting upon his own experience of senescence.

Tudor poetry participated ably in the dismissive mockery of age's crippling effects upon human sexual allure and potency. Earlier in the century,

Sir Thomas Wyatt rancorously attacked the erotic appetites of an aging woman at court:

> Ye old mule that think yourself so fair,
> Leave off with craft your beauty to repair,
> For it is true without any fable
> No man setteth more by riding in your saddle.   (1–4)

By contrast, the coy mistress of his "My lute awake" (as discussed earlier) excites the frustrated resentment of a deprived lover vengefully prepared to articulate her deserts before resigning his pursuit: "May chance thee lie withered and old, / The winter nights that are so cold," he anticipates, "Then shalt thou know beauty but lent, / And wish and want as I have done" (26–27, 34–35).[16] Fulke Greville's *Caelica* 19, which opens by asking "Ah silly *Cupid,* doe you make it coy / To keepe your seate in *Cala's* furrowed face?" reduces the entire prospect of aged sexuality to a sideshow spectacle of "traffique" between ludicrous elders.[17] Perhaps most egregiously, in his *Idea* 8, Michael Drayton grieves that his premature undoing will prevent him from witnessing his mistress's senescence, which he nonetheless imagines in grim detail:

> That where those two cleare sparkling Eyes are plac'd,
> Onely two Loope-holes, then I might behold.
> That lovely, arched, yvorie, pollish'd Brow,
> Defac'd with Wrinkles, that I might but see;
> Thy daintie Hayre, so curl'd, and crisped now,
> Like grizzled Mosse upon some aged Tree;
> Thy Cheeke, now flush with Roses, sunke, and leane,
> Thy Lips, with age, as any Wafer thinne,
> Thy Pearly Teeth out of thy Head so cleane,
> That when thou feed'st, thy Nose shall touch thy Chinne.   (3–12)[18]

In the hands of the post-Petrarchan lover, age becomes a brutally effective instrument of spite and self-vindication. But like their classical models, English poets played variations upon this more scurrilous theme. The voice of the aging lover at times served good homiletic use. Thomas, Lord Vaux, for example, takes the occasion of confronting his "limpyng age" to decry all youthful folly, and the speaker of George Gascoigne's "The Anatomye of a Lover" warns his readers against the passions that have left him superannuated, even as he discloses the enduring nature of his lusts.[19]

More self-reflexively still, in the autobiography he compiled around 1576, the musician and poet Thomas Whythorne professes his fascination with the "ages of man" motif from his teenage years on, when he writes:

"The pleaziurz that I tak / Now in my yowthfull yeerz / The sam shall mee forsak / When hoery age appeerz."[20] Whythorne's account, whose title announces him (at the age of forty-eight) as "entring into the old mans lyfe," simultaneously finds him avowing "I am not verye olde" from early in the narrative (pp. 1 and 4). A protégé of the prolific John Heywood, for whom he transcribed the then unpublished lyrics of Wyatt and Surrey, Whythorne portrays himself throughout his life as one immune to the erotic advances of various suitors, several much older than he, though more out of "bashfulnes" than piety (p. 33). Like Donne after him, the author also took delight in charting his own aging process in visual images as well as words, having had at intervals three portraits completed: as a youth (to accompany the verses quoted above); after the severe "ague" he suffered at age twenty-two; and again when he was "A dozen yeerz elder," this last of which he tags "As tym doth alter evry wiht / So evri age hath hiz deliht" (pp. 134–35). And though he goes on to expand this epigram into a "sonnet" bidding farewell to youth's joys before the approach of "kold weak age," he concludes by observing with satisfaction how "I waz judged of many which did not know my yeerz, to be alwaiz yoonger then I waz in deed" (pp. 135–36).

Later Elizabethan poetry takes up the subject in a more peculiarly inquisitive manner in verse that especially comes to expose mixed attitudes about the impact old age has upon the sexuality in which we largely ground our identities—a poetry that, by making sympathetic a plight we both hope and fear to share, becomes extraordinarily self-conscious about its impetus and implications. If we attribute the emergence of this perspective in part to the spectacle of an aging monarch celebrated in the most lavish Petrarchan terms, we may appropriately begin with the way in which Sir Walter Ralegh exploits the topic of age in the lyrics he composed to recover the queen's favor at various turns in his checkered courtly career.

Ralegh capitalized adroitly upon the convention of time's eroding power throughout his slim lyric output. It notably informs his well-known "Nature that washt her hands in milke," whose first three stanzas portray the crafting of a beautiful (though hard-hearted) mistress, only to deconstruct her in the subsequent three stanzas under the onslaught of "cruell Time," who "takes in trust / our youth, our Joyes, and all we have, / and payes us but with age and dust" (31–33).[21] His even more familiar reply to Marlowe's "Passionate Shepherd" likewise answers "the shepherd's amorous images of delight" (in Stephen Greenblatt's words) "with a melancholy vision of Time the Destroyer."[22] Age, more than death, significantly compromises the lover's promise, as we grasp in the final wistful thought that only "could youth last, and love stil breed, / Had joyes no date, nor age no need" (21–22), the speaker might consent to the lover's appeals. The passing years mock all human pretension to a point where the most florid poetic imaginings face substantial qualification, if not total *dis*-qualification. The stock sentiment Ralegh indulges in his epitaph on Sir Philip Sidney's premature death—"There didst thou vanquish shame and tedious age, / Griefe, sorow, sicknes, and base fortunes might: / Thy rising day, saw never wofull night" (33–35)—takes on a special resonance in the context of his larger oeuvre.

From this point of view, it becomes obvious why myths of eternal youthfulness should have served Ralegh as a supreme poetic compliment. His role as prime contributor to the celebration of Elizabeth as a perpetually rejuvenated Cynthia in the post-Armada years was no literary accident.[23] His paradigmatic "Praysed be *Dianaes* faire and harmelesse light" fastens the convention most forthrightly. "Eternity in her oft change she beares," he says of the sacred mistress: "Time weares her not, she dooth his Chariot guide, / Mortality below her Orbe is plast" (11, 13–14). "Now we have present made" similarly honors the "Bewty that cannot vade" of one "whose summer ever lastethe / tyme conquringe all she mastreth / by beinge allwaye new" (4, 10–12). Greenblatt's seminal reading of Ralegh's theatrical impulses, moreover, prevents us from disregarding this gesture as merely one more instance of mercenary flattery.[24] So intertwined was the courtier's personal plight with his imaginative constructions of the monarch that every trope he deployed consequentially reflected on his own self-image. This point comes home especially in the period of disfavor that Ralegh suffered in 1589 and (more severely) in 1592, when he augments his vision of the ageless queen with a counterimage of his own premature decay: the poet's denial of his lady's susceptibility to time's ravages is underlined by his own succumbing to this force. Extending the fiction in this manner, he enables a larger reflection on the painful experience of growing progressively more obsolete in the eyes of those to whom one looks for essential validation.

According to the medical wisdom of the day, few experiences accelerated the onset of old age more grimly than servitude at court. "One sees courtiers quickly worn and aged from running after posts, from being too often in a standing position without moving from their places," Laurent Joubert reports, "staying up late, eating on the run, having no fixed hours for meals, and doing other such hurried, urgent, and unreasonable tasks." The psychological stress of this lifestyle caused even greater damage, in the doctor's opinion: "Then there are the court jealousies, the yearnings, the concern for favor that rattles their brains with ambition, the avarice that gnaws at their hearts, the envy and hidden hatred, calumny, detraction, intrigue, and other court vices that eat out their insides. Who could live long and become old in such a captive and wretched existence?"[25] Ralegh was of course acutely sensitive to this reality, as his poem commonly titled "A Farewell to the Court" betrays in its speaker's announced intention to flee while there is still time, "Whom care forewarnes, ere age and winter colde, / To haste me hence, to find my fortunes folde" (13–14).

In "As you came from the holy land," Ralegh takes on precisely this guise of the superannuated but faithful retainer, whose function has declined with age, and who now shores up his dignity with an awareness of his loyalty in the face of estrangement from the cruel, unaging beauty that his decline has occasioned. Obsolescence naturally provides an ironic backdrop to the Walsingham ballad in its conjured recollections of the now defunct English shrine and the religious Marian folk tunes associated with it.[26] Having outlasted his usefulness, the speaker immediately reveals himself as one who lives in the past, for whom Walsingham remains a "holy land" despite the decrees of a new dispensation.

> As you came from the holy land
>   Of Walsinghame—
> Mett you not with my true love
>   by the way as you came—
> How shall I know your trew love
> That have mett many one
> As I went to the holy lande
> That have come that have gone.   (1–8)

A mournful double meaning inhabits his addressee's initial reply as well: ostensibly modifying the "many one" he has encountered on his travels, the final line's reflection on those who have come and gone also glances poignantly at the transience—of sacred institutions and lovers' favor alike—that comprises the poem's chief meditation. But this early signal still does not prepare us for the temporal disjunction between the main speaker's own conspicuous decay and his "true" love's immunity to this. Her appearance has not altered—"She *is* neyther whyte nor browne / Butt as the heavens fayre" (9–10; my emphasis)—while he wears his years for all to witness:

> I have lovde her all my youth
> Butt no[w] ould as you see
> Love lykes not the fallyng frute
> From the wythered tree.   (25–28)

Age, which cannot be masked, marks the "cause" of his abandonment by the woman now that he has wasted himself in her service.

The Maximianus-like self-pity driving the poet's lament turns ultimately upon the contrasting childlike status of love, whose carelessness and infidelity he or the interlocutor (the distinction becomes uncertain beyond line 28) indicts in the final movement. Against this entity's "dureless contente" (33), the lover poses his own truer "durable fyre," the abstract dedication—"never sicke never ould never dead / from itt selfe never turnynge" (43–44)—to which he clings despite the attenuation he owns. The gesture partakes of the usual effort to shame the cruel woman, here, into an appreciation of the gift she allegedly enjoys, since her resistance to age has desensitized her to the conscientious liberality she should therefore exercise toward her less fortunate servants. Still, his interior fidelity remains a function strictly "In the mynde ever burnynge" (42), in stark opposition to the aged outward form, which, "as you see," relegates him to a lonely recollection of times "that have come that have gone."

It remains unclear whether or not the Walsingham poem was a product of Ralegh's 1589 rustication, commemorated in Spenser's *Colin Clouts Come Home Againe,* the brief episode that likely saw the origins (at least) of his far more ambitious poetical work, *The Ocean to Scinthia.* We are confident, however, that the latter develops significantly during the potentially career-shattering disgrace he suffered three years later, when the queen discovered his secret marriage to Elizabeth Throckmorton. In this extended performance of almost 550 lines, the soliloquy of a devotee abandoned by his unaging mistress takes on a grander, mythic intonation, fitting the epic aspirations suggested by the pseudo fragment's (probably faux) titles: "The 21th and last booke of the Ocean to Scinthia," and its abbreviated sequel, "The end of the boockes, of the Oceans love to Scinthia, and the beginning of the 22 boock, entreatinge of Sorrow."[27] Ralegh's provocatively disjointed, often cacophonous delivery has not muted the allure of this work, wherein old age becomes a more subtle yet even more pervasive coordinating concern, threading eerily throughout its component movements.[28]

Significantly, the "fragment" Ralegh designs assumes a kind of engagement with the dead that we find in the *nekyía* of classical epic, like *Odyssey* 11 or *Aeneid* 6. A weird, netherworldly introversion sets the tone:

> Sufficeth it to yow my joyes interred,
> in simpell wordes that I my woes cumplayne,
> Yow that then died when first my fancy erred.
> joyes under dust that never live agayne:

> If to the livinge weare my muse adressed,
> or did my minde her own spirrit still inhold,
> weare not my livinge passion so repressed,
> as to the dead, the dead did thes unfold,
> sume sweeter wordes, sume more becumming vers,
> should wittness my myshapp in hygher kynd.   (1–10)

His address to moribund joys befits the death-in-life of obsolescence he has come to know, disclosed in his self-characterization as "the Idea but restinge, of a wasted minde,/the blossumes fallen, the sapp gon from the tree" (12–13). In the story we overhear at one remove, he desperately recounts his miseries despite the loss of all hope for rejuvenation. Mind without spirit and body without passion, the speaker finds himself drawn to memories he harbors for himself alone, rather than to the vital world of youthful potential he had previously known.

The appetite for narrative—one of the few hungers seemingly left to the aged in his bitter evaluation—itself becomes a recurring concern in his lament. On the threshold of death or the twilight of life, a frenzied, last-ditch compulsion, "the sowle yeven then departinge," to articulate "the weale, the wo, the passages of olde/and worlds of thoughts describde by onn last sythinge" (94–96) preoccupies the poet's imagination. More than simply hyperbolic metaphors for the futility of his desires, his images speak directly to the recuperative impulse we experience as night falls, when

> each livinge creature draweth to his restinge
> wee should beginn by such a partinge light
> to write the story of all ages past
> and end the same before th'aprochinge night.   (100–3)

Trapped now in an eternal retrospect, he recalls a misspent youth that proleptically intuited future misery but failed to appreciate his own pre-science. He reflects on the "twelve yeares of my most happy younger dayes," belatedly realizing how "I in them, and they now wasted ar/of all which past the sorrow only stayes,/So wrate I once and my mishapp fortolde" (120–23). Memory serves only as a source of pain and resentment against destructive age:

> the thoughts of passed tymes like flames of hell,
> kyndled a fresh within my memorye
> the many deere achivments that befell
> in thos prime yeares and infancy of love
> which to describe weare butt to dy in writinge.   (166–70)

The noble resolve of "true love" that closes the Walsingham poem, "from itt selfe never turnynge," transforms here to the bitter solipsism of his chthonic death-in-writing.

The principal nexus between Ralegh's ballad and the *Ocean to Scinthia*, however, remains the figure of the eternally youthful queen herself. Confronted by her unnatural preservation, the poet finds himself slave at once to his own old age and to the agelessness he beholds:

> Loves ground, his essence, and his emperye,
> all slaves to age, and vassalls unto tyme
> of which repentance writes the tragedye,
> But this, my harts desire could not conceve
> Whose *Love* outflew the fastest fliing tyme
> A bewty that cann easely deseave
> th'arrest of yeares, and creepinge age outclyme,
> a springe of bewties which tyme ripeth not
> tyme that butt workes onn frayle mortallety.   (178–86)

His intellectual grasp—informed by "strong reason"—that all are "slaves to age" collides with the countervision of unnatural preservation this woman poses. In her very defiance of "creepinge age," she herself appears to have arrested time's progress, outrunning her adversary's slow powers of attrition. Embodying the "vestall fier that burnes, but never wasteth," the "blossumes of pride that cann nor vade nor fall" (189, 192), she differs nonetheless from the Walsingham mistress in that she not only witnesses the decline of her vulnerable devotees but actually occasions this. When she "did but decline her beames as discontented," the "affection which our youth presented" withered, evidence of how "as tyme gave, tyme did agayne devoure" (251, 249, 247). As Robert Stillman has argued, "The Queen has come to embody devouring time itself." But where Stillman finds a "historical critique" of how "A queen's love will decay just as certainly as her empire," the speaker seems far too defeated and genuinely overawed by her power to register any outrage or resentment he feels, however subtly.[29] While her disfavor cannot temper his dedication, as before, it remains equally clear that "With youth, is deade the hope of loves returne" (287).

Ralegh himself reached toward a mythology of the damned when expressing his grief over the queen's enmity. When, during his arrest, he saw Elizabeth's barge on the Thames from his study window, according to Sir Arthur Gorges's often quoted letter, "soodaynly he brake owte into a great distemper, and sware that hys Enymyes hadd of purpose brought hyr Majestie thethar, to breake hys gaule in sounder with Tantalus Torment."[30] In a striking manner, he resorts to similar measures at the end of the *Ocean to*

Scinthia's Book 21, closing the *nekyía* frame with an allusion to Sisyphus's sufferings:

> Yet every foot, olde thoughts turne back myne eyes
> constraynt me guides as old age drawes a stonn
> agaynst the hill, which over wayghty lyes
> for feebell armes, or wasted strenght to move
> my steapps ar backwarde, gasinge onn my loss.   (510–13)

The reference provides an appropriate cap for the protracted (if "fragmentary") structure: far more than simply another metaphor in the vast accumulation Ralegh sweeps together, the figure's eternal plight affords a perfect analogue for the perpetual false starts and back-and-forth rhythm of the overall lament, even beyond the titular notion of a perpetual ebb-and-flow that Agnes Latham remarks.[31] Most subtly, Ralegh recovers Sisyphus as an expressly *aged* character, in line with the more obscure scolia on the myth. Despite his notorious cunning, which enabled his escape even from Hades, Sisyphus nonetheless eventually "died of old age," and upon his return to the underworld was as a result condemned to his famous punishment.[32] Like his legendary counterpart, Ralegh's speaker stands out as an old man doomed to an impossible task he never can accomplish, despite his witty resourcefulness and record of earlier victories.

Appropriately for the Sisyphean narrator, the resignation of the finality of "the 21th booke" yields to the resumption of the twenty-two-line coda that follows, a deliberately feeble parody of the gesture of renewal to which it (again) returns. The opening reflection on how the "springetyme joies" of the "risinge soonn of youth" now "in the yeveninge, and the winter sadd / present my minde, which takes my tymes accompt / the greif remayninge of the joy it had" (1–2, 4–6) terminates once more in a corresponding invocation of Scinthia's powers, "by vertu lastinge over tyme and date" (18). Lacking even his "shepherds staff" which "age hath brast," as he bemoaned at the close of the previous book (504), he attempts to fashion a new one that ultimately cannot uphold him. No more than the "unburied bones" stripped clean by "tymes tempestius" (20, 14), he still manages to summon the strength to voice his demoralization, perversely celebrating the very force of eternal youth that reduces and rejects him. In this, it concentrates most powerfully Ralegh's sense of our status as "slaves to age," who sooner or later discover ourselves "as old age drawes a stonn."

Amid all its intricacies, Ralegh's pose in these works still offers only a modification of conventional lyric portrayals of old age. His speaker is too emotionally broken to summon indignation against the mistress who has spent him, and too paralyzed to take comfort in the moralism of a lesson painfully learned. For a more radical departure, we must turn to the collection of poems that likely took shape in the 1590s and saw publication in 1609 as *Shake-speares Sonnets*. This sequence foregrounds the aging sonneteer's fraught self-consciousness about the threats of senescence he apprehensively anticipates, a concern that spills over into the narrative coda, *A Lover's Complaint,* that rounds out the volume. With stunning and provocative complexity, Shakespeare's speaker contends with a disdain for old age so powerful that it qualifies his sentiments even as the sexual passion he is experiencing holds out the brief promise of surmounting this deeply ingrained prejudice.

Whereas the "hot and bold" temperament of youth offsets the purportedly "weake and cold" character of age in *The Passionate Pilgrime*'s excerpt, this casual dismissal of elderly impotence is itself challenged in the poem that inaugurates Jaggard's anthology, justly famous for offering the first published glimpse of what would become Shakespeare's sonnet 138:

> When my Love sweares that she is made of truth,
> I doe beleeve her (though I know she lies)
> That she might thinke me some untutor'd youth,
> Unskilfull in the worlds false forgeries.
> Thus vainly thinking that she thinkes me young,
> Although I know my yeares be past the best:
> I smiling, credite her false speaking toung,
> Outfacing faults in Love, with loves ill rest.
> But wherefore sayes my Love that she is young?
> And wherefore say not I, that I am old?
> O, Loves best habite is a soothing toung,
> And Age (in Love) loves not to have yeares told.
>   Therefore Ile lye with Love, and Love with me,
>   Since that our faults in Love thus smother'd be.

Whether it represents an early draft or a garbled transmission, this sonnet has uniformly suffered by comparison to the quarto text, which in Colin Burrow's assessment turns "a poem on lying about your age into an edgy work on mutually knowing deception."[33] Whatever its provenance, the poem at very least suggests that preoccupation with the sonneteer's advanced age was integral to Shakespeare's conception from early on, just as the version of sonnet 144 ("Two Loves I have, of Comfort, and Despaire") that Jaggard also published anticipates the pivotal triangulation of poet, young man, and "Woman (colour'd ill)" configuring the final sequence's drama. Judged independently of its more nuanced successor, moreover, the *Passionate Pilgrim*'s "When my Love sweares that she is made of truth" maintains a performance more successful and fascinating than its critics have allowed.

Reading backward through the lens of the quarto, readers have found themselves posed by line 8's obscurity and disoriented by the following line's alleged incoherence. Arthur Marotti disregards "But wherefore says my Love that she is young?" as "a nonsensical version, since the mistress's age is not at issue in the poem, but rather her honesty."[34] We cannot, however, so casually presume outside the references of Q's larger sequence to equate the "truth" owned by the woman in the opening line with "honesty" in the sense of sexual continence or fidelity. More directly, in context, this initial assertion assures her lover of her candor, specifically (so the later lines discover) in her denial of their susceptibility to age. If we take line 9 at face value rather than as a corruption, the sonnet turns into an account of how this aging couple, who both feel the pull of time, mutually reinforce one another by means of a pacific—"soothing"—discourse. This, in turn, enables them to defy or "outface" time with the "ill rest" of nights given to a sexual consummation of which their years are supposed to have deprived them. The poet's knowing acceptance of his mate's (here benign) false assertions sustains the fantasy that her lie aims to foster; he shrewdly discovers the prospect of "lying about your age" as a complex affair. At the same time, their exercise still identifies age as a supreme "fault": the parentheses in line 12's "And Age (in Love) loves not to have yeares told" tellingly intimates that senescence becomes a stigma once elders transgress into erotic territory, however readily they may otherwise acknowledge their years. Developing such ambiguity even in this preliminary way, the poem stands as a worthy predecessor to the more tense dubieties of sonnet 138, to which I return at the close of this discussion as one of the most provocative reflections on "age in love" to survive from the period.

Sonnet 138 appropriately previews Shakespeare's sequence, since it also provides a telos of sorts to the preoccupation with age that distinguishes the larger work's design. The foundational paradox upon which the author builds his *Sonnets* is the way in which the society depicted therein demands, sponsors, and erects monuments to its own endurance (as 55, "Not marble nor the gilded monuments / Of princes shall outlive this pow'rful rhyme," famously ponders) while nonetheless expressing a collective disdain for the effects of longevity itself. Sonnet 17 closes the initial procreation sequence in a graphic articulation of this very point, with its troubled fantasy of the text's fate in a "time to come": "So should my papers, yellowed with their age," the poet reflects, "Be scorned, like old men of less truth than tongue, / And your true rights be termed a poet's rage / And stretched meter of an antique song" (17:9–12).[35] A figure of deceit and impotent fury, the garrulous elder is best dismissed, the yellowing pages of his legacy deservingly forgotten.

In his pioneering essay on how the matter of age "colors almost every motive and action in the relationships to which the *Sonnets* refer," John Klause reads the sonneteer's blatant inconsistencies and professed mendacity as a function of his advanced years.[36] The chronic self-abasement to which the speaker is given forms part of his strategy to "educate" love, an ambition to which his seniority confines him: "A young lover may try to win the admiration of a lady by parading his vigor, his potential, or his achievement. . . . An older man will have to be loved for different reasons: not for his prowess, but for his tenderness, understanding, constancy, generosity."[37] In order to realize his goal, he strives—ultimately without success—to distinguish himself "in selfless dedication," in a manner that recalls the stance prescribed for pastoral elders surveyed in the last chapter.

But it is less the callous young man's ineducatability that defeats the sonneteer in Shakespeare's formulation than the speaker's own investment in the bias against age he reflexively perpetuates. Klause accurately characterizes the poet-lover as one who "lives in open-eyed thrall to a passion which, as the young Hamlet believed, is supposed to be conquered by time," but we need to recognize how this fundamental gerontophobic bias definitively contours his crippling self-loathing.[38] Though he intuits otherwise, time (the speaker has been conditioned to believe) compromises our very humanity, a point Dympna Callaghan discerns in her analysis of "the sheer *speed,* the agitated urgency" that she identifies as "the hallmark of Shakespeare's sonnets": "the changes brought by nature and time resemble the sudden and startling transformations of Ovidian metamorphoses, when from one minute to the next perfectly attractive young people are reduced to animal life, or less."[39] Old age's debilities, which most graphically sponsor this declension, will be kept in view from the sequence's earliest moment to the final turn's depressed erotic resignations.

And beyond. Indeed, a starkly stratified instance of sexuality's generational "layering" extends outside the sonnet sequence proper in the 1609 publication to imprint the short verse lament appended to the poems, titled *A Lover's Complaint*.[40] There Shakespeare introduces the figure of a "reverend man," who, "privileged by age," approaches the disheveled young woman consolingly to hear her story of the youth who seduced and abandoned her (57, 62). The "privilege" enjoyed by the elder is that his years render him sexually innocuous, enabling the approach of one who "desires to know / In brief the grounds and motives of her woe" (62–63). In other words, the old man's "desire" is reduced to the wish to hear the lamentations of anguished youth. In contrast to this aged "Father" to whom the narrative's principal speaker unburdens herself, the young man who undid her stands as a figure of predatory self-indulgence: "His rudeness so with his authorised youth / Did livery falseness in a pride of truth" (104–5).[41] The young man's age itself sanctions the erotic misconduct and attitude that, as his victim suggests at the close of her own protracted lament, continue to prove irresistible and cut across both gender and generational boundaries: "he did in the general bosom reign / Of young, of old, and sexes both enchanted" (127–28). The sheer force of his sexual allure enables a forwardness of which the old man's modest compassion, characterized expressly as "the charity of age" (70), comes to seem in retrospect an aged, de-eroticized parody.

Perhaps most interesting amid these polarities of age and youth is the curious median position of the female speaker herself. We encounter her immediately in the second stanza as a peculiar figure of the *puella senex,* a "maid" whose youthfulness is belied by her atrophied appearance, "The carcass of a beauty spent and done": "Time had not scythed all that youth begun, / Nor youth all quit, but, spite of heaven's fell rage, / Some beauty peeped through lattice of seared age" (11–14). Equally arresting is the odd defensiveness of her response to the aged interlocutor. She insistently dispels any notion of the advanced years one might ascribe to her bedraggled appearance:

> "Father," she says, "though in me you behold
> The injury of many a blasting hour,
> Let it not tell your judgement I am old:
> Not age, but sorrow, over me hath power.
> I might as yet have been a spreading flower.   (71–75)

As surely as the experience of abandonment has shattered her vanity—or precisely because of this—she appears driven to dissociate herself from the old man whose kindness she perhaps appreciates but whose sexlessness she revealingly takes for granted. Prepared to confess her own folly, she is less willing to entertain the misconceptions about her age that her worn visage, a signature of the erotic trauma she has suffered, might prompt. Eros breaks down the body with a more terrible efficiency than time itself, but its corrosive effects evidently do not extend to the psychology that only clings all the more tenaciously to youth. It is as though she takes shelter in a "youthful" naiveté—or (as Shakespeare's sonneteer will put it in 138) an "untutored" status that, in turn, "authorizes" her—regardless of the humiliation it may entail for her public image.[42]

The premium expressly awarded to youth by the *Complaint*'s abandoned lover only takes up the profound celebration of youth at the expense of old age that fills out the preceding sequence. The procreation sonnets that begin the collection build their counsel to the young man less around any threat of "the grave" than around a fundamental fear of aging that augers a fate worse than death. The "forty winters" that promise in sonnet 2 to "dig deep trenches in thy beauty's field" suggest not so much mortality's imminence as a passing of physical attractiveness—an exclusive attribute of youth for this speaker—that chiefly determines one's worth, in a time when "Thy youth's proud livery, so gazed on now, / Will be a tottered weed of small worth held" (2:1–4). To find one's bodily appearance compromised is to be old, and to be old is to be without value, in need of "excuse" against the gerontophobic sensibilities that the speaker has absorbed and represents.[43]

The beauty of youth focuses a principal orthodoxy for the poet-lover, who correspondingly regards a decline into "feeble age" as an occasion for apostasy. The rising sun of sonnet 7, to whom "each under eye / Doth homage," configures for him the supersession that awaits us in later life:

> And having climbed the steep-up heav'nly hill,
> Resembling strong youth in his middle age,
> Yet mortal looks adore his beauty still,
> Attending on his golden pilgrimage.
> But when from highmost pitch, with weary car,
> Like feeble age he reeleth from the day,
> The eyes ('fore duteous) now converted are
> From his low tract and look another way.   (7:5–12)

The poem's inflections propose, moreover, that the aging subject himself bears responsibility for the indifference and rejection he must suffer. By sonnet 11, the speaker constructs age as itself a form of apostasy. Ardently encouraging the young man that "that fresh blood which youngly thou bestow'st / Thou mayst call thine, *when thou from youth convertest*," he emphasizes how "Herein lives wisdom, beauty, and increase; / Without this, folly, age, and cold decay" (11:3–6; my emphasis). As the opposition between beauty and age obtains in the lines' incremental pairings, the fear of what it means to face down time's encroachments dilates into an outright spiritual anxiety.

The speaker's apprehensiveness about unorthodox behavior or attitudes becomes a chief concern of sonnet 105, where he entreats, "Let not my love be called idolatry, / Nor my beloved as an idol show" (1–2). Yet the denial here becomes less conventional in the wake of the previous poem's critical return to the topic of agedness. Sonnet 104 offers an apology intended ostensibly to challenge or offset the collective pejorative emphasis of the procreation sequence. The opening reassurance will, however, terminate in an insecurity that cannot be altogether overcome; the speaker's subjective partiality might well be to blame, he speculates, since the survival of beauty in time evidently strikes him as the deepest of anomalies. Future, past, and present collapse within the lover's imagination in the three initial lines: "To me, fair friend, you never can be old, / For as you were when first your eye I eyed, / Such seems your beauty still" (104:1–3). As the seasons decline and regenerate around them, the (still) young man retains his physical appeal. No sooner does the poet put the youth's well-preserved beauty into words, however, than he turns to a more deep-seated "fear" that time's passing can bring no good:

> Ah yet doth beauty, like a dial hand,
> Steal from his figure, and no pace perceived;
> So your sweet hue, which methinks still doth stand,
> Hath motion, and mine eye may be deceived:
>   For fear of which, hear this, thou age unbred,
>   Ere you were born was beauty's summer dead.   (104:9–12)

Even though sonnet 22 had clarified the poet's personal stake in affirming the beloved's beauty—"My glass shall not persuade me I am old / So long as youth and thou are of one date" (1–2)—he still feels compelled to call the young man's "agelessness" into question. Once more, the larger gerontophobic sensibility triumphs, subverting any adjustments that the young man's impact on his own understanding might promise. In some respects, 104's compliment could be seen to enact the flattery that 138 will ponder from the opposite vantage point. Instead of the female lover assuring her aging partner that age has left him unscathed, the aging poet himself—far less disingenuously—celebrates his beloved's enduring youthfulness. Unlike the later mistress, however, the poet cannot sustain his performance convincingly to himself, despite all the evidence he so wonders at.

The speaker's nervous sensitivity to the reprobation threatened "when thou from youth convertest" stands out even more once we come to understand his own seniority. Just as old age had served as the principal emphasis of the poet's self-denigration in Ralegh's "Walsingham" ballad and

The Ocean to Scinthia, so does Shakespeare's speaker come to accentuate his advanced years apologetically in his efforts (as Klause proposes) to instruct the young man. But even the oft-quoted sonnet 73, which best crystallizes the moving paradox of how our very transiency intensifies rather than diminishes our emotional attachments, packs a potentially gerontophobic inflection in its couplet:

> That time of year thou mayst in me behold,
> When yellow leaves, or none, or few, do hang
> Upon those boughs which shake against the cold,
> Bare ruined choirs, where late the sweet birds sang.
> In me thou seest the twilight of such day,
> As after sunset fadeth in the west,
> Which by and by black night doth take away,
> Death's second self, that seals up all in rest.
> In me thou seest the glowing of such fire,
> That on the ashes of his youth doth lie,
> As the death-bed whereon it must expire,
> Consumed with that which it was nourished by.
>   This thou perceiv'st, which makes thy love more strong,
>   To love that well which thou must leave ere long.

The lyric summons the youth to appreciate one who expects soon to "expire," though he must do so despite the ruination by which he characterizes later life. The grim portrayal of age, however, also hearkens back to the procreation poems' early emphasis in implicitly recalling to the addressee the inevitability of his own decline into such a state.

Vicarious appreciation of another's plight, invited here, also becomes the poet's affair in sonnet 62, "Sin of self-love possesseth all mine eye." This performance builds its paradox around the self-evident absurdity of senescence vainly admiring its own attractiveness, amounting in his calculation to nothing less than "iniquity":

> But when my glass shows me myself indeed
> Beated and chopped with tanned antiquity,
> Mine own self-love quite contrary I read;
> Self so self-loving were iniquity.   (62:9–12)

The couplet's resolution, not surprisingly, discovers the elder's conceit as no more than his vicarious cosmetic overlay of the youth's admired appearance: "'Tis thee, myself, that for myself I praise, / Painting my age with beauty of thy days" (62:13–14), lines that could once more recall the reassurances of generational succession early on in the collection. To drive the point home more forcefully still, the following poem both extends 62's actual self-deprecation and reaffirms faith in art's preservative power "Against confounding age's cruel knife" by imaging their alignment and decay more graphically:

> Against my love shall be as I am now,
> With time's injurious hand crushed and o'erworn,
> When hours have drained his blood and filled his brow
> With lines and wrinkles, when his youthful morn
> Hath traveled on to age's steepy night,
>
> . . . .
>
> His beauty shall in these black lines be seen,
> And they shall live, and he in them still green.   (63:1–5, 13–14)

Celebration of eternal "greenness" relies in the poet's imagination on a honed sensitivity to time's inevitable blight on the human form: the victory boasted in the couplet is essentially controverted by the previous twelve lines' meditation, which captures, not the youth's splendor (as so many of the other sonnets had), but its "confounding" by relentless old age.

The sole moment of escape from this mindset by Shakespeare's speaker arrives in 108's project to count "no old thing old" through a new calculus of worth:

> So that eternal love in love's fresh case
> Weighs not the dust and injury of age,
> Nor gives to necessary wrinkles place,
> But makes antiquity for aye his page,
>   Finding the first conceit of love there bred,
>   Where time and outward form would show it dead.   (108:9–14)

For once, the wrinkles (whose "necessity" is never denied) are absorbed in a perspective that judges the body's attractiveness, not in terms of age's indelible signature, but through an affection that validates its appeal regardless of time—"love's fresh case." Although the final line still instinctively dissociates the prospect of love from age's "outward form," the translation of "antiquity" into a force that need not yield to youth marks a novel instant for this speaker, who throughout the balance of the young man poems has "weighed" little else in his strained and fearful regard for time's passage.

The momentary disavowal we witness here proves unfortunately transient for a poet-lover conditioned by the intimidating power of his society's prevailing disposition against advanced age. The young man's disorienting violation of these representative prejudices about aged decline, which had disturbed sonnet 104, closes out the poems dedicated to him. Despite 108's promise, the poet is left ultimately to warn the young man against his own promise in sonnet 126, just as he had chastened his solitariness at the outset: the youth, "Who hast by waning grown, and therein show'st / Thy lovers withering, as thy sweet self growest," should keep in mind that nature "may detain but not still keep her treasure. / Her audit, though delayed, answered must be, / And her quietus is to render thee" (126:3–4, 10–12). He still cannot effectively bring himself to accept the idea of growing "by waning." His incredulity, as much as any emotional trauma he may have suffered over the course of his evidently tumultuous relationship with the young man, inspires an almost hostile reluctance to give any more credit to the remarkable situation than his perceptions demand. Instead, he keeps his eye fixed on the final "quietus"—which here again looks less to death than to the physical attrition that age must inevitably bring. The experience will assuredly leave its mark on the self-image coloring 138, to which we now return.

Against the Young Man poems' gerontophobic cast, sonnet 138's more circumspect account of sexual potency's endurance unfolds an elaborate psychology that provocatively belies presumptions with which the speaker contends, where the stereotype of aged mendacity dilates into something more deliberated and strategic:

> When my love swears that she is made of truth,
> I do believe her though I know she lies,
> That she might think me some untutored youth,
> Unlearned in the world's false subtleties.
> Thus vainly thinking that she thinks me young,
> Although she knows my days are past the best,
> Simply I credit her false-speaking tongue:
> On both sides thus is simple truth suppressed.
> But wherefore says she not she is unjust?
> And wherefore say not I that I am old?
> O love's best habit is in seeming trust,
> And age in love loves not to have years told.
>   Therefore I lie with her, and she with me,
>   And in our faults by lies we flattered be.

The conventional target of public derision speaks up, keenly alert to and articulate about the personal and social implications of his experience. His searching observations disclose the full complexity of his self-regard, refracted through the multiple and not always compatible lenses of personal desire and public prejudice.

Although readers have long recognized the poem as one critically preoccupied with "lies," the concern with fabrication extends well beyond the notorious pun featured in its couplet.[44] More subtly, the sonnet contests the myth of aged impotence with the consummation its speaker disarmingly acknowledges, while betraying the fantasies of youthfulness that ironically enable this.[45] As Joel Fineman observes, the lyric "economically summarizes the May-December topos that informs the cuckoldry plots of Shakespearean comedy, tragedy, and romance, at the same time as it manages to give both to the dirty old man and to the licentious wench of fabliau a dignity that, at least for the moment of the poem, passes for worldly wisdom."[46] Shakespeare casts his persona not as the besotted, pathetic *senex amans* of tradition, however, but as a canny, sophisticated agent of his own desires, fully cognizant of and confident in the mental tactics he must employ to attain his erotic ends. Openly subscribing to professions of "truth" that he knows to be false, the aging lover plays to his mistress's fantasy that she can both sexually tutor her elder partner and get away with the deception. By means of feigned ignorance, he realizes the carnal knowledge that serves to substantiate the aged self-image so vitally at stake for him. In a supreme exercise of wit, the poet has it both ways. Not only does he both substantiate and violate his stereotypical status as an old man "of less truth than tongue," but his candid admissions renovate and "suppress" the "truth" of his advanced years. His very escape from the temporal attrition that he knows his body too plainly signifies will valorize the potential of the aged lover anew.

At the same time that the speaker's ingenuity finds expression in a practice of sustained disingenuity, however, his confessional performance—in which he "tells" years that he claims he would prefer to leave untold—betrays in a yet more telling fashion his incapacity fully to overcome the age bias he aims to subvert. While the consummated sexuality he enjoys challenges suspicions that "Age is weak and cold," his capacity to experience and satisfy sexual desire is contingent upon the cultivation of a youthful self-image in a setting where innocence and naiveté alone are eroticized. In other words, beneath the aged self-assertion that drives the poem resides an unnerving intuition of his failure to realize a corresponding desire to *un*learn a more pervasive bias against age to which he remains depressingly enthralled. Admitting his own fantasy that the woman "thinks me young" as "vain"—in the multiple senses of disingenuous, narcissistic, and futile—the skeptical speaker reveals his own actual credulity: while he doesn't believe the truth of her sincerity, he does subscribe to the gerontophobic view of age itself (especially "in love") as a "fault," its years something shameful, unworthy of being "told."

As the progress traced in the poem suppresses (that is, essentially *un-*makes) "simple" truth, more complex ones simultaneously emerge in the tenth line's pivotal question, "And wherefore say not I that I am old?" As multiform as anything else in the sonnet, the query stands as both a rhetorical setup ("Why don't I just admit my age?") and a more unsettling self-interrogation ("Why can't I recognize advanced years as anything but undesirable?"). He gives the lie, in other words, to prejudicial suppositions that "age in love loves not," only to give over in the line's complementary rejoinder ("to have years told") to a cultural fetishizing of youth's natural superiority. Shakespeare's persona ends, not by owning and celebrating a sexuality that (as he expressly demonstrates) can endure into late life, but by fostering an illusion of youthfulness that he covets even more ardently.

"Eche one doeth seeke and wishe for age, all while it is awaie," in Timothe Kendall's epigrammatic formulation, only to discover that "When age yet comes, eche doeth it lothe, and all doe it detest." In the sequence's dramatic eroticism, proverbial age comes to bear a subtle relationship to the lust characterized in sonnet 129: "Past reason hunted, and no sooner had, / Past reason hated as a swallowed bait, / On purpose laid to make the taker mad" (129:6–8). As he unfolds in sonnet 151's penultimate performance, his abjuration of conscience is expressly linked to his even greater lust for youthfulness: "Love is too young to know what conscience is" in his determination; so his eager surrender to his "gross body's treason" praises something much more than sexual, orgasmic satisfaction. "My soul doth tell my body that he may / Triumph in love; flesh stays no farther reason, / But rising at thy name doth point out thee, / As his triumphant prize" (7–10). The rush of youthful adrenaline that his transience signifies substantiates his youthful self-image, and so the "drudgery" of his condition becomes self-justifying.

Shakespeare's poet errs, to his own impoverishment, in "redesigning" youth in the image of a society that makes little actual room for the old, regardless of their creative potential. As lyrically fertile as the aged persona proves himself to be, Shakespeare endows him with a demeanor of deep personal dissatisfaction: fetishizing youth, he remains, for all 138's bravado, unable to respect his own worth. To grow old in his world is both to suffer and ultimately to become one of the "wastes of time" referred to in sonnet 12, where survival past one's "prime" to experience "sable curls all silvered o'er with white" only condemns the subject to an impending "hideous night." In this manner, Shakespeare brilliantly imagined perhaps the most deeply wrenching lyric persona of his time. In contrast to the dignified assertiveness of old Adam in *As You Like It,* or even to Falstaff's bold swagger, the sonneteer never allows himself the liberty of embracing senescence on his own terms and so takes his place among the sublimely heartbreaking characters who carry the mature tragedies.

Where Shakespeare's sonnets represent the period's most protracted engagement with society's bitter refusal to countenance beauty in age, it remained for John Donne to provide the most compressed dramatization of this in his elegy commonly titled "The Autumnall," dated variously from the late 1590s to the time of Donne's own death over thirty years later.[47] In some respects, the elegy endeavors to reverse the decline mocked in the "old strange thinges" of the earlier epigram: far from alienating people, age may actually refine intimacies. Yet, in its attempt to repair this breakage, the poem discovers a dividedness all its own. After challenging youth's prevailing "springe" and "summer" vanities in favor of an "Autumnall" subject's superior beauty for thirty-six lines, the poet shears abruptly into a devastating reflection on the bodily decay that awaits a "winter" of advanced senescence. The apology for age's discrete charms ends up foregrounding—as apologies so often do—the very objectionable characteristics it struggles to ameliorate.[48] Although readers have long admired the lyric's refreshingly novel celebration of a beautiful elder woman, thought by many since the seventeenth century to be Lady Magdalen Herbert, even the most sympathetic find it awkward to negotiate what remains an essentially fractured performance. Uncomfortable suspicions linger that "The Autumnall" falters as an encomium gone awry amid its own earnest but risky strategies, or as a sophistic paradox whose cleverness cannot effectively redeem its crueler impulses.

   In order to appreciate more fully the poem's remarkable achievement, I think we need to concentrate precisely upon the glaring fault lines to which the poet deliberately draws our attention rather than trying to talk around or explain these away. Donne's central purpose seems to have been to force a confrontation with the very ambivalence afflicting our regard for old age, something he boldly dramatizes in the performance. Any effort to refamiliarize an audience with the substantial graces that late life potentially harbors will also, he intuits, bring to the surface deeply sublimated anxieties about age's corrosive effects on the body, and the social consequence of these changes. As he does frequently in his poems, Donne (like Shakespeare) holds up for scrutiny his own speaker's professed attitudes along with the cultural mores that gave them shape.

   Although the aging woman's beauty transgresses against time's caustic threats to inspire the poet's self-consciously unorthodox apology, it also reawakens anticipatory fears over a deferred yet immanent decrepitude that proves far more unnerving than the anticipation of death itself. Initial efforts to suppress this darker perspective can result, he realizes, in the explosive reassertion of a gerontophobia that compromises his more benign intentions. This divided experience will further bring the speaker to terms with the equally unyielding limits of his larger poetic ambitions. Neither a perversely ingenious homage to the late splendors of Lady Herbert's (or any other individual's) enduring attractiveness nor a glib satiric indulgence, "The Autumnall" boldly anatomizes impulses that its persona both challenges and betrays.

Predictably, the radical internal disjunction that folds "The Autumnall" back against itself has frustrated efforts to formulate a unified critical response to it. Any immediate reflex to dismiss this feature as merely one more example of Donne's trademark delight in paradox fails to address the excessive brutality it indulges.[49] The generic mockery directed at old age in the poet's formal paradox "That old Men are more Fantastique then younge" strikes us, by contrast, as good-humored to the point of benignity.[50] Perplexed by the elegy's severity, readers have often ventured outside, seeking to mend its weird disparity with the convenient patch of biographical surmise. Mary Alice Greller, for instance, offers a representative view that Donne's insensitive allusions in the poem to age's impending ravages actually were "a compliment to Mrs. Herbert's intellectual and aesthetic perceptiveness, to her sense of humor, her appreciation of wit, her relish for irony, above all, to her realistic and mature acceptance of the stage of life in which both poet and patroness found themselves"; supposedly, "she would have enjoyed the understated compliment of this elaborately wrought conceit much more than fulsome and unambiguous praise."[51] Besides asking a great deal of the patroness's taste or generosity toward the full and unambiguous revulsion for aged flesh ultimately expressed in the poem, such an approach builds its case upon a dangerously speculative foundation.[52]

Somewhat more plausibly, others have examined the poem's surface for clues. Alan Armstrong explains the disjointedness in formalist terms. He reads the sharp turn toward extreme old age's debilities as part of the structural symmetry integral to the paradoxical artist's witty display: Donne plots to distinguish his autumnal subject from this bleaker "third state," which contrasts with her visage just as the "youthful beauty" of the earlier movement had done.[53] This argument likewise proves unsatisfactory, however, since it is the evident *im*balance of the life course so aggressively sketched out in "The Autumnall" that renders the poem's argumentative design so deeply problematic. For all the heady excesses of youth's "infla-meing tyme," the "growing beauties" nonetheless retain their own undis-puted virtues and at least anticipate the prospect of one day knowing a more temperate season's joys, in harsh contrast to the emphatically irre-versible and terminal miseries to which our "winter" existence is subject. Were symmetry the principal concern here, surely the poet might have tempered his characterization of life's final stage to bring it into line with his regard for youth's significant (if lesser) delights, and so offset more gently and effectively the middle ground he is celebrating. Instead, sen-sual, intellectual, and spiritual joys all are utterly canceled in his portrait of elderly decrepitude. This foreclosure of all promise in time overshadows the rhetorical effect monstrously, blocking efforts to explain the disruption simply as a structural device.

Those few who have delved further into the persona Donne crafts for his idiosyncratic presentation have come closest to grasping the elegy's fuller complexity. In her suggestive effort to place Donne's poem amid the "ugly beauty" tradition available to his generation, Heather Dubrow proposes that the speaker's "largely successful" attempts to stave off fears of decay and death by means of the poet's "usual linguistic games" bring his own empowerment into view: "the emphasis on the speech acts of naming and calling reminds us that the poet himself is engaged in such acts, with his ability to name and call, rather than any objective assessment, determin-ing how this autumnal beauty is viewed. . . . Donne at once expresses and contains anxieties that an autumnal beauty is in fact, or will soon become, wintry—and does so by drawing attention to his own ability to construct that beauty as he pleases."[54] But even Dubrow's sensitive interpretation ul-timately misreads his gestures, since it remains, as I will argue, the speaker's *failed* presumption to rhetoricize age away that animates his performance. He deploys his considerable verbal talents to counter the gerontophobic prejudice that would disqualify his subject from such praise only to have this very bias reassert itself, with a vengeance, from within the reservoir of prejudice he shares with those whom he would challenge. The persona's ultimate engagement with his own shortcomings completes a rich psycho-logical drama that marks the elegy as one of Donne's most sophisticated accomplishments.

In the philosophical and clinical literature on the topic at his disposal, as we have seen, Donne might easily have found ample sanction for the divided conceptualization of old age that marks his poem. Among the various models of life's multiple stages that had survived and developed from antiquity, the progress traced from "springe" and "summer beautie" that the poet qualifies, to the "Autumnall" moment he valorizes, to the "winter" he abhors would have found uncontroversial support in Donne's day. Henry Cuffe's *Differences of the Ages of Mans Life,* composed sometime during the final years of the sixteenth century and released posthumously in 1607, exploits the seasonal analogy, eliding autumn and moving directly from the late summer of "our *Manhood,* the most constant and setled part of our life," to winter, subdivided into "degrees or parts":

> the first wherein our strength and heat are evidently impaired, yet not so much, but that there remaineth a will and readinesse to bee doing. . . . The second part of this last part of our life, which they call decrepit old age, is when our strength and heat is so farre decaied, that not onely all abilitie is taken away, but even all willingnesse, to the least strength and motion of our bodie: and this is the conclusion and end of our life, resembling death it selfe, whose harbinger and fore-runner it is.[55]

Even for those hardy or fortunate enough to enjoy the gradual, virtually "insensible" attrition of physical capabilities into late life, a more sudden moment of catastrophic decline awaits. At most, glorification of life's autumn—what we now colloquially term "Indian summer"—only defers, and so potentially compounds, the anxiety of imminent old age. A source of simultaneous desire and terror, age comes to present the ultimate challenge to the composure and continuity of one's self-image.

The stark contextual juxtaposition we encounter in "the Autumnall" suggests a speaker—and by extension the milieu he represents—caught in the double grasp of an *ars amatoria* that seeks to embrace every type of conceivable partner in its omnivorous sexuality and a *remedia amoris* that aims to cancel affection by describing the most distasteful characteristics of any match. It is as if Donne's persona could justify his obsession with this "vintage" figure, but just as readily disengage by contemplating what she will become. The few surviving counter-instances acknowledging an aging female's enduring sexual charms that Donne may have encountered in translated excerpts from *The Greek Anthology* did little to stem the prevailing tide.[56]

Fully cognizant of the constraints these circumstances placed upon his undertaking, Donne managed the delicate adjustment in his poem's opening movement. From its earliest gesture, "The Autumnall" preemptively qualifies its subject's erotic allure by translating venereal attraction into a decorous "reverence": "If t'were a shame to love, t'were here noe shame," the poet proclaims, "Affection here takes reverences Name" (4–5). He cautiously disentangles the pleasure one takes in this woman's company from all fleshliness: her presence, where one may enjoy "noe voluptuousnes, yet all delight," instead excites a more cerebral array of pleasures from which to choose. Mature attractiveness more precisely resides in the distinctive charm of the masculine persuasive force he attributes to her tempered appearance: "Yong beauties force your love," he insists, "and that's a Rape; / This doth but Councell, yet you cannot scape" (3–4). Beyond the violence of youthful passion, her charismatic appeal at once confirms her own intellectual agency and in turn grants a greater sense of agency to the audience, as her no less intense magnetism asks them to think, in the speaker's assessment, rather than merely to feel. "In all her words, unto all hearers fitt / You may at Revells, you at Councell sitt" (22–24). The dignified praise the speaker forges effectively subtends the epiphany for which his argument reaches at lines 33–36:

> If wee love things long sought, age is a thinge
> Which wee are fifty yeares in Compassinge.
> If transitory things, which soone decaye,
> Age must bee loveliest at the latest daye.

In many respects, the passage's benign wisdom constitutes a perfect aphoristic denouement to the entire performance.

The poet's effort to read his subject's seductive intelligence on to her material being—the peculiarity of this "one Autumnall face" that marks his encomium's point of departure—itself faces challenges that soon significantly tax his ingenuity. The seasonal analogy from which his presentation derives its grace cannot altogether mask the indelible physical signature of time that his culture regards with such trepidation. In the words of a sixteenth-century German proverb, " 'Das Alter hat den Kalender am Lieb' (age has the body as a calendar)," and the vulnerable corporeality highlighted in this notion cannot for long be denied in Donne's construct.[57] No sooner does he allow his imagination to play across the very skin that, as Elizabeth Harvey has recently argued, "provides a more complex border between inside and outside, one that emphasizes the shifting, dynamic relation between the two," than the poet's expression begins to lose its own elasticity.[58] The literal texture of the lady's aging visage inspires metaphors whose cosmetic effects fail to eclipse an instinctual impulse to align these features with references to sickness and death that intrude well before the poem's explicit "turn."

Though the woman's "Faire eyes" emit only sufficient heat to sustain the "habitable Tropique Clyme" of advanced age (10), he declares, "who askes more heat then comes from hence, / Hee in a feaver wishes Pestilence" (11–12). Couched sufficiently in the qualified manner of Petrarchan convention, the reference seems innocuous enough. In the ensuing lines, however, the encomiast's inability to dissociate age and decline becomes evident in his peculiarly defensive compulsion to rehabilitate the significance of her tempered "habitable" appearance. "Call not those wrincles Graves," he instructs; instead, we must regard the pronounced age lines to which he calls attention as trenches where Cupid stations himself "like an Anachorite" (13, 16). Not content to de-eroticize the woman, the poet recommissions the god of love himself, who trades in his weapons for implements better suiting his peculiar change of vocation: "And here, till her, which must bee his, death come, / Hee doth not digg a Grave, but build a Tombe" (17–18). Retired to the convent of her chaste older appearance, Cupid abjures the indignity of grave-digging duties, opting instead for the more distinguished yet no less unwonted pastime of erecting mausoleums. However witty, the architectural transition from graves to tombs hardly obscures the more unsettling mortal thoughts that her furrowed skin evidently provokes for the speaker, and (he presumes) anyone else who might behold her.

Between the genteel opening tribute and the sentencious resolution of lines 33–36, a figural static comes to distort the poet's edgy metaphors, down to the dissonant analogy of the Platane tree and its representation of "Ages glorie, Barrennesse" (32). Nothing quite prepares us, however, for the precipitous fall into what Seneca had called the "decrepit and spent" state that the poem so abruptly takes at line 37:

> But name not winter faces, whose skinn's slack,
> Lanke, as an unthrifts pursse; but a soules sack,
> Whose eyes seeke light within, for all here is shade,
> Whose mouthes are holes, rather worne-out, then made,
> Whose every tooth to a several place is gone,
> To vexe their soules, at Resurrection;
> Name not these liveing deaths-heads unto mee,
> For these not antient, but antiques bee.   (37–44)

Especially for one who professes in the next line to "hate extreames," the severity of his imprecations against the superannuated human body nullifies any suppositions about the passage's playfulness. The fragile earlier compliments are frightfully shattered against this extravagant description of physical breakdown. Retrospectively, the placid, sentencious wisdom offered in the immediately preceding lines comes to sound sophistic; it cannot compete with the palpable emotional disgust suddenly unleashed in this brutal dismissal.

Most interestingly, the outburst's invective recapitulates only to invert the argument's previous images and allusions, suggesting that these anxieties that now rush to the surface had always been present, only suppressed. First, his earlier imperative to "Call not" this woman's wrinkles unsightly echoes more distressingly in his repeated preemptory injunctions to "Name not" the grisly winter visages whose identities he refuses to acknowledge even as he so brutally anatomizes their features. In stark contrast to the "one Autumnall face" he singles out for praise, their plurality blurs into a grim generic face*less*ness: even gender distinctions collapse in the passage's pronominal neutrality. Next, where even the alluring "wrincles" of his autumnal subject had retained sufficient firmness to serve as Cupid's "standing house," winter flesh distends into a mere "soules sack," barely fit for habitation by the wizened spirit dwelling feebly within. Moreover, if the "Golden age" of youth had earlier found itself reinvested in an autumnal state of "gold ofte try'ed, and ever newe" (7–8), the old discover themselves in time's bitter economy irreversibly spent, "Lanke, as an unthrifts pursse," altogether non-negotiable. Likewise, the "Faire eyes" of the first movement, which warmed those upon whom they gazed with a temperate heat, are blinkered by the literal and figurative "shade" of blindness and neglect. Desperately seeking light "within," they go without their society's sympathy, finding comfort—if at all—only in being spared a glimpse of their own deformity. Desiccated dwellers-in-darkness, they ironically parody the happier autumnal state of "noe voluptuousness, yet all de[-]light." Finally, the previously endorsed eloquence of "her words, unto all hearers fitt," where "You may at Revells, you at Councell sitt" (23–23), fades into the toothless mumble of "worne-out" holes over which their passive owners, denied even the agency to "make" their own mouths, exert no human control.

   In short, upon closer scrutiny we discern how the lines' explosive spontaneity brings about a rather precise undoing of the earlier presentation's witty defenses. Beyond the revelry and counseling sobriety that lingers on in the elder woman's face lurks the darker solemnity of funereal decline that will not for long be kept at bay. Bitterly prefiguring the dispersal of these decrepit characters' teeth as a breakdown of physical integrity that will "vexe their soules, at Resurrection," this speaker suggests that his fear of old age far outstrips his fear of mortality. The ghostly prospect of what comes after the grave (which as his audience well knew might yawn unexpectedly before any individual, regardless of age) at least held out the solace of potential spiritual redemption and rejuvenation; but in the mortality that their memento mori faces presage, the undeniable afflictions threatening age were, by contrast, all too palpable.

In the consolatory literature of the period, one of death's abiding virtues was its promise of release from the infirmity of age.[59] Carried on the wings of unmitigated disgust, the speaker conspicuously invokes the "soul" twice, and the day of Resurrection itself, only to add greater ferocity to his ridicule. So exclusive is his fixation upon time's decimating power over the human form that it obscures any vision of release from bodily vexations on a day of spiritual rejuvenation, the only real event left for these benighted "antiques" to look forward to. Revealingly, the offhand allusions lock us ever more depressingly into the kind of sentiment expressed in Erasmus's poem on senescence, published in his *Epigrammata* of 1518, that "before his fleeting years have finished the fifth decade, old age does not hesitate to assail the immortal part of a man, the part descended from the heavens; even this she boldly challenges and has no fear of assaulting the sacred sinews of his inner nature" (46–51).[60] Mocking the retreat to a glowering "light within" that age allegedly compels, the poem simultaneously betrays its own darker inward turn, to a state of mind where compassion subsides as spirituality itself degenerates into a joke.

In his closing command to "Name not these lieving deaths-heads *unto mee*," the speaker revealingly puts his signature to the preceding gerontophobic rant. This "personalizing" gesture reaches back to the individuated perspective announced at the start—"Noe springe, nor summer beautie, hath such grace / As *I* have seene in one Autumnall face" (my emphases). On the threshold of the final stand succeeding the turn and counterturn of the poem's earlier movements, the culminating effort to discriminate dismissively between the "antient" he reveres and the "antiques" (punning on antics or grotesques) he despises sounds glib and feeble. Though the earlier tribute had dramatically traced the cosmetic power of verse, capable of translating boldly invoked "wrincles" into Cupid's "trenches," the more disturbing later movement discovers the limits of poetic resourcefulness in his imaginative incapacity to locate some redeeming quality in the deep winters of our existence, should we find ourselves so unfortunate (in his implied view) to survive into such a state. Compelled to glance upon the picture of bodily decomposition graphically alive in his mind's eye, the poet experiences a furious reassertion of barely suppressed anxieties over the devastating effects of age. In light of the abrupt about-face the poem unexpectedly makes, we come to realize with violent immediacy that the speaker's efforts to compartmentalize the life course serve less to flatter his aging subject than to pacify his own less easily appeased anxieties about an inevitable slide into a bitter twilight of physical decline, and the loss of identity that attends it. These fears can be contained only briefly and at great expense before they violently reclaim his imagination, as they do here. Like the "Rape" that a young beauty metaphorically enacts upon the erotic imaginations of her audience, the more literal carrying-off of physical sensation becomes, for him, a plight we "cannot scape" except through the dubious channel of premature demise.

The rigid demarcation between autumnal splendor and winter disgrace set down by the speaker, in other words, brings him into stark confrontation with the boundaries of his own rhetorical capacities: his contraventional valorization of later life cannot hope to prevent—or even defer—a physical debility more intimidating than the prospect of death itself. If death can take no pride in its presumed mastery over all things mortal, as one of Donne's most famous holy sonnets will protest, age can inspire a dread far more substantial, because palpable (ironically) for everyone but the vegetating elder him- or herself. And just as the very inefficacy of that sonnet's arguments "improves the poem," as John Carey has so provocatively argued, "for it shows how little its reasonings have impinged on the speaker's basic fears," so does the elegy's argumentative dissolution enrich rather than compromise its effectiveness.[61] However creatively he may convert wrinkles into Cupid's "Graves," the encomiast's writing cannot effectively compete with the chiaroscuro artistry of the supreme deconstructive agent, time itself, whose physical inscriptions on the surface of the subject's aging skin will always prevail. He cannot *en*grave her well-preserved attractiveness against the lines time will continue to engrave ever more deeply in her skin, or delay the grave significance of this inscription for long.

Working on twin registers determined by the persona and the poet who fashions him, "The Autumnall" folds together a dual intention to console and chasten its audience with the prospect of time's effect on sexuality, prestige, and the self-image grounded in these social experiences. The speaker's aberrant gesture expresses confidence that time need not diminish us—since even a woman (he intimates), whose appearance determines so much about her position in the masculine world she inhabits, can continue to exert an allure into advanced years—only to terminate this hope in the terrifying caricature that he abruptly and impulsively sketches. The poem's chief dramatic effect lies in his very inability to sustain a complimentary sense of "reverence" for long, as his endeavor of encomiastic persuasion or self-reinforcement crumbles under the weight of disgust he ultimately cannot ignore. As is typical of Donne—especially the Donne of the *Elegies*—the speaker's naked psychology takes center stage, exposing our deepest fears of the aged state we struggle to deny. When the would-be celebrant of age resigns himself with the words "I hate extreames; yet I had rather staye/With tombes, then cradles to weare out a day" (45–46), he transparently confesses that his resolution at best is making a virtue of necessity. After the ringing disparagement unleashed in the preceding passage, as graceless as the face he had set out to honor was purportedly graceful, he surrenders himself to a "descending" love, "ebbing" on the road back to a home that promises little reassurance. Sadder and perhaps wiser as the result of his previous efforts, he betrays in the "naturall lation" or process to which he refers a poignant disenchantment:

> Since such Loves naturall lation is may still
> My Love descend, and journey downe the hill
> Not panting after growing beauties, soe
> I shall ebbe on, with them whoe homeward goe.   (47–50)

We may find in these words a tacit concession that "ancient" and "antique" states admit a much greater proximity within the scope of life's "natural" process than he had attempted to deny. Refusing to embrace our existence's terminal stage, he had essentially devalued the very autumnal moment whose enchantments he set out to promote; arriving finally at an unretouched affirmation of his own breathless "descent," he departs with a sobered, far more substantive tribute to the capacities and the dignity of late life. In this fashion, the final movement quietly realigns the speaker's polarized impulses, imparting to the poem a profoundly emotional, dramatic completeness.

These closing lines display both a recovered composure and a chastened perspective, available only through the poet's frank confrontation, face to aging face, with his complicity in the gerontophobia he had set out to refute. An awareness, however begrudging, tempers the passage and (retrospectively) the entire performance: the "extreames" of cradle and tomb, between which we all wear out days that in turn wear us out physically, mark the essential though unsettling terminuses of our experience. Only by acknowledging the terrors of our own decline that refuse to be rhetoricized away, and the defensive cruelties to which these drive us, can we savor more fully the fall beauty this woman embodies. Yet the larger effect Donne achieves in "The Autumnall" transcends even this *carpe vesperum* advisory to cherish life's penultimate moments while we may, to realize the urgency of a more inclusive fellowship, especially with those who are as we may one day be. Unlike the Hamon epigram, "The Autumnall" will escape the estrangement from other and self threatened by age precisely through the speaker's parting determination to keep company "with them" whose fate, however unnerving, he consents to share. The chillier shade of winter may not afford as much shelter as "Zerxes strange Lydian Love, the Platane tree" (29), but it offers as much as we can hope for along our "barren" path leading to the security of a final "home." The oft-tried counsel he discovers for himself at last, like the conciliation it enables, can prove ever new and just valuable enough to sustain the most destitute unthrift. Supremely eager to confront that most suppressed of all "natural" and inevitable apprehensions, Donne candidly engages and reconfigures in his elegy the gerontophobic urges that subtly and overtly plagued the sensibilities of his day, and our own.

Acutely sensitive to matters of corporeality and appearance, as critics have long observed, Donne's companion Ben Jonson was as aware as his fellow poet of the limits that age placed upon the individual. At the beginning of his play *Epicene,* Jonson ironically appropriates his friend's expression to mock the "grave and youthful matron, the Lady Haughty": "A pox of her autumnal face, her pieced beauty," the character Clerimont exclaims (1.1.80–81). Moreover, opening his lyric collection *The Forrest* with the poem "Why I Write Not of Love"—perhaps a good-humored swipe at his colleague, whose secular poetry spoke of little else—Jonson grounds his recusancy in his agedness: "Then wonder not," he advises, "my numbers are so cold, / When *Love* is fled, and I grow old" (10–12).

But the poetry I have invoked here offers another prospect, one that glances less resignedly, and more compassionately, at the endurance of passion into late life. Let me leave off with a short piece included in the anthology *Englands Helicon,* published in 1600. There the anonymous "Olde *Melibeus* Song, courting his Nimph" (attributed at one point to Greville) sounds a curious variation on the Venus and Adonis myth that had dominated Jaggard's offerings of the previous year. Disillusioned by her amorous obsession with the beautiful but disdainful young hunter, the goddess seeks temporary shelter in the affection of age, much to the elder speaker's bemusement:

> Loves Queene long wayting for her true-Love,
>   Slaine by a Boare which he had chafed,
>   Left off her teares, and me embraced,
> She kist me sweete, and call'd ne new-Love.
>   With my silver haire she toyed,
>   In my stayed lookes she joyed.
>   Boyes (she sayd) breede beauties sorrow:
>   Olde men cheere it even and morrow.
>
> My face she nam'd the seate of favour,
>   All my defects her tongue defended,

My shape she prais'd, but most commended
My breath more sweete then Balme in savour.
Be olde man with me delighted,
Love for love shall be requited.
With her toyes at last she wone me:
Now she coyes that hath undone me.[62]

Up until the final line's sad reversal, the poem reads like the ultimate mythic fantasy of aged love, where Venus translates the physical attributes that the speaker himself still identifies as "defects" into virtues preferable to youth's fleeting attractions. Although she abandons Melibeus once she has reduced him to the status of one more of her playthings, the still incredulous *senex amans* recalls the passion to which he succumbed against his better judgment with a wonder that both ameliorates and enhances his sensitivity to the constitution that can still somehow substantiate love's attractions. His experience arouses an awareness of the potential he had presumed forsaken, and the subsequent abandonment he suffers cannot altogether counteract the bittersweet self-discovery that survives. The encounter does not so much remind him of what it was like to be young as it imparts a new vision of what age can still sustain, physically and emotionally.

Refusing to dismiss the rich complexity of aged sexuality, or to objectify its agents as old things, the period's verse fruitfully confronts the gerontophobic urges that literally set the stage for the gravest reflection on what it means to attempt a defense against "old age" in all of our drama, *King Lear*.

CHAPTER FIVE

"Confin'd to Exhibition":
King Lear through the Spectacles of Age

O F ALL THE LYRIC MEDITATIONS on the plight of old age to survive from antiquity, none confronts anxieties over dependency in a more stark fashion than the brief fragment attributed to Theognis:

> Men get a fair share, from the gods, of youth
> And horrid age and many another thing.
> But one thing's worst of all, more terrible
> Than death or any sickness: when you raise
> Children and give them all the tools of life,
> And suffer greatly getting wealth for them,
> And then they hate their father, pray he'll die
> And loathe him as a beggar in their midst.[1]

As a folkloric topos, the provider's reversion to the status of *ptōchós* or "beggar" takes many forms. One of these, the pseudo-historical narrative of the British King Leir, lent the *Sonnets*' author raw material for what we often regard as his greatest tragedy. Acutely sensitive to this threat of diminution, Shakespeare's royal character reflexively stages a mock-enactment of pathetic indigence as the actual prospect of suing to his offspring first becomes disturbingly real. When Regan proposes that her father return to Goneril and patch things up with her, Lear retorts "Do you but mark how this becomes the house! / 'Dear daughter, I confess that I am old; / Age is unnecessary. On my knees I beg / That you'll vouchsafe me raiment, bed, and food'" (2.4.153–56).[2] As if to preempt the child who he declares has "strook me with her tongue, / Most serpent-like, upon the very heart" from cursing him further, Lear follows his sardonic obsequiousness with his own poisonous words, calling on the heavens to "Strike her young bones, / You taking airs, with lameness!" (2.4.160–61, 163–64). Disgusted by his histrionics,

Regan upbraids her father for making a spectacle of himself: "Good sir, no more; these are unsightly tricks" (2.4.157). However, embarrassing the audience—transferring the shame onto the spectator by making his daughter the focus—is precisely the elder's intention. His "unsightly" gestures aim to turn the witness's Medusa gaze back upon herself.

The beggar's spectacular deployment of his own body and its disruptive effect on the social world he marginally inhabits, as William Carroll's searching anatomy of Tom o'Bedlam's role in the play has established, help to orient *King Lear*'s "persistent interrogation of the human body's place in the natural and social orders."[3] Insofar as the old king and mock beggar fuse theoretically in Lear's charade before Regan, and literally bond in the subsequent scenes on the heath, the aging body likewise occupies a central place in our comprehension of the dramatic issues that Shakespeare explores as a similar object of a public gaze. Even under the most generous circumstances, senescence faces the humiliating prospect of subjection to the "scornful eyes" that Lear so quickly comes to know (2.4.166). This very fear accents George Whetstone's commonplace in his "Verses written of 20. good precepts," published in *The Paradise of Daintie Devises* of 1576, which winds up its list of counsels by looking to life's decline:

> *Provide for age*[,] or looke to dye with greefe,
> Some forst thro[ugh] shame ther aged freends do ayde:
> But O sowre lookes, *so salves this sweete releefe*[,]
> As day and night, with sighes they are dismayde.[4]

Even should others follow their better instincts by extending support and comfort to the old, the kindness will come, in the poet's view, at the cost of the "sowre lookes" that conventionally accompany whatever "releefe" to which others begrudgingly find themselves constrained.

If matters of aged self-image and the larger societal witnessing that helps to shape it have seemed less critically urgent than they obviously should in a tragedy that has chosen senescence so profoundly and distinctively as its central topic, this has much to do with the play's peculiar refusal to enact explicitly the physical curtailments commonly associated with old age. Whereas Edgar's begrimed and mutilated torso remains before us both verbally and visually, other characters' professions of decrepitude seldom square with the vigorous physical activity that accompanies these references. The king declares his elderly decline in the opening scene, for instance, only to indulge a fit of physical rage unbefitting one prepared to "crawl toward death." In the Royal Shakespeare Company's 2011 production of

the play, Greg Hicks's Lear returns from the hunt in act 1, scene 4 leading his raucous attendants, the boar's carcass hoist across his own hardy
shoulders. Similarly, his final broken confession, "I am old now," comes
in the wake of his dispatching the henchman who has executed Cordelia.
Yet this tremendous resilience of the aged bodies envisioned throughout
serves provocatively to foreground the physical, psychological, and (above
all) social apprehensions that cluster around the figure of the elder. Kent's
epitaph upon his departed master, "The wonder is he hath endur'd so
long, / He but usurp'd his life" (5.3.317–18), reverberates as both an expression of disbelief that a human constitution could show such stamina and a
telling refusal to accept the legitimacy (that finest of words in this play) of
what he has just witnessed. The vision of age Shakespeare creates at once
commands our wondrous gaze and excites our denial.

The denial—in the sense of an unwillingness to acknowledge conspicuous realities in order to shelter oneself psychologically—that significantly
informs a good deal of the play's overall dynamic also understandably
comes to trouble audience response to the extremes of human experience
that Shakespeare aims to depict. Most notoriously, Nahum Tate's radical
revision of *King Lear*'s spectacular ending illustrates a prevailing reluctance
to confront the physical and metaphysical horrors highlighted in Shakespeare's version of the story. Similarly, the critical tradition's evident reluctance to engage what the play has to say precisely about the experience
of senescence also stems from a pervasive nervousness or embarrassment
about the topic that hampers direct investigation. Although virtually all of
the vast commentary pays some kind of lip service to the king's advanced
age as a singular aspect of his character, the record has taken too little care
to address this feature in a sustained way, opting instead to deflect discourse onto other, related matters.[5] Almost paradoxically, the question of
age goes begging through a largely uncharted landscape.

In one of the play's most chillingly proleptic lines, the Earl of Gloucester announces to his son Edmund that he will "not need spectacles"
(1.2.35). His unwitting remark is rendered ironic not only by the agony of
his impending blindness but by the fact that he will himself soon become
a show, turned loose by his tormentors upon a world always in need of
spectacles—particularly, as I argue in this chapter, spectacles of old age.
Several lines earlier, Gloucester had wandered onto the scene reflecting
aloud to himself about the troubling prospect of the old king "Confin'd
to exhibition" (1.2.25). By the strict inflection of the term's primary usage
in 1605, "exhibition" here refers to the pension to which the monarch

has shamefully been reduced; but it also reaches back etymologically to its Latin root *ex* + *habere,* to "hold forth" or (in the recovered modern sense) "display." In this construction, the expression perfectly captures the predicament in which both he and Lear will find themselves ensnared. As embodiments of old age, they must contend with the literal obscenity of their "unsightly" statures before a society that nonetheless fears the inevitable reality they represent and wishes to consolidate its power (while shoring up its self-image) by preserving them as controlled spectacles. The title character's struggle to marshal his own formidable constitution against the public and private roles that the ascending generation would constitute for him in particular emerges as one of the tragedy's most potent dramatic achievements.

Of all the period genres, Elizabethan drama represented old age most frequently and casually—more so than pastoral or lyric, certainly; yet the form also carried the heaviest topical baggage, supplying Shakespeare and his contemporaries with a well-developed array of stock figures from which to draw. Most notably, the ubiquitous *senex* of Latin comedy established the pattern of senior folly and obstructionism that stands behind characters as diverse as *A Midsummer Night's Dream*'s Egeus, Juliet's father, Capulet, or even Shylock. Closer in time, the "pantaloon" of Italian commedia dell'arte reinforced dramatic caricature of crabbed (though largely impotent) elder authority.[6] By virtue of their oppositional parental status, regardless of the chronological age they may manifest, these figures step forward as exponents of aged privilege, and so in their retrenchment come to be regarded as superannuated both by the younger company who typically triumphs over them (morally if not actually) by play's end and by the audience who witnesses this enactment of generational conflict.

Alongside the classical and continental sources, a developing tradition supplied Elizabethan playwrights with alternative popular incarnations of old age. The eponymous comic heroine of the university play *Gammer Gurtons Nedle* of "Mr. S," for instance, projected a kinetic, knockabout image of senescence fully capable of delivering on her threats of physical violence against anyone who would dare attack her as an "old gyb" or "withered witch."[7] Similarly, the title character of John Lyly's *Mother Bombie,* as a "cunning woman," struggles to parry with dignity the charges of witchcraft that her efficacious prophecies earn her along with a more callous general gerontophobia that typifies the play's younger cast: "though you bee as olde as you are," one of them addresses her, "yet am I as younge as I am, and because that I am so fayre, therefore are you so fowle; & so farewell frost, my fortune naught me cost."[8] On a more tragic plane, the nameless "Old Man" of Marlowe's *Doctor Faustus* seeks to offer redemptive solace as a "sweet friend" to the reprobate hero as the pious embodiment of aged holiness. Although his gentle guidance cannot finally rescue Faustus, this fatherly *senex* stands up righteously against the devils who arrive to menace him. In such roles, the elders featured on the Elizabethan stage could strike defiantly self-reliant—if ultimately no less formulaic—poses.

In the main action and subplots of his *Endimion* (1588), Lyly contrived a somewhat more gnarled presentation of senescence. The principal threat edging the play toward tragedy is the curse Endimion suffers, whereby he falls asleep as a youth only to wake decades later as a decrepit old man: "thou shalt sleep out thy youth and flowring time, and become dry hay before thou knowest thy selfe greene grasse," the aged sorceress Dipsas pronounces, wringing a pained lament from her own assistant Bagoa, "O faire *Endimion!* how it grieveth me that that faire face must be turned to a withered skinne, & taste the paines of death before it feele the reward of love" (2.3.32–34 and 46–49). Even the goddess Cynthia—a transparent representation of Elizabeth herself—who will at last remedy his plight in her eternal capacity to regenerate, cannot suppress her grief at the sight of the transformed youth: "Hollow eyes? gray haires? wrinckled cheekes? and decayed limmes? Is it destinie, or deceite that hath brought this to passe?" (4.3.75–77). This portrayal of old age as a fearsome state of pitiful decay is compounded, moreover, by the young braggart fool Sir Tophas. His erotic infatuation with Dipsas sets the stage for an expansive mock-encomium of the disheveled crone, whose chin (we are informed) "almost toucheth her knees" (5.2.56–57). Yet against this harsh comedy Lyly poises the patient compassion of her long-suffering husband Geron, with whom the reformed Dipsas reunites in the final scene, again through Cynthia's sponsorship. Lyly's juxtaposed visions of senescence as either a horrid though ultimately ridiculous state of spiritual and physical corruption or a time of passive dignity and disdained wisdom bespeaks the playwright's own conflicted perspective. Performed (as we are told on the title page) "before the Queenes Majestie at Greenewich on Candlemas day at night, by the Chyldren of Paules," the original production must have further ironized this representation of late life with young boys in the roles of the diverse elders.

One of the most curious dramatic reflections on matters of old age and generational conflict occurs, however, in the anonymous interlude *New*

Custome, a work possibly of Edwardian origin but significantly redacted sometime after 1570 and published in 1573.[9] This brief morality play crystallizes a striking example of the redefined relationship between youth and senescence that accompanied emerging Protestant ideology, which (as historians have long observed) "characterized the older generation as a race of exhausted old men, spiritually worn out."[10] The attitude finds spirited expression in Henry Smith's sermon "The Young Mans Taske," where the preacher casts modern youth in the role of the spiritually wise, against the retrenchment of an elder Catholic generation. Smith likens sin itself to "an olde man, so tough and froward, that he will not heare," lamenting in the same breath how difficult it is "to reclaime one of these olde sinners, or grande Papists, which are incorporate into poperie."[11] He saves his most severe imprecations against the senior establishment for his sermon's climactic closing movement:

> The yong men follow Christ, the yong men heare the word, the yong men sanctifie themselves, the young men stande for the church, the yong men beare the heate of this day: olde Noah is drunke, old Lot is sleepie[,] olde Sampson hath lost his strength. Once the yonger brother did steale the blessing from the elder, & now he hath got it againe, as the malice of Esau shewes, which persecutes him for it. . . . What mervaile then if they be not reverenced, but mockt and pointed at, when Sem and Iaphet had need to come againe, and cover their nakednesse? . . . Which made an olde Father of this Citie say, which now is with God, that if there were any good to bee done in these dayes, it is the yong men that must doe it, for the olde men are out of date, their courage stoopes like their shoulders, their zeale is withered, like their browes; their faith staggereth like their feete, and their religion is dead before them. (pp. 473–75)

Protestantism's ascent—grounded in its ambition to recover the faith's purer, "primitive" spirit, and its corresponding self-image as a force of rejuvenation—would come at the expense of an attenuated elder authority that masked its actual "upstart" illegitimacy behind a façade of sage maturity.

It is precisely this reformist self-conception as *puer senex* that *New Custome* enacts. The "enterlude," whose opening line announces, "Al things be not soe as in sight they doe seeme," traces the persecution and ultimate vindication of "New Custome, a minister," at the hands of two elder church officials, named (unambiguously enough) "Perverse Doctrine" and "Ignoraunce."[12] Even before the action begins, the Prologue sets forth the conceptual confusion that results when

> the Primitive constitution whiche was fyrst appointed
> Even by God him self, and by Christ his annoynted:

Confirmed by thappostles, and of great antiquitie:
See howe it is perverted by mannes wicked iniquitie,
To be called newe Custome, or newe Constitucion,
Surely a name of to muche ungodly abusion.

When in the action proper New Custome takes his seniors (who jealously claim religious doctrine as their exclusive domain) to task with his charge "New fashions you have constitute[d] in Religion," they immediately indict his youthful pretension:

Pervers d. Whie, how olde art thou, tell mee I pray thee hartely?
New cust. Older then you I perceive.
Pervers d. What older then I?
           The younge knave by the masse not fully thirtie,
           Woulde [b]e elder then I that am above sixtie?
New cust. A thousande, and a halfe, that surely is my age.
           Aske and enquire of all men of knowlage.
Pervers d. A thousand yeares olde? precious sowle I am out of my wittes.
           Hee is possessed of some devyll or of some evill sprites.
           Why thou art a young knave, of that sorte I saye,
           That brought into this realme but the other daye,
           This new learning, and these heresies, and suche other things moe,
           With strange guises invented no[t] long agoe.   (pp. Biii r–v)

As an upshot of their violent exchange, New Custome discloses his actual identity as "Primitive Constitution," a name lost to those who now deem "olde to be newe, and new to be olde" in their deceitful teaching. As Smith had so vehemently argued, youth has come to reanimate primal religious truths, much to the shame of a splenetic and decrepit seniority too far gone to recognize its own enfeebled wrongheadedness.

By the play's close, the newly titled Primitive Constitution reclaims his ancient entitlement. Despite the assistance of Cruelty and Avarice— whose methods, interestingly enough, include hanging their victims "privilie, / Saying that them selves so dyed desperately," and the sponsorship of fratricidal betrayal in order to cheat the true heir out of "all his lyvinge" (pp. Ciii verso and Civ)—Perverse Doctrine cannot wear down his patient adversary, through whom he is at last converted by the character Light of the Gospel's superior instruction. Beneath this propagandistic wish fulfillment, however, resides a more disturbing justification and translation of gerontophobic resentment. Requisitioning a truer ecclesiastical doctrine as "constituted" by the early church, the interlude's staid but nimble hero retains his conspicuously youthful constitution even as he arrogates to himself an authority grounded in "antiquity" and so triumphs over the perverse and ignorant elders who would presume to hold him down. An amalgam of the best of both worlds, youth displaces arrogant senescence by paradoxically turning a more genuine reverence for aged prerogative against it.

Himself an aggressive and voracious young student of the dramatic models that his contemporary cultural scene increasingly presented, by the 1590s Shakespeare demonstrated his own capacity to depict old age in a variety of conventional and innovative forms. As noted above, the obsession with fatherly prerogative displayed by Egeus and "Old Capulet" helps drive their respective comedy and tragedy. While seniority anchors the privileges claimed by these figures (despite the actual indeterminacy of their calendar ages), anxieties about the onset of old age conversely trouble heroes from Titus Andronicus to Othello. At the same time, we have noted how Shakespeare followed Lodge's championing of senescence in *As You Like It,* dignifying old Adam even against the gerontophobic caricature that Jaques parrots. In particular, the history plays that especially distinguish this first half of his career feature an array of valiant, aged councilors—from the Talbot and Clifford of the *Henry VI* plays to *Richard II*'s John of Gaunt—who are exemplary in their stamina and integrity. Over all these, however, bulks the playwright's most complex and inventive portrayal of charismatic old age, the great anti-councilor Falstaff.

A conspicuous reversal of the *puer senex,* Falstaff conducts himself throughout the *Henry IV* plays as a Silenus-like *senex elementarius,* or "old man young." At least well into his sixties (if we are to judge from the comic understatement hedging his self-characterization as "his age some fifty, or, by'r lady, inclining to threescore" [*1HIV* 2.4.424–25]), and possibly approaching eighty (by the calculations available in *2HIV* 3.2), Falstaff displays a sustained exuberance even as he ages before our eyes across the play's second part. From the mock-denials of his senescence before the Chief Justice in *2HIV* 1.2, where he asserts, "The truth is, I am only old in judgment and understanding" (191–92), to his later solitary acknowledgment "Lord, Lord, how subject we old men are to this vice of lying!" (3.2.303–4), he remains fully cognizant of how the stereotypes he so often violates do (or can) stick. His bold self-defense before the prince during their theatrical tavern charade becomes in many respects a signature apology for old age's reassuring vitality. "If to be old and merry be a sin, then many an old host that I know is damn'd," he proclaims, and celebrates himself as "more valiant, being as he is old Jack Falstaff . . . banish plump Jack, and banish all the world" (*1HIV* 2.4.471–72 and 477–80). The heartbreak that infuses Hal's ultimate decision to make good at the close of Part II on his somber reply to all this, "I do, I will," is rendered all the more bitter by the young king's explicit attack on his old companion's senescence:

> I know thee not, old man, fall to thy prayers.
> How ill white hairs becomes a fool and jester!
> I have long dreamt of such a kind of man,
> So surfeit-swell'd, so old, and so profane;
> But being awak'd, I do despise my dream.   (*2HIV* 5.5.47–51)

As Herbert S. Donow has perceptively remarked, "Falstaff is rejected not so much because the old man is a sinner but because the sinner is an old man, and because the old man has failed to adapt successfully."[13] Like New Custome, Henry vanquishes his superannuated antitype in the name of a superior maturity he self-consciously appropriates. Reaching far beyond the morality play's narrower homiletic purpose, however, Shakespeare's tragicomic resolution here forces a more direct confrontation with the troubling ageist implications of this self-righteous gesture.

The far less complicated defeat that Falstaff suffers in *The Merry Wives of Windsor* suggests Shakespeare's willingness to flatten his masterful comic invention into a stereotype of aged folly, "One that is well-nigh worn to pieces with age" (in the disgusted indictment of his matronly love interest Mistress Page) who is out "to show himself a young gallant" (2.1.21–22) or (in her husband's final summary) "Old, cold, wither'd, and of intolerable entrails" (5.5.153–54). Stripped of the witty resourcefulness evident in the history plays, and subject (as Anthony Ellis has argued) to an effeminizing melancholy that is literally manifest in the humiliating cross-dressing to which he submits, *The Merry Wives'* Falstaff seems to occupy a conventional role in an orthodox comedy that "projects the cause of bodily disorder onto the *senex,* and the control of performance to the younger characters who stage-manage his correction."[14] Yet even here the playwright betrays a certain discomfort with the subjection of old age to the "correction" of "younger" hands. Not only are the agents of Falstaff's punishment older figures who regard themselves as defenders of mature sobriety, but one of these, Francis Ford, shows himself subject to destructive jealous passion. Should we put any stock in the anecdote that Shakespeare composed the play as a hasty response to the queen's own desire to see Falstaff "in love"—an equivocal commission if there ever was one—then he might be seen as erring on the side of caution, celebrating mature chastity at the expense of aged infatuation: the old knight in any case proves far more in love with himself than with either of his erotic interests. In typical style, he takes shelter in the discomfiture he shares with so many of his adversaries—young and old—in the play's comic resolution, as his final words acknowledge: "When night-dogs run, all sorts of deer are chas'd" (5.5.238).

Whatever provocation or inspiration Elizabeth provided Shakespeare and his fellow dramatists in life, her death in 1603 elicited a more general retrospective. As Curtis Perry has so cogently demonstrated, a rich and multivalent "nostalgia" for the queen—which would prove a bane of the Stuart monarchy throughout the following century—took shape in the early years of her successor's reign.[15] Explicitly, works like Thomas Heywood's *If You Know Not Me, You Know Nobody* plays of 1605 and 1606 revisited the years leading up to Elizabeth's accession and her (idealized) relationship with London's merchant class later in the century. Such nostalgic impulses, however, needed to reckon with more somber recollections of the acrimonious generational conflict that had scarred the queen's final decade, along with the bitter fact that so many of her subjects (as we have heard Camden report) "were weary of her long government, (for things of long continuance, though good, are tedious)." At the dawn of James's reign, with the battle lost and won, some found themselves contemplating Elizabeth's protracted tenure more abstractly, to significantly different effect. It seems no coincidence that at this particular moment the Lear legend, with its account of an ingratitude more nightmarish than anything lamented by Elizabeth's sympathetic historians, would reenter the national imagination with such force. Although in no way a direct "commentary" on the recently deceased queen, Shakespeare's great tragedy (like the anonymous play that immediately preceded it) is nonetheless crafted in the refracted afterglow of her own confrontation with the hazards attending her very endurance in the face of younger forces ever eager to claim the political stage. In this respect, *King Lear* looks back upon the spectacle of a recent past to ask what it means to grow old in power.

Shakespeare wrote for an audience earnestly conditioned to moralize the ubiquitous spectacles it beheld. For the sensitized witness, everyday experience translated into opportunities for instruction no less than the most formal displays engineered to edify a populace. The playwright had gently sent up this sensibility in *As You Like It* when the report of a stricken stag expiring mournfully next to a brook prompts Duke Senior to inquire, "But what said Jaques? / Did he not moralize this spectacle?" (2.1.43–44). However routine, such interpretive impulses remained troubled by anxieties over misconstruction, fears neatly accommodated in English by the homonymic connection between "spectacles" as objects of public vision and "spectacles" as the eyeglasses or corrective instruments through which we often need to view the former in order to avoid error. The popularity of this verbal linkage is apparent in the widespread punning that we encounter across an array of contemporary literary registers. A broadside issued in 1589 by William Fulwood offers a minor yet strikingly graphic instance. *A Spectacle for Perjurers* sets out to publicize its author's vindication: Fulwood, who had been indicted on charges of "conspiracie" based on the bogus testimony of one John Jones, is exonerated when Jones is discovered to have perjured himself in a subsequent case. Fulwood ostensibly circulates the report as proof of how God beholds the crimes that men commit and as an admonition to those who deceive themselves into thinking otherwise. Despite his righteous confidence, however, Fulwood cannot help but close with a nervous glance at how depressingly "any man may be condemned in any cause whatsoever" by means of false witness. To offset this apprehension, his printed "spectacle" illustrates its contention that *Deus Videt* (God oversees) by placing the words inside a pair of spectacles adorning the page's upper border (see fig. 2). The account's proper moral of divine vigilance is one that the reader unequivocally perceives, but only through the literal lenses of this emblem.

Such "spectacular" mentality is likewise evident on a more bookish level in Lodowick Lloyd's rambling compendium *Linceus Spectacles*—coincidentally set to press by the publisher Nicholas Okes almost in tandem with his 1608 quarto edition of *King Lear*—where the pun on "spectacles" obtains from the title on throughout the didactic scenes culled indiscriminately from scriptural, historical, and literary sources.[16] At one model turn, Lloyd proclaims his overriding thesis that "*Exempla magis movent quam verba* [the (visual) example moves more than the word alone]" by invoking the custom of ancient drama, where "*Priamus Deiphobus,* and many other Greeks and Trojans were brought in upon a stage, ugly, guastly, and bloudy to persuade men that live ill, to live better by the terrible and horrible sights of such great men, beeing dead, & in hell punished" and wishing "such were plaid on their stages in London."[17] Like Fulwood, Lloyd at the same time betrays an awareness of the more complex matter of directing or determining audience response to the very spectacles he foregrounds, remarking on the way figures throughout history had disregarded or willfully misread their own exemplary circumstances, for "these had not *Linceus* Spectacles on" (p. 26).

The connection between spectacles as objects of attention and as the glasses through which we look to perceive these exhibits' significance properly finds its most florid expression in John Lyly's *Euphues and his England*

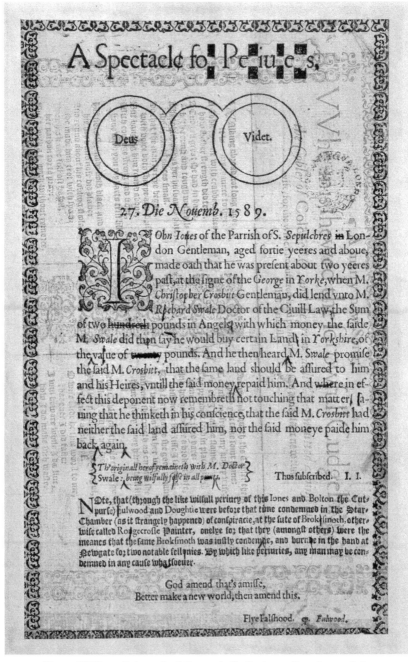

Fig. 2. William Fulwood, *A Spectacle for Perjurers* (London, 1589).
Copyright the Society of Antiquaries of London.

(1580) when toward the close the title character designs a "Glasse" for "the Ladyes and Gentlewomen of Italy," comparing them unfavorably with the virtues of his own countrywomen: "But your eyes being too olde to judge of so rare a spectacle," he challenges them, "my counsell is that you looke with spectacles," and then proceeds to specify that "The spectacles I would have you use, are for the one eie judgment with-out flattering your selves, for the other eye, beliefe with-out mistrusting of me" (2:189–90). Behind the conventional wordplay rests the serious notion that a spectator is always potentially implicated in the spectacle he witnesses. Unable to rely upon his audience's capability or acquiescence to see things his way, a broker of spectacles like Lyly's Euphues faces an enduring threat of myopia and misprision in those he would endeavor to instruct.

Lyly's address to his "too olde" audience further offers a glimpse of the casual association of eyeglasses with advanced age, more familiarly portrayed in Jaques's iconic "lean and slipper'd pantaloon, / With spectacles on nose, and pouch on side" (*As You Like It,* 2.7.158–59). While senescence is characterized as particularly reliant upon this means of visual assistance, it can also become the peculiar object of an evaluative public gaze and a focal subject of moral reflection. Such is the case in *King Lear*'s most starkly concentrated moment of elderly victimization, the horrific spectacle of Gloucester's blinding in act 3, scene 7. In the Quarto's extended version, two servants linger to ruminate over the catastrophic violence they have just witnessed: a venerable old man tortured gleefully and one of their own company treacherously slain when he fruitlessly attempts to answer the victim's appeal, "He that will think to live till he be old, / Give me some help!" (3.7.69–70). The revulsion they express in their nine-line exchange looks beyond the immediate scene to its unnerving long-range consequences, as the specter of cruelty's triumph over inefficacious virtue leaves their moral sensibilities severely shaken. "I'll never care what wickedness I do / If this man come to good," the second servant says of Cornwall, to which his companion rejoins, "If she [Regan] live long, / And in the end meet the old course of death, / Women will all turn monsters" (3.7.99–102).

Although evil ultimately undoes itself in the play—the "hurt" that Cornwall departs the scene nursing itself proves mortal, we soon learn—this comes at a staggeringly high cost, captured in Kent's signature exclamation at the tragedy's close, "Is this the promis'd end?" (5.3.264), a remark that glances back to the appalled servants' incredulity. Of all the horror they have beheld, moreover, it is the picture of old age abused that especially troubles their imaginations. To subject an elder to such brutality is to forego one's own claim to longevity or "the old course of death," and they direct their (now admittedly guarded) pity in kind to "the old Earl," whose "bleeding face" they dress before turning him over to the care of mad Tom (3.7.103, 107).[18]

Even in its chronicle form, the Leir story shapes up as a fitting *speculum* well suited to its place in the *Mirror for Magistrates* of 1574. The most immediate dramatic source for Shakespeare's play, the anonymous *True Chronicle Historie of King Leir* (1605), participates fully in this "exemplary" tradition, faithfully enacting in its portrayal of aged resignation's hazards at the hands of ambitious, predatory youth a neatly didactic instance of how (in the words of the play's Gallian King) "Nor never like impiety was done, / Since the creation of the world begun" (2281–82).[19] As radically as Shakespeare's version departs from its received models, *King Lear* stands out most for the way in which it relentlessly poses the question "What does old age look like?" and, more consequentially, "How might it govern its image and reception, preserving the dignity that attends such agency?" As we have seen throughout the previous chapters, efforts to marginalize or sequester the elder frequently provoke an ongoing competition between broader, typically younger designs to determine how old age should comport and regard itself, and senescence's more individuated ambition to sustain or reclaim dominion over its own destiny. In *King Lear,* this "spectacular" dynamic plays out with a supremely complex ferocity.[20]

We may trace the origin of this informing preoccupation, moreover, to Shakespeare's other chief literary source for his play, the revised version of Sidney's *Arcadia.* As is commonly recognized, Sidney's tale of the Paphlagonian king's usurpation and blinding by his bastard son, Plexirtus, in the romance's second book, and the character's eventual rescue and restoration by the legitimate son, Leonatus, whose life he had unjustly sought, provided Shakespeare with the plotline he would refashion into the plight of Lear's ill-fated minister. A far more vital legacy of the *Arcadia* episode is its remarkably penetrating reflection on the nature of spectacle itself, and the elder's efforts to contend with this. Sidney's attention to the nature of exemplary display—especially as this pertains to vital matters of *self*-revelation and autonomy—subtly imprints his successor's own tragic spectacle of old age.

Sidney crafts his fiction of the Paphlagonian king expressly as an exemplary narrative, one "worthy to be remembered for the unused examples therein, as well of true natural goodness, as of wretched ungratefulness" (*NA,* 179). The contrasting responses to senescence that it juxtaposes fit conveniently into Shakespeare's principal dramatic story line, mirroring the dichotomy between the elder daughters' predatory victimization of their father and Cordelia's pious devotion. As the young prince Musidorus recounts to his beloved Pamela, the adventure begins when he and his companion Pyrocles, sheltering from a storm, come upon a blinded old man being led by a youth. After overhearing a part of their pathetic exchange, the princes step forward to offer their comfort. At that time, Leonatus, the old man's son, explains how his illegitimate brother had wickedly deposed their father the king and subsequently put out his eyes. Refusing to grant the elder's wish that he help him to commit suicide, the good son enlists the princes' aid to succor him in his grief. At this point the old king intervenes to reveal how his own gullibility had not only empowered Plexirtus but turned him against the son who, despite the injustice he suffered, returned from exile at his own risk to aid his former persecutor. When Plexirtus arrives amid the old king's confession to dispatch his brother, the princes join forces with Leonatus and, after summoning allies to stage a campaign against the tyrant, manage to overthrow him and restore the rightful king. At the public ceremony where he surrenders the crown in turn to Leonatus, publishing his own previous injustices, the old man "even in a moment died—as it should seem, his heart, broken with unkindness and affliction, stretched so far beyond his limits with this excess of comfort, as it was able no longer to keep safe his royal spirits" (*NA,* 185).

Beneath the transparent relevance of this romance to his own designs, a more discreet feature takes on renewed significance in Shakespeare's play. At the core of Sidney's tale lies the Machiavellian purposefulness of Plexirtus's decision to release rather than simply to murder his blinded father: the old man relates how, "proud in his tyranny," the bastard son "let me go, neither imprisoning nor killing me, but rather delighting to make me feel my misery" (*NA,* 182). Far more than the sadistic pleasure he takes in subjecting his father to the physical torments of exposure and the mental anguish of bad conscience, however, Plexirtus displays the terrible spectacle of his ruined parent as an instrument of his own political terror. The elder's tormented body serves as an example of the tyrant's cruelty, cowing his subjects into further submission. Whereas the old king's aged folly had cost him the sympathy of his previous subjects, he reveals, even those still aroused to compassion by his terrible state feared to express it "scarcely with giving me alms at their doors . . . nobody daring to show so much charity as to lend me a hand to guide my dark steps." As Leonatus summarizes, "though nothing is so needful unto us as pity, yet nothing is more dangerous unto us than to make ourselves so known as may stir pity" (*NA,* 180).

Most provocative of all is how Sidney's old king, reduced in this fashion to the status of an applied spectacle, boldly moves to reclaim his own narrative. "[N]othing is so welcome to my thoughts as the publishing of my shame," he asserts, as he takes Leonatus's edited account of their misadventure to task; "how evil an historian are you," he chides before the princes, "that leave out the chief knot of all the discourse—my wickedness!" (*NA,* 181). The elder's aggressive self-abnegation harbors a self-assertive, even competitive, drive to set straight the public record of his fall in terms that he alone authorizes. In turn, his supplementary account manages through its own professedly censored details to deflect attention away from Plexirtus's all-encompassing evil onto his victim's foolish complicity, to establish what the old man regards as a truer representation of events. He suppresses the acknowledged catalogue of "poisonous hypocrisy, desperate fraud, smooth malice, hidden ambition, and smiling envy" that Plexirtus had deployed to pit him against Leonatus, since "No remembrance, no, of naughtiness delights me, but mine own; and methinks the accusing his traps might in some manner excuse my fault, which certainly I loath to do." Whereas the good son's grace serves his father as a "glass even to my blind eyes of my naughtiness," and the comfort he selflessly tenders magnifies the undeserving parent's shame (in Sidney's gripping metaphor) "as if he would carry mud in a chest of crystal," the elder's self-laceration affords him the paradoxical means to recover lost dignity (*NA,* 182).

The Paphlagonian king's poignant confession before the princes is only a rehearsal of the grander public resignation that caps his history and his life. Upon his restoration by Leonatus after the eventual defeat of Plexirtus (who himself returns to the scene as both "actor and spectator"), the old man performs the transfer of power as a spectacle of his own infamy, virtually scripted as a definitive final act: "the blind king, having in the chief city of his realm set the crown upon his son Leonatus' head, with many tears both of joy and sorrow setting forth to the whole people his own fault and his son's virtue, after he had kissed him and forced his son to accept honour of him, as of his new-become subject, even in a moment died" (*NA,* 184–85). Leonatus's heroic capacity to sustain his father throughout their wanderings at last finds its limit, and the elder ends by realizing his destiny as cautionary display—but one over which he exercises full authority. However humiliating his self-demotion as a "new-become subject," whose restorative experience of unmerited "comfort" at last breaks his heart, the old king departs asserting dominion over this one residual element of his existence in a setting of "unkindness and affliction" that had exploited his monarchical apprehensions to deprive him of all else.

In his final act of public expiation, Sidney's fallen elder ekes out a personal victory of sorts through the recuperation of his own agency. This brand of closure proves far more elusive for the protagonists Shakespeare fashions from his romance source, though they are no less preoccupied with the self-assertion that the blinded monarch pursues so doggedly. This is owing in part to the way the playwright curiously inverts the dynamic of Sidney's presentation. The story of the Paphlagonian king's dreadful fall starts out as selectively edited reportage but concludes as a matter of public witness; the origin of Gloucester's disaster, in contrast, is fully dramatized, wherein his crucial death scene dwindles to the peculiar "brief tale" Edgar delivers (5.3.182). More fundamentally, the resignation spectacle engineered by Sidney's king resonates with the Leir story's opening divestiture ceremony. Despite the vast difference between the Paphlagonian king's dying ambition and the British ruler's political designs, both strive to cement their legacies in a final public, executive act as they take the initiative to empower a younger generation to whom they defer. At the beginning of his tragedy, Lear finds his audience less compliant and tractable than the Sidneian elder had at the close of his, and this critical discrepancy affords Shakespeare another point of departure for his distinctive version of the legend.[21]

Shakespeare conspicuously suppresses the precise motivations behind the love contest that Lear enfolds in his initial ceremony's "darker purpose," something the *True Chronicle Historie*'s preliminary scene had fully delineated.[22] As a result, where the anonymous play's audiences might call into question Leir's strategic skill, critics and directors alike have found ample grounds to challenge the executive competence and even the mental capability of Shakespeare's aged monarch. No less a reader than Northrop Frye regards Lear and his minister Gloucester as "a couple of incredibly foolish and gullible dodderers," and the tendency to see Lear's actions as a function of "senile folly" enjoys a healthy scholarly and performance history.[23]

However understandable such attacks may seem from the perfect hindsight of the king's impending catastrophe, magnified by the Fool's running indictments, we need to keep in view the potential soundness of the controversial political designs Lear brings to the opening ritual.[24] The transitional spectacle that he convenes on the one hand assays to accommodate younger capabilities and aspirations in a fashion laid out, for instance, in Stefano Guazzo's *Civile Conversation,* where the discussion of family politics faults "when eyther thorow the authoritie of olde age, or thorow ambition, or covetousnesse, or too good opinion in his own sufficiencie, the father is so desirous of keping his paternall jurisdiction, that though his children bee arived to mans estate, and be perfectly accomplished every way, yet he will alowe them neither more living, nor more liberty then they had when they were children."[25] Against this, Guazzo's interlocutor poses "the sweet rest and contentment" that arises from a timely transfer of authority, "which the father injoieth in his old yeeres, both for that he feeleth himselfe rid of all incombrance and vexation, and besides seeth his sonne by his example governe his house orderly" (2:68). Simultaneously, by invoking his daughters' unscripted but no less obligatory declarations of love, Lear seeks to balance the ritual rhetorically, through their public affirmation that the respect is mutual. In this transaction before his court, Lear underlines in spectacular fashion the liberality of his gesture—he partitions his kingdom freely, not out of necessity or coercion—even as he binds his offspring's ascent to their own public profession of familial love and political allegiance. Although the preordained divisions of his realm denote that he takes this worthiness as a foregone conclusion, their participation in the theatrical moment he orchestrates remains integral to his project of honoring their "merit" while retaining the privilege he deems his right by "nature"—aims that he clearly does not regard as antithetical.[26]

Lear had intended to stage his final royal performance as a public illustration of his autonomy even at the very moment he conceded dominion. By authorizing the transfer of his own authority, he in effect aims to write the final chapter of his reign as he "publishes" his daughters' domestic and political dowries. The old king seeks neither to deny the mortality he is approaching nor to embrace the "deleterious stereotype of old age as second childhood" as some have proposed, but rather to navigate between these hazards, renegotiating dependency and autonomy on his own terms.[27] Far from an "indecorous" response to "the indecorum of age,"[28] Lear's ceremony aims creatively to work free of protocols and conventions, to empower youth and liberate old age by implementing what Paul W. Kahn aptly calls "a rational plan to reorder law in a way that simultaneously secures political stability and familial love."[29] Cordelia's unexpected refusal to assume her implicit role in the performance and Kent's corresponding challenge excite his outrage primarily because their recalcitrance in effect usurps the very narrative he had sought to control, placing them (as he pointedly charges Kent) "betwixt our sentence and our power" (1.1.170). In a sudden reversal, Lear finds himself the one put on the spot to declare his love—"I lov'd her most, and thought to set my rest / On her kind nursery," he exclaims in his wounded fury (1.1.122–23)—no longer in charge of his spectacle's unfolding. The delicate balance he had aimed for now hopelessly upset, he impulsively yields to the fatal overreaction of writing both Cordelia and Kent out of the story.

While Lear's abortive venture in the opening scene largely determines the play's tense emotional ambience, the latent fears it uncovers carry over most immediately in Gloucester's nervous disorientation. To comprehend the full trajectory of the earl's tragedy, we must first recognize the fateful conclusion to which he jumps in act 1, scene 2 as continuous with the opening scene's thwarted ceremony and its consequences—a spectacle from which he is largely absent. His early departure from the previous scene removes him from much of this inaugural show of aged resignation and its fearsome price; he therefore comes before us again as one testily scrabbling for "news," returning in disbelief to a court suddenly emptied of "honesty," its absentee monarch "Confin'd to exhibition." Rightfully apprehensive about the precedent Lear's action sets for the retention of aged privilege and authority, he enters into a state of "ripeness" (in a setting where, as his youthful guide will soon instruct him, this condition "is all") for defensive retrenchment against whatever ambitious, ageist policies the new order may threaten.

Awakened to a freshly inverted generational economy, Gloucester demands, "Let's see, let's see," when he notices his bastard son putting away the letter, a reflex that stems from his refusal under the circumstances to grant youth a superior perspective (1.2.43). Fully attentive to the moment, Edmund knows how to play to the "credulous" mindset in which events have cornered his father. The schemer's forgery targets precisely the elder's sudden anxiety over lost agency, as the domestic harmonies of generational order are untuned into "the oppression of aged tyranny" that governs only "as it is suffer'd" (1.2.49–51). Anxious about how others now perceive him, Gloucester cannot abide this notion of age's merely cosmetic authority; inclined to guard with an ever greater jealousy the more substantive powers in which he grounds his dignity, the old earl in assuming the role of senescence's paternal champion unwittingly opens himself to his illegitimate offspring's machinations.

Although it is easy to regard Gloucester's impulsive manner as the function of a stereotypical elderly suspiciousness he shares with his prince, his reactions emerge directly from the troubled politics that Lear's actions have enabled. If anything, the councilor's willingness to believe the worst of Edgar seems altogether uncharacteristic, inspired by and a function of his temperamental rebellion against his master's designs which he, like the other senior minister, Kent, finds so objectionable. The chief irony of his fall stems from the way in which his initial refusal to mimic Lear's voluntary consignment of his "revenue" to "younger strengths"—evident in his violent contempt for Edgar's alleged contention "that, sons at perfect age and fathers declin'd, the father should be as ward to the son, and the son manage his revenue" (1.2.72–74)—in fact steers him to follow the king's course, and at the very price of filial alienation that Lear also will end up paying. When he declares, "I would unstate myself to be in a due resolution" (1.2.99–100), his phrasing itself recalls the king's expressed "darker purpose" to surrender his throne as a means of avoiding "future strife" (1.1.36, 44). Gloucester, of course, loses hegemony over his own earldom, as he comes to face the "resolution" (here in the word's alternate sense of decomposition or *dis*solution) of the same elderly prospects he had aimed to preserve.

For all his prodigious ability to read and manipulate his father, Edmund misconstrues Gloucester's harried invocation of "These late eclipses in the sun and moon" (1.2.103) when he regards the old man's musings as an instance of "the excellent foppery of the world" that passively ascribes our behavior to "an enforc'd obedience of planetary influence" (1.2.118, 124–25). Although Gloucester relates the distressing developments he faces politically and personally to the "sequent effects" of astronomical phenomena, he remains far too invested in an urgent self-assertiveness to evade responsibility in the way Edmund contemptuously suggests. The aggravated challenges the old man has come to believe one encounters late in life—a senescence he maps onto history itself when he anguishes, "We have seen the best of our time" (1.2.112)—motivate his frenetic efforts to address and countermand the "ruinous disorders" that "follow us disquietly to our graves" (1.2.113–14). His campaign to apprehend the fugitive Edgar belies the aged weakness and demoralization he voices in act 2, scene 1 when he laments to Regan, "O madam, my old heart is crack'd, it's crack'd!" (90). Prompted to act, he finds himself trapped between the urge aggressively to resume control of his domestic affairs and the shame he suffers before the publicity this very activity necessitates. When Regan inquires, "What, did my father's godson seek your life?," he can only reply, "O lady, lady, shame would have it hid!" (2.1.91, 93), fearing to "monster" further the generational strife of the times and craving to dodge the spotlight into which Cornwall's solicitous attention throws him. As he soon discovers, his guests' darker resolutions allow little opportunity for him to escape their keen vigilance.

In *King Lear*, the younger generation's drive to assume power over their elders' activities finds expression in an avid willingness to project their own image of senescence onto the aged subjects and to exhibit them accordingly, whether to punitive or redemptive ends. While Lear's elder daughters match a "counternarrative" of decline to their father's self-image, both Kent and Gloucester, the two other elders who significantly contribute to the action of Shakespeare's play, are transformed into spectacles by their youthful adversaries.[30] Though one maintains his independence while the other succumbs to their demoralizing, violent designs, both suffer humiliation for trespassing the boundaries deemed suitable to their time of life.

Amid the divestiture scene's rapid disintegration, Lear cannot grasp the full extent of his project's failure, although the oath he utters upon his dismissal of Cordelia, "So be my grave my peace, as here I give / Her father's heart from her" (1.1.125–26), ominously betrays an intuition that he will hereafter find solace only in death. But as the king's command over his own exposition slips, we see him even before the opening scene's completion as the subject of a rival decline narrative that instantly begins to pervade the play. Upon their father's departure from the stage, the two elder daughters waste no time before conspiring to forge a gerontophobic diagnosis of what they have just witnessed. "You see how full of change his age is," Goneril posits, and when Regan extends her observation retrospectively, " 'Tis the infirmity of his age, yet he hath ever but slenderly known himself," she seizes upon this to feed a revisionary history already in progress: "The best and soundest of his time hath been but rash; then must we look from his age to receive not alone the imperfections of long-engraff'd condition, but therewithal the unruly waywardness that infirm and choleric years bring with them" (1.1.288, 293–99).

The self-serving bias that informs the sisters' charges has not prevented some audiences from investing in the possible validity of their claims, even though other characters' responses subvert or at least seriously challenge such suspicions. The inept and insubstantial personality that Goneril and Regan indict would not likely sustain the impassioned allegiance of figures like Gloucester or (especially) Kent, whose outspoken assault on his lord's actions seems provoked precisely by their anomalous nature.[31] Indeed, the essential point that Shakespeare manages to convey is just how immaterial the facticity of the daughters' allegations about their father's past behavior becomes for their own current project. Fearing how "this last surrender of his will but offend us" (1.1.305–6), they script a narrative that best suits their youthful convenience and act together to make it official, for all practical purposes.

Not surprisingly, the vigorous activity to which Lear commits himself amid his newly attained leisure exacerbates rather than mitigates his daughters' charges of impairment. As early as act 1, scene 3, Goneril's indictment of the "Idle old man, / That still would manage those authorities / That he hath given away" (16–18) shapes her readiness to affirm that "Old fools are babes again, and must be us'd / With checks as flatteries, when they are seen abus'd" (19–20). Her determination "I will not speak with him," calculated to force an occasion "That I may speak" (1.3.8, 25), sets the stage for the following scene's confrontation where, after returning from the hunt and suffering Oswald's effrontery (which only compounds the "most faint neglect" [1.4.68] he has begun to sense well before this), Lear squares off with her. Throughout their exchange, her airing of grievances rapidly escalates from turgid circumlocution (the "redresses" that his faults demand, in her view, "Might in their working do you that offense, / Which else were shame, that then necessity / Will call discreet proceeding" [1.4.210, 212–14]) to patronizing cajoling ("As you are old and reverend, [you] should be wise" [240]), to a more blatant threat:

> Be then desir'd
> By her, that else will take the thing she begs,
> A little to disquantity your train,
> And the remainders that shall still depend,
> To be such men as may besort your age,
> Which know themselves and you.   (247–52)

Exasperated by Lear's refusal to adopt the retiring manners she would assign to men of his age, Goneril opportunistically assails his knights as "Men so disorder's, so debosh'd, and bold, / That this our court, infected with their manners, / Shows like a riotous inn" (1.4.242–44)—a charge directors have, oddly, seemed all too ready to take at face value, given that the few retainers who speak lines betray a decorum fitting the "men of choice and rarest parts" Lear praises (263). The disgruntled daughter intends to displace the soldiers' more formidable defensive strengths on behalf of a diminished, compliant company that better "besorts" her notion of senescence to justify the social segregation she would impose on her inconveniently frenetic parent.

Lear's impassioned flight to what he thinks will be the refuge of his other daughter's care culminates in an equally frank encounter with ageist condescension. Regan's self-interest inspires her to reiterate her sister's perspective:

> O sir, you are old,
> Nature in you stands on the very verge
> Of his confine. You should be rul'd and led
> By some discretion that discerns your state
> Better than you yourself.   (2.4.146–50)

For Regan, it seems, Goneril's design to relegate the old king to a harmless circle of his peers names her own very deed, only it falls too short; the younger sibling would assign their father to the passive charge of those who know not merely "themselves and you," but his actual "state," better than he. Given the siblings' early commitment to array themselves against "what most nearly appertains to us both" (1.1.283–84), she seems bound to join in concert with her sister who arrives mid-scene, to aver communally that (in Goneril's words) "All's not offense that indiscretion finds / And dotage terms so" and (as Regan portentously trails off) "those that mingle reason with your passion / Must be content to think you old, and so—" (2.4.196–97, 234–35).

As their coordinated dismissals make clear, Goneril and Regan archly resent the display of robust, "anomalous" aging into which their father throws himself, and their alliance ultimately drives Lear to his "high rage" (2.4.296).[32] Against his rejection of the aged subservience he lampoons before Regan in act 2, scene 4 (cited earlier), the sisters enact the very repudiation best distilled in Edmund's forgery: "This policy and reverence of age makes the world bitter to the best of our times; keeps our fortunes from us till our oldness cannot relish them. I begin to find an idle and fond bondage in the oppression of aged tyranny, who sways, not as it hath power, but as it is suffer'd" (1.2.46–51). Whatever agency an older generation retains, in their construction, it retains exclusively at their behest. Mere tolerance of the elder by the younger has become the order of the day, and youth has reached its threshold. No sooner does Lear's effort to commandeer his own spectacle of aged transition crumble than an alternative account, spinning the construction of events to its own advantage, moves in to take its place. Again, in Edmund's succinct delineation, "The younger rises when the old doth fall" (3.3.25).

Like that of his master, Kent's physical vigor distinguishes his fortitude. This, no less than his moral determination to stand by the king who banished him, likewise secures the disfavor of the new order he contemptuously opposes. The multiple beatings to which he subjects Goneril's sycophantic courtier Oswald make plain his hearty constitution, as does the speed with which he delivers Lear's correspondence: he foregoes sleep to honor the king's command and outpaces the younger steward who arrives "Stew'd in his haste, half breathless, panting forth" (2.4.31). The altercation with Oswald that takes place in front of Gloucester's castle issues in the stark, emblematic moment of Kent's punishment in the stocks, where he remains throughout much of the second act—a literally foregrounded spectacle of the immobilized elder. Notably, what appears most to offend his hostile superiors in the scene, more than his aggressive conduct or his disrespectful plainspokenness, is the fact that someone of his years would dare to display these traits. Upon Cornwall's intervention, Oswald indicts his attacker as an "ancient ruffian . . . whose life I have spar'd at suit of his grey beard" (2.2.62–63), and the duke likewise assails him as a "stubborn ancient knave" and "reverent [i.e., aged] braggart" (126). Kent's seniority renders his assertive demeanor doubly repugnant to the gathering, which gladly seizes the opportunity to condition his "overlusty" legs through the confinement of "wooden nether-stocks."

Given the choleric disposition of "the firey Duke," and the brutality of which we shall soon come to know him capable, we might in retrospect be startled at the leniency of the penalty he inflicts on Kent: uncomfortable as the exposure that the older servant suffers may be, his misery is more a matter of public humiliation than physical torment. Kent gruffly parries Cornwall's heated threat "We'll teach you" with "Sir, I am too old to learn. / Call not your stocks for me" (2.2.127–28), but in the atmosphere that Shakespeare here generates, teaching the elder to act his age in an appropriately subservient manner is a primary office of those in their violent youth. Cornwall aims to bring his aged antagonist to "heel," as the Fool might say. In fact, the Fool alone—so often a step ahead—seems to grasp the full import of Kent's punishment when he jests to the stocked figure, "We'll set thee to school to an ant, to teach thee there's no laboring i' th' winter" (2.4.67–68). Apart from the fable's suggestion that winter labor (as the provident ant knows) yields no profit, Kent must come to terms with the social convention that the winter of life permits no decorous self-assertion—a lesson that the subjects of this new regime are deemed never too old to learn.

The irascible Cornwall is not rash in the sentence he hands down; rather, the mortifying public display is shrewdly calibrated for the benefit of a target audience, the old king himself. Gloucester's attempted intervention against this "purpos'd low correction," since "The King must take it ill / That he, so slightly valued in his messenger, / Should have him thus restrained" (2.2.142, 145–47), fails to comprehend that royal insult is exactly Cornwall and Regan's "purpos'd" intent. Displaying solidarity with Goneril before the king by punishing her man's attacker, they compound the pressing threat to diminish his retinue by symbolically hobbling his most aggressively self-sufficient retainer. In so doing, they demonstrate for Lear the practical effects of opposing his daughters' wills. Lear's explosive outrage, grounded in his ready capability to see himself vicariously demeaned in his servant's confinement, makes it clear that the point is by no means lost on him.

Kent is effectively silenced in the scene once Lear and his daughters engage, his voice lost amid the gathering tempestuous emotions and the corresponding literal tempest that drowns out his mishap. He emerges from the experience undiminished, however, as his subsequent efforts confirm. Simultaneously the subject of ridicule—adumbrated in the Fool's initial, resonant laughter, "Hah, ha, he wears cruel garters" (2.4.7)—and sympathetic indignation, he weathers the storm. Similarly, the bitter spectacle fails to shatter Lear's own oppositional drive, even as the old man's wits begin to yield to the trauma he endures. Such will not be the case for the king's other aged supporter, Gloucester, who in a torturous collapse is reduced to a monstrous (in the full sense of this word), blinded witness to his own multiple reconstructions as spectacle.

At one moment in his confinement, the demeaned but resilient Kent prays, "All weary and o'erwatch'd, / Take vantage, heavy eyes, not to behold / This shameful lodging" (2.2.170–72). His compatriot Gloucester is not granted even this little solace, despite the fact that the horrific torture he undergoes will claim the very organs with which he might witness his own degradation as he "smell[s] / His way to Dover" (3.7.93–94). While public exposure of his ruined, aged body fails to achieve the political ends that his tormenters had intended, we may equally question the efficacy of Edgar's more personal, spiritual designs for his father's spectacular recovery, as the old man is called upon to "Look up" and behold a miraculous redemption staged expressly for his benefit.

Gloucester's deep-seated fears that an institutionalized "reverence of age" but thinly masks the young's disdainful tolerance are realized for him throughout the second and third acts, over the course of Regan and Cornwall's visit. Although they arrive deferentially seeking from "Our good old friend" the "needful counsel to our businesses, / Which craves the instant use" (2.1.125, 127–28), by the close of act 2 they reveal how they in reality are pursuing a predetermined agenda. Discouraging his compassionate move to succor the outcast king, they are the ones to advise the elder: "Shut up your doors, my lord," as Cornwall menacingly proposes, " 'tis a wild night. / My Regan counsels well. Come out o' th' storm" (2.4.308–9). Gloucester's failure to comply quickly excites their less equivocal assertions of mastery. "I like not this unnatural dealing," he confides to Edmund in act 3, scene 3, "When I desir'd their leave that I might pity him [Lear], they took from me the use of mine own house, charg'd me on pain of perpetual displeasure neither to speak of him, entreat for him, or any way sustain him" (1–6). Yet, as his agency grows increasingly compromised, the covert activity he pursues to assist Lear highlights his vitality no less than his

commitment to the old king.[33] In a world where detestation of the elder
has become the norm—where, in his blighted view, "Our flesh and blood
. . . is grown so vild / That it doth hate what gets it" (3.4.145–46)—Gloucester sternly refuses to "suffer" the daughters' hard commands "to bar my
doors, / And let this tyrannous night take hold upon you" (3.4.150–51), or
to surrender to the ascendant will of youth. The more literally and figu-
ratively excluded old age becomes under the new regime, the more dramatically caught up Gloucester gets in a frantic movement of defensive
displacement.

Gloucester's "treason" culminates, as we know, in the spectacular undoing that Cornwall and Regan oversee, in a scene from which Edmund is
ironically excluded: the duke dismisses him beforehand, advising how "the
revenges we are bound to take upon your traitorous father are not fit for
your beholding" (3.7.7–9). As had been the case with Kent in act 2, scene
2, the focus once again falls upon the subject of old age, from the binding
of the elder's "corky arms," to Regan's mocking incredulity as she plucks his
beard, "So white, and such a traitor?" as if his seniority alone should have
excluded him from such activity (3.7.29, 37). Discovering himself "tied to
th' stake" like a bear on display in the pit (3.7.54), Gloucester takes up their
emphasis. When called upon to justify why he had assisted the king against
their "interdiction," the old man casts his reply not only as a loyal subject
but as a sympathetic fellow elder:

> Because I would not see thy cruel nails
> Pluck out his poor old eyes, nor thy fierce sister
> In his anointed flesh rash boarish fangs.
> The sea, with such a storm as his bare head
> In hell-black night endur'd, would have bouy'd up
> And quench'd the stelled fires,
> Yet, poor old heart, he holp the heavens to rain.   (3.7.56–62)

So saying, he sets the terms for their cruelly precise sentence: because he
would not stand by willingly as an audience to their abuse of old age, they
take his eyes and thrust him into the blasted, featureless landscape from
which he had sought to protect Lear, determined to permit him never to
"see / The winged vengeance overtake such children" (3.7.65–66).

The elder's public exposure, as Regan discovers and confesses, proves
counterproductive: "It was great ignorance," she observes to Oswald in act
4, scene 5, "Gloucester's eyes being out, / To let him live; where he arrives
he moves / All hearts against us" (9–11). Despite all his strenuous efforts
to defend his king, the loyal retainer arguably does his greatest good as a
spectacle, passively stirring sympathy for Lear's cause. The irony is some-

thing Gloucester apprehends, for the demoralization he suffers henceforth concentrates upon his utter loss of agency, something he projects onto the heavens. The earl's best-remembered pronouncement, "As flies to wanton boys are we to th' gods, / They kill us for their sport" (4.1.36–37), fastens his newly discovered and intolerable status as a passive show for the amusement of (notably) youthful deities. "Turn'd out," he shuns even the assistance of the "Old Man" who professes to "have been your tenant, and your father's tenant, / These fourscore years" (4.1.13–14). What begins as a concern for the faithful companion's welfare—"Good friend, be gone," he directs, possibly regarding him as an image of his own futile efforts to sustain a fellow elder, "Thy comforts can do me no good at all; / Thee they may hurt" (4.1.15–16)—soon dwindles to apathetic indifference: "Do as I bid thee, or rather do thy pleasure; / Above the rest, be gone" (4.1.47–48).

Gloucester's chief dismay lies, however, in his own capacity for endurance. The suicide on which he resolves comprises the old man's final, desperate attempt to reclaim agency, only to have even this elude him. Set free in a setting over which he exercises no power, he quests for the "confined deep" in which to drown his now oblivious existence (4.1.74). When his passive reliance on mad Tom's guidance to the cliff from which he intends to jump issues in his uninjured reawakening upon the beach, the beneficiary of Edgar's device to "cure" his despair experiences only intensified anguish: "Is wretchedness depriv'd that benefit," he exclaims, "To end itself by death? 'Twas yet some comfort, / When misery could beguile the tyrant's rage, / And frustrate his proud will" (4.6.61–64). Rather like the victim of some mythic curse than a beneficiary of divine favor, Gloucester comes to feel the misery he is destined to suffer as itself deathless.

Compounding his wretchedness, Gloucester's constitution preserves him as a blind witness to the very king he had sought to protect, the "ruin'd piece of nature" in whom he perceives an image of universal senescence: "This great world / Shall so wear out to nought" (4.6.134–35). Although he prays for patience, much to his son's approval, the elder easily regresses, surrendering gladly to Oswald's murderous intentions, bemoaning to the end the sturdiness of his mental and physical stamina alike. Thinking on Lear's madness, he reflects

> how stiff is my vild sense
> That I stand up, and have ingenious feeling
> Of my huge sorrows! Better I were distract,
> So should my thoughts be sever'd from my griefs,
> And woes by wrong imaginations lose
> The knowledge of themselves.   (4.6.279–84)

The final line given him in the Folio—the four-word rejoinder to Edgar's assertion "Ripeness is all," "And that's true, too" (5.2.11–12)—bespeaks less acquiescence to the statement's sententiousness than an ironic recollection of his naive "ripeness" or vulnerability at the start. After all the moral wavering he exhibits up to the point of his death, Gloucester's ultimate experience is that someone of his crippled fortune cannot even "rot" in peace.

Given his failed attempts to reclaim, in the manner of his Sidneian prototype, some dominion over his own narrative, it seems fitting that Gloucester's tragedy closes with the old man's relegation to another's "brief" account. As we now commonly acknowledge, Edgar's description of his father's last moments, like his urgent and tenacious project to rehabilitate him from his profound resignation generally, speaks to a vision of redemption he just as desperately requires. The sight of his elderly parent's abused body stirs in Edgar feelings of protective compassion despite the injustice he has endured at the senior figure's hands, which offset the predatory disregard that Edmund, his royal paramours, and their company display. Nonetheless, his self-ordained role as age's champion is also deeply rooted in a sense of superior youthful direction that must take over when age falters. Edgar eagerly assumes responsibility for the elder's story, fretting openly at one point that he perhaps underrated the power of his beleaguered father's imagination, suddenly fearing after Gloucester's intended fall from the cliff, "And yet I know not how conceit may rob / The treasury of life, when life itself / Yields to the theft" (4.6.42–44). He requisitions command over his father's moral sensibilities, commending ("Well pray you, father" [4.6.219]) or chastising ("What, in ill thoughts again?" [5.2.9]) as the old man's responses demand, and never adequately sensitive to the source of the other's despair, from which he boldly claims to have "sav'd him" (5.3.192). In his strange, dreamlike narrative of Gloucester's death, Edgar betrays the personal "fault" he smells about his own belated revelation to the old man that seems to hasten his end.[34] As the dying Edmund himself observes, his brother always seems to have "something more to say" (5.3.202). Edgar's stringent need to weave necessary stories around the spectacle of the elder ironically eclipses Gloucester's chance to express himself at last as his own person—a destiny that, in Shakespeare's retelling, his king will not share.

To rescue his aged parent, the destitute Edgar must rely upon his unaccommodated wits and fortitude. Cordelia, in contrast, who presumably stands behind the French invasion of her homeland provoked by intelligence of the "hard rein" to which her sisters and their husbands have subjected the "old kind King" (3.1.27–28), has an army at her disposal. Nevertheless, she demonstrates in similar fashion that she can understand her father only in terms of his victimized weakness. She calls him "child-changed," referring both to his transformation at the hands of his unscrupulous and more powerful daughters and to his reversion to infancy in his elderly dementia (4.7.16). Her eulogy of the sleeping king upon his recovery inverts her sisters' gerontophobic reflexes but replaces their contempt only with the pity that the sight of old age ought to excite in its audience:

> Had you not been their father, these white flakes
> Did challenge pity of them. Was this a face
> To be oppos'd against the warring winds?
> To stand against the deep dread-bolted thunder?
> In the most terrible and nimble stroke
> Of quick cross lightning? to watch—poor perdu!—
> With this thin helm?   (4.7.29–35)

The powerful image Cordelia conjures of Lear's formidable constitution, capable (as we have seen) of braving the tempest's elemental opposition, strangely serves to rhetoricize the primary, virtually maternal sense of his pathetic frailty by which her own heroic selflessness (like Edgar's) is significantly conditioned. In an appropriately ironic reversal, upon their defeat she tries to console Lear with the assurance, "For thee, oppressed king, I am cast down, / Myself could else out-frown false Fortune's frown" (5.3.5–6), only to be silenced by her father's own more lyrical convictions. These overwhelm his daughter's depressed or "cast down" utterances with matching assurances of the two's ability to endure within the confines of their "wall'd prison" (5.3.18)—an impulse that proves of a piece with his ardent refusal to cede dominion over his own image from the onset of their final catastrophe.

However miserably Lear's opening spectacle had failed to realize its desired effect, the king's old age, like Gloucester's, clearly possesses "charms" that threaten to undo the military triumph that his adversaries ultimately achieve. Having learned from Regan and Cornwall's misguided decision to release his own blinded father, or simply more politically savvy than they, Edmund grasps this point and its consequences when he responds to Albany's demand for custody of the captives:

> Sir, I thought it fit
> To send the old and miserable King
> To some retention and appointed guard,
> Whose age had charms in it, whose title more,
> To pluck the common bosom on his side,

> And turn our impress'd lances in our eyes
> Which do command them.   (5.3.45–51)

Lear himself invests steadfastly in the mystique of his old age throughout his fall, no less convinced of its efficacy than he is of his title as "every inch a king" (4.6.107). Where his initial divestiture had aimed to grant "younger strengths" the executive power they covet in a way he optimistically hoped would not detract from his dignity as elder and king (whose "additions" he thought to retain), once this project falters he turns to a melodramatic exploitation of a pathetic aged status.[35] The display of self-pity he indulges in throughout much of the ensuing action significantly contours our own responses to his manner.

No sooner does Lear meet with his elder daughters' "checks" and reprisals than he shows himself sharply sensitive to their predatory reductiveness, "capable" (in Helen Small's penetrating analysis) "of smelling out the bad faith that speaks in injunctions to be patient, when what is intended is that one should surrender meekly to injustice."[36] His responses, at first imperiously irascible, quickly give way to histrionic posturing. As he incredulously confronts the indifference or hostility of those to whom he plays, he summons the gods themselves as witnesses to his victimization. "O heavens!" he cries upon Goneril's approach, "If you do love old men, if your sweet sway / Allow obedience, if you yourselves are old, / Make it your cause; send down, and take my part" (2.4.189–92). Where the conditional clauses that Lear strings together here serve chiefly a rhetorical effect, his discourse erodes as the old man's confidence in divine sympathy begins to falter: "You see me here, you gods, a poor old man, / As full of grief as age, wretched in both" (2.4.272–73). In what unsettles him as a kind of disastrous cosmic replay of the opening ceremony's failed spectacle, he discovers yet again his inability to depend upon the compliance of an audience, human or divine.

In her obsequious opening pledge, Goneril had vowed to love her father "Dearer than eyesight, space, and liberty" (1.1.56). Of the play's three principal elders, Gloucester suffers the loss of his eyes and Kent must await liberation from the stocks; Lear, for his part, vigorously traverses the seemingly boundless space of his realm, in which he remains "at large" in every sense of the word throughout most of the action. In increasingly desperate fashion, he meets a threatened relegation to the "confine" on whose verge he purportedly stands with an even more frenetically mobile course of "exhibition" in nature, as he takes his show of demoted senescence on tour, so to speak, out into nature itself. He presents his aged form to the storm's "eyeless rage," striving (as one of his faithful retainers reports to Kent) "in his little world of man to outscorn / The to-and-fro-conflicting wind and rain" (3.1.8, 10–11). Lear girds his octogenarian's physique to contend with the elements as if to reaffirm his own constitutional strength even as he amplifies his outraged self-pity before the deities from whom he dissociates himself:

> I tax not you, you elements, with unkindness;
> I never gave you kingdom, call'd you children;
> You owe me no subscription. Then let fall
> Your horrible pleasure. Here I stand your slave,
> A poor, infirm, weak, and despis'd old man;
> But yet I call you servile ministers,
> That will with two pernicious daughters join
> Your high-engender'd battles 'gainst a head
> So old and white as this. O, ho! 'tis foul.   (3.2.16–24)

He exonerates the gods only to mock their apparent willingness to pander to younger powers, something he now adamantly refuses to do even in such a "poor, infirm, weak, and despis'd" condition—adjectives which, in the new dispensation his daughters would enforce, inherently modify senescence. Struggling to shame heaven itself, Lear offers a spectacle of endurance and injustice, collapsed in a frame both professedly "infirm" and yet able to withstand the "high-engender'd" siege of which he proclaims himself the victim.

Even as his wits disintegrate, Lear maintains a self-consciously theatrical role that showcases his vigor and martial authority. His initial ravings alternate between spectacular self-pity and affirmations of strength. Before the hovel, he rages with the storm, to no one in particular,

> filial ingratitude!
> Is it not as this mouth should tear this hand
> For lifting food to't? But I will punish home.
> No, I will weep no more. In such a night
> To shut me out? Pour on, I will endure.
> In such a night as this? O Regan, Goneril!
> Your old kind father, whose frank heart gave all.   (3.4.14–20)

His dementia turns him even further toward theatrical metaphors, which hold a special fascination for him. Reunited with Gloucester, he begins to sermonize that "When we are born, we cry that we are come / To this great stage of fools"; the notoriously unclear interjection with which he breaks his lesson, "This' a good block" (4.6.182–83), signals Lear's delight in this commonplace analogy of the world as a showing place: "*There's* a good conceit," he seems to muse approvingly, regarding this as best suited to his own spectacular progress. From this platform, he voices his disdain for the audience who encouraged his performance of a role they actually despised. "They flatter'd me like a dog, and told me I had the white hairs in my beard ere the black ones were there," he recalls, noting how in their obnoxious offense his juniors had pretended to hold the signs of late life as objects of respect when in fact, for them, "'Tis a lie." In his twilight, the king finds himself neither revered nor "ag[u]e-proof," immune to the afflictions and marginalizations that are bitterly due senescence (4.6.96–98, 105). When his blinded fellow elder begs to kiss his hand, Lear replies, "Let me wipe it first, it smells of mortality," disdaining what he has come to regard as the stink of aged flesh, in a sarcastic nod to his victimizers' cynical disgust (4.6.133).

When, in his mad state, he faces "capture" by his actual supporters, Lear again ties his liberty to his stamina, taunting the company as he flees: "Come, and you get it, you shall get it by running. Sa, sa, sa, sa" (4.6.202–3). Yet just as Gloucester had said of the "Madman and beggar" Poor Tom, "He has some reason, else he could not beg" (4.1.30–31), so the old king harbors sufficient remorse to avoid an audience with the returned Cordelia up to the time of his forced recovery in act 4, scene 7. Thoughts of "his own unkindness" to the faithful daughter, Kent reports, "sting / His mind so venomously, that burning shame / Detains him" (4.3.42, 45–47). Defenseless in the disorientation he experiences as he emerges from his breakdown, the old king—"still, far wide," in Cordelia's view (4.7.49)—struggles to gain some perspective on his state, as he discovers himself the object of his own gaze: "Where have I been? Where am I?," he puzzles, "I am mightily abus'd; I should ev'n die with pity / To see another thus. I know not what to say. / I will not swear these are my hands. Let's see" (4.7.51–54). Finding himself on the receiving end of a question he had himself posed so often before, his daughter's benign "Sir, do you know me?" (4.7.47), and for the first time unable to verify his own vision, Lear can only feebly approximate his former dynamism. As he began in a failed strategic effort to predetermine his life's final phase, he is left at this penultimate turn to wish "Would I were assur'd / Of my condition!" (55–56).

Emerging from the mental fog in which his traumatic fall has enveloped him, Lear strains to recover and replay flashes of his past experience, reworking these with a remarkable dexterity for one in his exhausted condition into neatly inflected restorative patterns. At the pivotal moment of reawakening in the presence of one whose sight inescapably recalls to him his own injustice, Lear reenacts the aged self-abnegation he had mockingly performed before Regan in act 2, scene 4, only now with a demoralized sincerity, a humiliated parody of his former parody. "Pray do not mock me," he entreats, "I am a very foolish fond old man, / Fourscore and upward, not an hour more nor less" (4.7.58–60). Although the confession looks like the old man's surrender to the elder daughters' gerontophobic perspective, his echoing of their "causeless" indictments is more cathartic than broken. He offers this verdict to Cordelia as a judgment that would be just from her subjective standpoint, even though the linkage of senescence and folly carries no objective validity for him: "You have some cause," he goes on to say, "they have not" (4.7.74).

More subtly still, the peculiarity of Lear's declaration of his age in the Folio—a detail that has gone oddly unremarked—as "Fourscore and upward, not an hour more nor less," stands out as a tellingly weird conjunction of vagary and precision: he's on the far side of eighty, down to the exact hour. In fact, the expression recovers (even as he prays her not to "mock" him) one of Cordelia's own cadences, recollected from the very moment of their fateful rupture, when she had insisted that she loved her father "According to my bond, no more nor less" (1.1.93). Taking up her expression of what he now recognizes as dignified youthful defiance, he returns it to her as an offering he hopes will recement their "bond" and win her pardon. The royal figure who had sought at that remote turn to "unburden" himself does so now emotionally, directly pointing out how "You must bear with me. / Pray you now forget, and forgive; I am old and foolish" (4.7.83–84). Again, the final remark sounds less like a condemnation of senescence as inherently foolish than an effort to dissociate these states: "Forget I am old," he appeals, "even as you forgive my folly," something that need not rest exclusively or even primarily within the province of old age.

In context, the Doctor's measured caution to Cordelia that "yet it is great danger / To make him even o'er [i.e., relive or fill in] the time he has lost" (4.7.78–79) sounds especially ironic. Even at this point of reentry, Lear has already begun to reinvent himself and, now with Cordelia's blessing, to rescript his story. Report, as Kent wryly remarks a few lines on, "is changeable" (91), something of which his master had never lost full sight. Although the military reversals suffered by Cordelia's forces preempt the happier, restorative outcome at which she too had aimed, Lear emerges from their defeat determined not to relinquish his newly recovered command over his own narrative, as his assertions early in act 5, scene 3 strikingly demonstrate. However odd audiences may find the rejuvenation that Lear conspicuously displays upon his reentry, this stands as an essential effect of his reemergence: he is decidedly no longer the decimated figure of aged folly he had effectively cast out in the previous scene.

Within the literal confines of their captivity after the battlefield debacle, the "child-changed father" in effect trades places with his daughter's more defiant posture, as he initiates the final chapter of their history. Against Cordelia's closing demand—"Shall we not see these daughters and these sisters?"—her final words in the play, he poises his vigorous reconstruction of their state together:

> No, no, no, no! Come let's away to prison:
> We two alone will sing like birds i' th' cage;
> When thou dost ask me blessing, I'll kneel down
> And ask of thee forgiveness. So we'll live,
> And pray, and sing, and tell old tales, and laugh
> At gilded butterflies, and hear poor rogues
> Talk of court news; and we'll talk with them too—
> Who loses and who wins; who's in, who's out—
> And take upon 's the mystery of things
> As if we were God's spies; and we'll wear out,
> In a wall's prison, packs and sects of great ones,
> That ebb and flow by th' moon.   (5.3.7–19)

In the poetic vision he crafts to reassure her, Lear collapses the functions of spectacle and spectator: on display to entertain others, "like birds i' th' cage," they will in fact "entertain" or gaze back in evaluative consideration at their beholders, attaining finally a semidivine perspective of "God's spies." He imagines a fiction of Cordelia and himself as subjects of their own "old tales"—caught not in a mere retrospect of past events but generating tales across generations about growing old, and what this means—while in turn contemptuously regarding the "great ones" whose ascendency has transformed them into spectacles. "The good-years shall devour them, flesh and fell, / Ere they shall make us weep," he concludes, "We'll see 'em starved first" (5.3.24–25). Again the source of much interpretive controversy, the "good-years" allusion sounds like yet another age reference, as the elder glances cooly to the way the captors' "good-years" shall feed upon their vain youth, simultaneously consuming and starving them, as this audience will eventually "see." To the last, endurance remains the keynote. Against Edmund's dark assertion several lines later that "men / Are as the time is" (30–31), Lear preemptively seeks to recast the time as uniquely his and Cordelia's own, regardless of the years.

Amid the clutter of act 5, scene 3's almost relentless compression, Lear's discourse of confined exhibition and spectacular audience reversal must still compete with others' more sinister narrative designs. Edmund's own "writ" upon their lives intends to reconstruct and publish its violence as self-inflicted: the order is "To hang Cordelia in the prison, and / To lay the blame upon her own despair, / That she fordid herself" (5.3.246, 254–56). The terrible events of murder and revenge are enacted offstage, just beyond our view, though still in the presence of witnesses. After having "kill'd the slave" that hanged Cordelia—"'Tis true, my lords, he did," the attending gentleman confirms (5.3.275–76)—Lear returns to the stage carrying her body, directing this last horrific spectacle's audience to "Howl," and calling for a mirror or speculum by which he hopes, fruitlessly, to detect some indication of his daughter's survival. In his last gestures, he recalls his own present visual impairments, even as he reminisces about the bygone day he has "seen":

> I have seen the day, with my good biting falchion
> I would have made them skip. I am old now,
> And these same crosses spoil me. Who are you?
> Mine eyes are not o' th' best; I'll tell you straight.   (5.3.277–80)

Though his own present "dull sight" conditions his responses, he is still able to identify those around him ("Are you not Kent?" [5.3.283]). Yet the visions he at last surveys hold little interest for him: from his first word in the initial scene, "Attend," to the Folio's closing "Look there, look there" (5.3.312), he ends as he began, directing the notice of his audience.[37] Lear dies prompting those he ultimately disregards as "dead and rotten" for all practical purposes to attend to a vision he alone can fully discern and construe.

In death, the aged king of course leaves it to others to reassess the spectacle of old age that his career has presented. In his own final entreaty for others to unbutton him, Lear takes the opportunity (as he had on the heath) to present his form to the world for an evaluation to which he nonetheless remains indifferent. The strength he displays—a factor that some hail as the chief component of his tragedy—itself poses his "bootless" spectators to the end, all of whom are unable to process his fate in a competent or plausible fashion.[38] Edgar's command for Lear to "Look up" (5.3.313), whatever efficacy it might have had for Gloucester back at the imagined cliff, rings especially hollow now, just as Albany's feeble efforts to reassign royal office seem, for all the urgency of dominion in this play of failed authority, "but a trifle." Kent, the sole surviving elder, resolves to maintain the itinerancy of senescence that the play has so relentlessly depicted, resolving upon the unspecified "journey" he will undertake on behalf of his "master." The spectacle defies moralization, having deconstructed our presuppositions—both pejorative and reverent—about the old age it has watched pass.

As Lodowick Lloyd observes at one point in his *Linceus Spectacles,* "*Aristippus* being asked to what purpose do men bring up their children in learning, answered, that when they come to sit [i]n *Theaters,* to see games & playes, *ne lapis super lapidem sederet,* that one stone should not sit upon another" (p. 5). When Lear indicts his followers upon his final entry, "O, you are men of stones" (5.3.258), it is not just the shrill, heartbroken cry of one crushed beneath his own tragic experience, in which he knows himself to be complicit. The elder's keening also gives voice to an outraged senescence railing against the ignorance and insensitivity of youth. Haranguing his audience, the old king bids one last time to script and direct the narrative and scene he so poignantly claims as his own: "Had I your tongues and eyes, I'd use them so / That heaven's vault should crack" (5.3.259–60). Unable to usurp the viewers' perspectives as he would like to do—as he had hoped to command speech from his daughters at the start—he retreats inward toward a state that leaves even his most sympathetic witnesses with a sense that "He knows not what he says" or (in the Quarto's variant) "He knows not what he sees" (5.3.294).

In either version, Albany is, typically, altogether off the mark: "Confin'd to exhibition," even as he retires to an individuated inaccessibility, Lear has never been more fully attuned to his surroundings, or their insignificance, which are *all* "but a trifle here," as the survivors' awkward final pronouncements implicitly reaffirm. We might do well to hear, in Kent's pointed summation "He but usurp'd his life" (5.3.318), the emphasis fall, not on the verb, but on the direct object. In death, the king forcibly lays claim to and closes the book on the autonomous command of his life story that he had so feared to lose. Having arrived at his mortal destination at last, fully "Unburthen'd," Lear bequeaths the "weight of this sad time" to "younger strengths" to carry. His reclamation leaves the surviving audience to affirm that "The oldest hath borne most, we that are young / Shall never see so much, nor live so long" (5.3.324, 326–27), dreading that they might survive long enough ever again to need such spectacles.

If *King Lear* bears a coda-like relationship to Elizabeth's reign, as I proposed early on, a trend in editorial scholarship on the play dating to the late 1970s draws out this connection well into her successor's regime. A number of prominent Shakespeareans maintain that the Folio version of *Lear,* which features a significant number of textual departures from the original version published in the 1608 quarto, actually marks the play-wright's wholesale revision of the work into what is essentially a new play.[39] Such an argument, moreover, redates the revised tragedy to 1610, ensconc-ing it among the late romances—plays that both dwell on a different kind of spectacular "wonder" and repeatedly build their plots around aged (or at least aging) figures. Although the theory on one level proves attractive for my own thesis, since it could be marshaled to suggest that the author continued to rework his play as the cultural nostalgia for Elizabeth itself evolved in the ways Curtis Perry describes, it also rests upon critical prem-ises that in fact distort *King Lear*'s affiliation with the late plays that in this textual reconstruction it purportedly complements.

Of all the formidable objections that have successfully undermined this dual-text approach, the most insightful and provocative is provided by Gordon McMullan in his study of Shakespeare and "late writing." In McMullan's diagnosis, the theory is symptomatic of a critical longing to re-gard *King Lear* as a late play—a product of Shakespeare's own "old age"— and to couch the work's unrelenting bleakness within the romances' more redemptive urges. Moreover, the juxtaposition better enables us to think about characters like Leontes, Pericles, and Prospero as old men, when in fact they need be no older than in their mid-forties. The discussion, McMullan speculates, "is dependent upon an unvoiced desire to make this play about an old man an old man's play, a kind of grim counterpart to, or forerunner of, the retirement motif of *The Tempest*. If Shakespeare writes a play about old age, in other words, it must be associated as closely as pos-sible with the plays which embody that old age dramatically—that is, the late plays." In his view, "Not only does the tacit incorporation of *King Lear* into the late plays offer a glimpse of a salvation that is not in fact avail-able, then, it also implicitly turns the late plays into something they are not—plays of old age, written by an allegedly 'ageing' playwright who was not in fact 'old' at all."[40]

McMullan's compelling critique does well to reinforce what I take to be an essential distance between Lear and the "mature" romance protagonists who follow in his wake. In his "Fourscore and upward," the old king de-signedly occupies a stage of life far beyond those who, even by the harshest contemporary standards, are barely past their prime. Although the spec-tacles engineered by Paulina or Prospero succeed where Lear's abortive opening show had not, their victories mark the achievements of those still in life's middle years, for all the trauma they suffer or have suffered. De-spite any tendency to resign themselves to the "grave," they in fact enjoy the potential prospect of many more years ahead of them, something that

Lear under the best of alternative circumstances could not, as Lyle Asher reminds us. We cannot, in other words, measure their victories or endurance fairly against the struggles of one who has lived, in Edgar's words, "so long." However frequently Shakespeare returned to matters of aging in his subsequent plays, and to whatever effect, *King Lear* stands alone as his paramount, sustained meditation on actual senescence and is unique within both his own oeuvre and the period's drama overall.

As the "pattern" of an empowered "aged princess," Elizabeth at the last left an indelible impression on Shakespeare and all her subjects, whether they recalled her fondly or bitterly. It seems fitting, therefore, that she should herself have made a belated appearance in one of the playwright's final collaborative endeavors, *Henry VIII* (1613), as the infant whose birth signals the "Holy-day" that concludes the action. This arrival—announced by the "Old Lady" in act 5, scene 1—takes on an especial poignancy, of course, in the wake of Queen Katherine's demise. Her lament, "I am old, my lords" (3.1.120), augmented by her departing prayer on behalf of her daughter Mary, "She is young, and of a noble modest nature, / I hope she will deserve well" (4.2.135–36), comes as close to the play's emotional core as we can get. The dramatic irony enabled by the audience's historical hindsight, furthermore, darkens the otherwise comic exchange between Anne Bullen and the Old Lady, who rebuts the young woman's claim "By my troth and maidenhead, / I would not be a queen" with the assurance "A threepence bow'd would hire me, / Old as I am, to queen it" (2.3.23–24 and 36–37).

Yet all the pain threatened by time's passage fails to dampen the enthusiasm that charges Archbishop Cranmer's closing prophecy over Henry's new daughter:

> This royal infant—heaven still move about her!—
> Though in her cradle, yet now promises
> Upon this land a thousand thousand blessings,
> Which time shall bring to ripeness. She shall be
> (But few now living can behold that goodness)
> A pattern to all princes living with her,
> And all that shall succeed.
>
> .   .   .   .
>
> She shall be, to the happiness of England,
> An aged princess; many days shall see her,
> And yet no day without a deed to crown it.   (5.5.17–23 & 56–58)

If any more positive image of genuine senescence in the later plays gestures to contrast the devastation of *King Lear*, we find it, not in the romances, but here in the prophetic vision of a monarch whose old age would come to be equated with a nation's happiness. Time and age alone could bring to ripeness whatever promised blessings she would realize as a model for those who look to "succeed" amid all the difficulties that we know await. Elizabeth's capacity to negotiate her own old age substantiated such promise: something the tragedian recognized as no mean feat.

EPILOGUE

Figures of Retire

FROM A CERTAIN VANTAGE POINT, Shakespeare's great tragedy of old age can be (and largely has been) seen as bearing out the grim conclusion drawn by Simone de Beauvoir at one turn in her pathbreaking study *The Coming of Age:* "Whether we like it or not, in the end we submit to the outsider's point of view."[1] *King Lear's* elders find themselves subject to the pervasive adjudicating gaze of an ascendant younger generation that regards them with either violent, self-serving disdain or a piteous "nursery," each threatening its own brand of confinement. As I have argued, however, the play simultaneously examines an enduring, constitutionally determined subjectivity that goes far to shield these older characters, for all the victimization they suffer, from the bad faith that Beauvoir seems to think of as a depressingly unavoidable component of the aged experience.[2] In the vision Shakespeare summoned, inauthenticity more often becomes the bane of a younger company that, even with the best intentions in sight, must remind itself of the need to "Speak what we feel, not what we ought to say" (5.3.325). In this regard, he brought his version of the story into alignment with the patterns of resistance I have chosen as examples from throughout the final phase of Elizabeth's reign. In all cases, though to various ends, senescence entails negotiation between opposing "constitutional" understandings of what old age may and may not allow. However much the "outsider's point of view" may attempt to govern behavior, the individual's more intimate awareness of a bodily constitution to which she or he alone enjoys complete access provides critical recourse against such encroachment.

The case studies I have pursued across the preceding chapters serve collectively to illustrate and confirm my sense of this fruitful tension between competing notions of our behavior's constitutional alignments in old age that arose in England uniquely toward the close of the sixteenth century.

In scrutinizing the ways in which the queen's own vigorous management of her public and private demeanor as she progressed into later life coincided with a growing cultural reconception of senescence, grounded in turn in a developing sense of a subject's individual bodily constitution, I have attempted to identify a clearer foundation for the increasingly greater publicity old age thereafter came to receive. Beyond the period surveyed, documentary evidence regarding cultural conversations about senescence became surprisingly plentiful. From the deeply sympathetic cast of Thomas Middleton, William Rowley, and Thomas Heywood's collaborative drama *The Old Law* (1618–19)—which Anthony Ellis deems "early modern comedy's most original defense of old age, a searing indictment of the mistreatment and undervaluation of the aged that can occur within materialistically inclined societies, where the elderly are only seen as unproductive impediments to the next generation's prosperity"[3]—and Thomas Sheafe's tract *Vindiciæ Senectutis, or, A Plea for Old-Age* (1639); to the more clinical discussions featured in Robert Burton's *Anatomy of Melancholy* (1621) and Francis Bacon's *Historia vitae & mortis* (1623); to the pseudo-biographical and autobiographical accounts of John Taylor's *The Old, Old, Very Old Man* (1635) and the papers of Archbishop William Stancroft (d. 1693); to the profusion of poems, broadsides, homilies, treatises, conduct books, and legal commentary now available in the corresponding volumes of Lynn Botelho and Susannah R. Ottaway's expansive *History of Old Age, 1600–1800,* literary critics and historians have enjoyed ample source material from which to undertake the tremendous amount of scholarly work in the field that remains to be completed.

I hope my own assessment of the emerging perspective evident in the pastoral reconfigurations of old age that Spenser and Sidney designed, the (more fraught) lyrical explorations of anxieties surrounding age that troubled the composure and self-image of the era's love poets, and Shakespeare's dramatization of the tragic consequences that can issue from explosive gerontophobic resentments played out in circles of political power will add some insight to this long-range endeavor. We can comprehend the various ways in which old age is conceived and represented throughout the later phases of early modernity only after we have attended to the preliminary shift that Elizabeth's reign had both enabled and witnessed—a shift that cannot be seen but as having a significant and lasting impact on all layers of future discourse on the topic.

"But what else is language and utterance, and discourse and persuasion, and argument in man," George Puttenham asks in his closing apology for the poetic artifice that his *Art of English Poesy* systematizes, "than the

Fig. 3. Andrea Alciato, from *Emblemata* (Lyon, 1550).
By permission of University of Glasgow Library,
Special Collections.

virtues of a well-constituted body and mind?"[4] And although artifice can aid and even at times surmount nature, as the physician is "able not only to restore the decayed spirits of man and render him health, but also to prolong the term of his life many years over and above the stint of his first and natural constitution" (p. 383), it is to this determinate inner makeup that he gives ultimate priority. When Puttenham emblematizes the eloquence promoted in his handbook, he can do no better than to invoke the commonplace beloved by early humanists, Lucian's well-known portrait of Heracles in his essay of that name—an image familiar to his audience throughout the century from the multiple editions of Andrea Alciato's popular *Emblemata* (see fig. 3). To justify his own reentry into the lists of public oratory late in life, the ancient Greek author recalls how the Celts portray Heracles—for them a more appropriate icon of rhetorical persuasiveness than Hermes—as a "lusty old man," who despite his wrinkles still bears the club, bow, and lion's skin of the mighty demigod, as he draws to himself an assembly of men by means of a delicate chain, one end of which is fastened to their ears and the other to his tongue.

Puttenham glosses the reference well beyond his source text, elaborating on how the Celtic emblem's design "to show more plainly that eloquence is of great force and not (as many men think amiss) the property and gift of young men only, but rather of old men, and a thing which better becometh hoary hairs than beardless boys" affirms their conviction that "age (say they and most truly) brings experience, experience bringeth wisdom, long life yields long use and much exercise of speech, exercise and custom with wisdom make an assured and voluble utterance. So is it that old men more than any other sort speak most gravely, wisely, assuredly, and plausibly, which parts are all that can be required in perfect eloquence" (p. 226).

Far more revealing than the routine attribution of wisdom to senescence—a presumption that carries, as we have seen, its own potential hazards—is Puttenham's claim for the "assurance" and "volubility" that the elder alone brings to the forum, traits that readily contest the misplaced perception of "many men" prone to favor the capabilities of "young men only." The "hoary hairs" he celebrates root their natural confidence not merely in a seasoned discursive facility but (as his choice term "voluble" expresses) in a serpentine agility or witty "Quickness in turning from one object to another" (*OED*, 1.1): a "lusty" circumspection, in short, which youth has simply not had time to develop.

Boldly reentering a public arena he had long since forsaken, armed with the encouragement of this Herculean precedent, Lucian's rhetor cuts a decidedly *un*retiring figure. Yet his gesture itself speaks to the fuller meaning of the term "retire," which can signify an enforced or voluntary withdrawal, but also a return or recovery. It is more to this latter sense of the word that Puttenham alludes when, among the "figures sententious" he compiles in the *Art*'s third book, he lists "*Epanodos,* or the Figure of Retire," a trope that undertakes "the resumption of a former proposition uttered in generality, to explain the same better by a particular division." More specifically, it "resumes both the matter and the terms, and is therefore accounted one of the Figures of Repetition" (p. 306). The expansive embellishment or revisiting of an earlier rhetorical locus, much like the elder's alleged tendency to dwell upon the past, here implies neither a tedious reiteration nor a sad escape from an impotent present, but a desire to explicate and make clearer sense of a time that is perhaps only now genuinely one's own, as it exists in the fuller context of hindsight and accumulated experience.

Even though the alignment of old age and "retirement" as a sanctioned, expected, or even obligatory graduation from a public workforce, as historians of the early modern period commonly emphasize, would not broadly emerge until well after industrialized Europe had redefined its own social landscape in the late nineteenth and early twentieth centuries, it has nonetheless formed an understandable association with advanced stages of life since antiquity, which recognized time's corroding power over a subject's physical (if not mental) capacities as an excuse from the ardors of more strenuous tasks, like military service.[5] All of the subjects to whom I have attended in this study, both literal and literary, confronted a vista of retirement that accompanies old age, both as a retreat and return. They might, with Cicero's Cato or Plutarch of the *Moralia,* vehemently resist any such removal from the arena of public responsibility, or they might strategize in more subdued ways to retain their influence, presence, and dignity.

For Elizabeth herself, as for Spenser's Thenot or Sidney's Geron, "retirement" at the behest of prejudicial outside forces or pressures was little more than a figure, and the threat it posed as such only an occasion for a self-affirming opposition all their own. Yet, as some of the lyric poetry we have examined demonstrates, the formative social bias that constructs this figure can prove formidable, especially when it comes to be internalized by the aging subject him- or herself. Although Beauvoir's vision of our inevitable surrender to "the outsider's point of view" finally proves too categorical to represent plausibly the rich diversity of late-life experience, it provides a salutary caution against our all-too-human propensity to capitulate before the intimidating directives of entrenched orthodoxy. In many ways, *King Lear* enacts how brutal the retaliation may turn when one presumes even to attempt a negotiated settlement with such external agencies, especially when these anchor whatever privileged self-image they promote in their target's docile acquiescence.

Students of gender, race, and class have long recognized how the chauvinisms afflicting these categories work their most insidious damage when members of the victimized group come to subscribe to the very ideological bigotry at whose hands they suffer. If anything, such a hazard pertains even more distressingly to matters of old age. "If people are culturally conditioned to expect to be dependent and helpless past a certain age," Thane sums up, "they are more likely to become so, with consequences for their own lives and those of others."[6] As sensitive as we have grown to the inequities and injustices that inhere within so many of our foundational cultural institutions, the gerontophobia that pervades our thinking and discourse goes virtually unchecked. Throughout the United States' presidential election of 2008, where racist or sexist jokes at the expense of the African American candidate or his female running mate met with speedy condemnation, the widespread ridicule of his elderly opponent's advanced years excited no such outrage; in fact, the older figure was often expected to participate in the mockery, presenting himself as a self-deprecating caricature of senescence. In the early modern period as now, across the literary record of late Elizabethan England and well beyond, it becomes clear that the greatest opportunity for the ageing subject's defeat arises when he or she comes to internalize this broader prejudicial disregard, allowing such external perspectives to overwhelm and redirect more "authentic" sensibilities. This, even more than the curtailments of physical decline, poses the most insidious threat to the composure of our subjective twilight. With this in mind, I close with brief reference to two items—one obscure and one familiar—that appeared in English during the final years of Elizabeth's reign.

The anonymous fragment "Concerning olde Age," published in the anthology *A Poetical Rapsody* (1602), presents an eclogue whose "beginning and end," as the editorial title announces, "are wanting." The poem casts its debate as a rustic exchange between two elders, one of whom, named Perin, has come to abhor the existence to which his advanced years have brought him. Although he begins in mid-sentence, he argues a foregone conclusion: "For when thou art not as thou wont of yore, / No cause why life should please thee any more."[7] Beholden strictly to the evaluative gaze of his "Shepheards Peeres," he discovers himself locked into a depression of nostalgic self-contempt:

> Whilome I was (in course of former yeeres,
> Ere freezing Eld had coold my youthly rage)
> Of mickle worth among my Shepheards Peeres.
> Now for I am some-dele ystept in age,
> For pleasance, strength, and beautie ginnes asswage.
>   Ech litle Heard-groom laughs my wrinkled face,
>   Ech bonny lasse for Cuddy shunnes the place.

To challenge this bleak assessment, his companion Wrenock, "in thilk estate," faults Perin's impulse "to blame that blamelesse seems to me, / And hurtlesse Eld to sneb" (1:50–51). When Perin retorts that Wrenock's ample wealth and comfortable lifestyle color his cheery "fained words"—if the senility of "rusty Eld" itself isn't prompting him to "doat"—and points to the frisking "Lambkin" and the aged "Ewe from whom all Joy with youth is fled" as suitable emblems of life's hopeless decline, his antagonist points out that they are equally well off materially, and dismisses the facile comparison of men and beasts (1:51–52). Human beings, endowed uniquely with an "inward light" that "neither Age nor Time can weare away," are warmed in his view by "Sike fire as Welkin showes in winter night." This inner fire, moreover,

> waxeth bett for use as Shepheards Crooke,
> That ever shineth brighter day by day:
> Al so though wrinkled seeme the aged looke,
> Bright shines the fire that from the stars we tooke.   (1:52)

We might just as easily regard the melancholy older sheep, in his witty counter-analogy, as lamenting the "paine" that the lamb will likely experience throughout its "wanton" youth.

Although the conversation breaks off without realizing further development or achieving resolution, leaving Perin caught in an enraptured vision of youth's "peerelesse pleasures" whose loss he so deeply mourns, the chief thrust of his friend's ameliorating counsels obtains (1:53). "The faults of men thou lay'st on Age I see," Wrenock succinctly assails Perin, whose willful refusal to acknowledge late life's unique virtues in favor of youth's preferred pleasures has made him his own worst enemy (1:51). Refusing in kind to deny or disavow the wrinkles he bears, regardless of the way these may excite the scorn of the world's Cuddies, Wrenock exhibits a substantiating inner composure that supports old age like the "Shepheards Crooke" on which he leans that shines more brightly with use (1:52). He valorizes their shared time of life precisely by disdaining a nostalgia for youth that plays into the biases of a younger generation and inevitably predetermines the elder's blasted self-image.

Significantly, Wrenock's select rebuttals display exactly the circumspect assurance and dexterity that Puttenham assigns to natural eloquence, those very attributes that elevate the shepherd's sentiments above a resigned preparedness merely to make the best of the situation his interlocutor grieves. If these supportive gestures falter before the allure of youthful approval that his mate covets, this speaks more to the sad elder's flawed priorities than to any inadequacy inhering in senescence itself. A curious final slip (whether of the author or the character remains uncertain) marks Perin's parting reverie, when he addresses Wrenock as "Thenot," which is suggestive of just how pervasively Spenser's pastoral champion of old age had come to represent this form of advocacy (1:53).

The pastoral lyric's irresolution holds in a tense, uneasy balance visions of senescence's embittered self-abnegation and contented self-confidence. Far more prominently, one of Michel de Montaigne's best-known later essays, Englished in 1603 as "Of Repenting" in John Florio's widely influential translation, confronts the experience of late life with the same candor and irony for which the author's earlier reflections are justly celebrated. Decidedly no "golden ager," Montaigne, who had remarked in the essay "Of Age" which concluded his collection's first volume, that our most worthy attainments are typically reached by age thirty, affirms at last how the years have afforded his discourse even more latitude: "for it seemeth, custome alloweth old age more liberty to babble, and indiscretion to talke of it selfe."[8] Although he deliberately leaves unstated whether this privilege derives more from respect or from indifference, the distinction carries little significance for him, as he makes most unequivocally clear his own antipathy to public opinion, especially amid the decay that this external perspective concurrently suffers. "To ground the recompence of vertuous actions upon the approbation of others is to undertake a most uncertaine or troubled foundation," he asserts, "namely in an age so corrupt and times so ignorant as this is: the vulgar peoples good opinion is injurious" (3:23). Moreover, it is fundamentally this larger company's inherent inability to see through our "outward apparance" to our "inward constitution" that most disqualifies their assessments (3:26). Even as he strives to "represent" himself in all the rich inconsistency and mutability that will inform his experience up to the moment of his death, the essayist refuses to acknowledge the external world's capability to comprehend or define him fully.

The very authenticity that audiences continue to recognize and appreciate in Montaigne's work is owing chiefly to his stirring ability to hold in check those forces of tradition or society that might presume to rein him in, even as he assails the equally insidious inner demons that persistently threaten to constrain him. True to form, Montaigne trains a no less critical eye on old age than he does on the myopia of external agencies, especially because he regards senescence's truest weakness as the self-betrayal to which it too often leaves us vulnerable. The most justly remembered point of attack in "Of Repenting" is the one upon the propensity late in life to regret our earlier years and the hypocrisy this typically entails, as older generations take youth to task for vices from which "impuissance" (Florio's wonderful term) alone excludes them. For such "accidentall repentance which olde age brings with it" he reserves his special contempt, sneering that "I shall never give impuissance thankes for any good it can do me" (3:33). Making a virtue of incapability is every bit as gross a surrender to bad faith as Perin's self-pitying malaise. Never denying the "care and weaknesse" or the "misery and mishap" that advanced age may bring, Montaigne grants these "importunate diseases and imperfections" little sway over his constant late "discretion" (3:34–35).

"[W]hatever some say," Montaigne declares with confidence and equanimity, "Retired lives sustaine [i.e., fulfill] . . . offices as much more crabbed and extended than other lives doe" (3:26). Nowhere does this notion better apply than to the kinds of retreat and return that senescence at least enables, if it (given the discrete circumstances of one's constitution) does not necessitate. As we observed earlier, old age in Montaigne's final summation "sets more wrinckles in our minds then on our foreheads," and for this reason rare are the "spirits," in his contentious late view, "which in growing old taste not sowrely and mustily" (3:36). But his very recognition of this bespeaks the self-awareness and self-possession that constitute our best inner strength at any time in life. In the end, such potency may manifest in a way that even those outside of us must perceive and reckon with. This is something that Lucian—in so many ways Montaigne's classical progenitor—pointedly suggests as he concludes the essay that Puttenham invoked with his own allusion to Homer's Odysseus, at the moment when the hero's still formidable strength glimmers through the ancient beggar's shabby appearance on his arrival back at Ithaca. Smilingly, the rhetorician muses how an audience to his aged efforts just may find themselves compelled to remark, as the startled and impressed suitors had done in their hushed realization, "See what limbs the old man's rags have uncovered."[9]

Notes

1. Age, Agency, and Early Modern Constitutions

1. Timothe Kendall, *Flowers of Epigrammes* (1874; repr., New York: Burt Franklin, 1967), pp. 150–51.

2. Margaret Morganroth Gullette, *Aged by Culture* (Chicago: University of Chicago Press, 2004), p. 122. See esp. her discussion of this "master narrative" on pp. 132–39. As I use the terms throughout, "gerontophobia"—a psychologically and socially ingrained repugnance for the aged body—and "gerontophobic" encompass interrelated exterior and interior sources for antipathies to old age. See Kathleen Woodward's entry in *Feminism and Psychoanalysis: A Critical Dictionary,* ed. Elizabeth Wright (Oxford: Blackwell, 1992), pp. 145–48; and Richard Freedman, "Sufficiently Decayed: Gerontophobia in English Literature," in *Aging and the Elderly: Humanistic Perspectives in Gerontology,* ed. Stuart F. Spickler (Atlantic Highlands, N.J.: Humanities Press, 1978), pp. 49–61.

3. Anthony Esler, *The Aspiring Mind of the Elizabethan Younger Generation* (Durham, N.C.: Duke University Press, 1966), p. 223.

4. Ibid., p. x.

5. A historical context that witnessed what Esler refers to as a younger generation "so vigorously and ubiquitously in evidence" (ibid., p. xviii) not surprisingly marked the emergence of "fairly reliable estimates of life expectancy" in England: see Pat Thane, *Old Age in English History: Past Experiences, Present Issues* (Oxford: Oxford University Press, 2000), p. 20.

6. A clear example of this transition is available in the Dutch doctor Levinus Lemnius's tract, translated by Thomas Newton in 1576 as *The Touchstone of Complexions,* which professes on its title page to teach its readers to "throughly know, as well the exacte state, habite, disposition, and constitution, of his owne Body outwardly: as also the inclinations, affections, motions, & desires of his mynd inwardly." Though Newton will deploy the terms interchangeably throughout the text, he specifies constitution's novelty at one turn, when he alludes to "the constitution of the bodye (which the Greekes do call *krāsis,* and the common sort, Complexion)" (p. 32v).

7. Thomas Fortescue, *The Foreste* (London, 1571), pp. 46r–v. Subsequent in-text citations from Fortescue refer to this edition.

8. The most concise modern survey of these schemas remains Samuel C. Chew's chapter in his *The Pilgrimage of Life* (New Haven: Yale University Press, 1962), pp. 144–73. For a thoughtful and exhaustive discussion of the topic's prominence and implications down to early modernity, see J. A. Burrow's excellent *The Ages of Man: A Study in Medieval Writing and Thought* (Oxford: Clarendon Press, 1986).

9. William Harrison, *The Description of England,* ed. Georges Edelen (Ithaca, N.Y.: Cornell University Press, 1968), pp. 448–49.

10. Thane, *Old Age in English History,* p. 27.

11. See the chart Peter Laslett reproduces in his "Necessary Knowledge: Age and Aging in the Societies of the Past," in *Aging in the Past: Demography, Society, and Old Age,* ed. David I. Kertzer and Peter Laslett (Berkeley: University of California Press, 1995), p. 19.

12. Keith Wrightson estimates that "the population of 2.98 million in 1561 had grown to over four million by 1601" (*Earthly Necessities: Economic Lives in Early Modern Britain* [New Haven: Yale University Press, 2000], p. 159). See also Laslett's graph, esp. table 1.3 and figure 1.6 (pp. 19 and 26).

13. Steven R. Smith, "Growing Old in Early Stuart England," *Albion* 8 (1976): 126.

14. *Tudor Economic Documents,* ed. R. H. Tawney and Eileen Power, 3 vols. (London: Longmans, 1924), 3:418.

15. Thane, *Old Age in English History,* p. 3.

16. Ibid., p. 19.

17. Creighton Gilbert, "When Did a Man in the Renaissance Grow Old?" *Studies in the Renaissance* 14 (1967): 7–32.

18. Thane, *Old Age in English History,* p. 24.

19. Along with the book, see Thane's subsequent article "Social Histories of Old Age and Aging," *Journal of Social History* 37 (2003): 93–111, which touches in summary form on many of the larger work's chief theoretical concerns and identifies the outstanding research to be done in what "remains a new topic area" (106–7); and the handsomely illustrated trade book *The Long History of Old Age* that she more recently edited (London: Thames and Hudson, 2005).

20. Anne M. Wyatt-Brown, "Literary Gerontology Comes of Age," in *Handbook of the Humanities and Aging,* ed. Thomas R. Cole et al. (New York: Springer, 1992), pp. 331–51.

21. The topic has enjoyed its most extensive attention of late from classicists: see esp. Tim Parkin, *Old Age in the Roman World: A Cultural and Social History* (Baltimore: Johns Hopkins University Press, 2003); and Karen Cokayne, *Experiencing Old Age in Ancient Rome* (London: Routledge, 2003). For analyses of later periods, see (for instance) Shulamith Shahar, *Growing Old in the Middle Ages: "Winter clothes us in shadow and pain,"* trans. Yael Lotan (London: Routledge, 1997); David G. Troyansky, *Old Age in the Old Regime: Image and Experience in Eighteenth Century France* (Ithaca, N.Y.: Cornell University Press, 1989); Susanna R. Ottaway, *The Decline of Life: Old Age in Eighteenth-Century England* (Cambridge: Cambridge University Press, 2007); and Kathleen Woodward, *Aging and Its Discontents: Freud and Other Fictions* (Bloomington: Indiana University Press, 1991).

22. Helen Small, *The Long Life* (New York: Oxford University Press, 2007), pp. 1–15. See esp. her early observation that "in the main, philosophy . . . has been far more interested in 'mortal questions.' Living to be old has historically been seen as exceptional, the questions it raises supererogatory to the main arguments to be had about lives, and goods, and values" (p. 1).

23. On Burckhardt and contemporary period scholarship, see William Kerrigan and Gordon Braden, *The Idea of the Renaissance* (Baltimore: Johns Hopkins University Press, 1989), esp. chaps. 1 and 2, pp. 3–54.

24. Keith Thomas, "Age and Authority in Early Modern England," *Proceedings of the British Academy* 62 (1976): 205–48.

25. Georges Minois, *A History of Old Age: From Antiquity to the Renaissance,* trans. Sarah Hanbury Tenison (Chicago: University of Chicago Press, 1987).

26. Lynn Botelho and Pat Thane (eds.), *Women and Ageing in British Society since 1500* (Harlow, Essex, Eng.: Longman/Pearson, 2001).

27. Erin J. Campbell (ed.), *Growing Old in Early Modern Europe: Cultural Representations* (Aldershot, Hampshire, Eng.: Ashgate, 2006).

28. Philip Sohm, *The Artist Grows Old: Arts and Artists in Italy, 1500–1800* (New Haven: Yale University Press, 2007); Anthony Ellis, *Old Age, Masculinity and Early Modern Drama* (Farnham, Surrey, Eng.: Ashgate, 2009); Maurice Charney, *Wrinkled Deep in Time: Aging in Shakespeare* (New York: Columbia University Press, 2010). For a selected bibliography of the (few) early items on Shakespeare and old age, see Charney, pp. 168–69n10.

29. Lynn Botelho, Susannah R. Ottaway, and Ingrid H. Tague (eds.), *The History of Old Age in England, 1600–1800,* 8 vols. (Biggleswade, Bedfordshire, Eng.: Pickering and Chatto, 2008–).

30. Nina Taunton, *Fictions of Old Age in Early Modern Literature and Culture* (London: Routledge, 2007), p. 77.

31. Ibid., p. 82.

32. If anything, sex (and its procreative payoff) only gets better. Copulating less frequently, old men produce sperm "more elaborated and refined," conducive to the generation of masculine offspring. Young husbands, by contrast, tend to beget female children, since "when their irons were hotter, they never stopped beating them on their anvils and never did anything right." Laurent Joubert, *Popular Errors,* trans. Gregory David de Rocher (Tuscaloosa: University of Alabama Press, 1989), p. 117. The original French refers to *Erreurs populaires au fait de la medicine et régime de santé* (Bordeaux, 1578), p. 193.

33. He goes on to assert, "It is useful to keep track of years for the payment of rent, but with people, years mean nothing in the consideration of one's state and present disposition (*disposicion presante*), which are more or less what makes a person last" (p. 119; *Erreurs,* p. 201).

34. Joubert, *Popular Errors,* p. 120; *Erreurs,* p. 203.

35. Leslie A. Fiedler, "Eros and Thanatos: Old Age in Love," *Aging, Death, and the Completion of Being,* ed. David D. Van Tassel (Philadelphia: University of Pennsylvania Press, 1979), p. 236. See also his "More Images of Eros and Old Age: The Damnation of Faust and the Fountain of Youth," in Kathleen Woodward and Murray M. Schwartz (eds.), *Memory and Desire: Aging—Literature—Psychoanalysis* (Bloomington: Indiana University Press, 1986), pp. 37–50.

36. Throughout this book, unless otherwise noted, all quotations from the plays refer to *The Riverside Shakespeare,* 2nd ed., ed. G. Blakemore Evans et al. (Boston: Houghton Mifflin, 1997).

37. Haim Hazan, *Old Age: Constructions and Deconstructions* (Cambridge: Cambridge University Press, 1994), pp. 2, 13.

38. Gullette, *Aged by Culture,* p. 130. Emphasizing that "No other construction concerns every one, or concerns each one so nearly," Gullette argues stridently for a refreshed discourse wherein "It becomes harder to blame the body in itself, harder to displace economic or sociopolitical problems onto age, and harder to call age and aging wholly 'natural'" (pp. 97 and 103).

39. Thane, *Old Age in English History,* p. 5.

40. Jenny Hockey and Allison James, *Social Identities across the Life Course* (Basingstoke: Palgrave, 2003), pp. 134, 135; Richard Jenkins, *Social Identity,* 2nd ed. (London: Routledge, 2004).

41. Michael C. Schoenfeldt, *Bodies and Selves in Early Modern England: Physiology and Inwardness in Spenser, Shakespeare, Herbert, and Milton* (Cambridge: Cambridge University Press, 1999), esp. chap. 1, pp. 1–39.

42. Cicero, *Of Old Age,* trans. Thomas Newton (London, 1569), fol. 4. While I retain the period spellings of the original texts I cite throughout this book, I have silently modernized the u/v and i/j conventions of Tudor usage.

43. Cokayne, *Experiencing Old Age in Ancient Rome,* p. 93.

44. Shahar, *Growing Old in the Middle Ages,* p. 72.

45. Woodward, *Aging and Its Discontents,* p. 62. See also Sohm's discussion of "Gerontophobia and the Anxiety of Obsolescence" in his *The Artist Grows Old*: "We accumulate

our prejudices about our bodies—gender, race, age—when we are young, when negative stereotypes of the elderly help us to form our emerging identities, but unlike racists and sexists, every ageist turns into the object he fears, should he be lucky enough to live so long. A recent survey of more than 17,000 people shows a dramatic drop in self-esteem in old age. Age turns us against ourselves" (p. 19). For more general discussions of the disparity between bodily self-perception and identity construction in old age, see esp. Mike Hepworth, "Positive Ageing and the Mask of Age," *Journal of Educational Gerontology* 6 (1991): 93–101; and Simon Biggs, *The Mature Imagination: Dynamics of Identity in Midlife and Beyond* (Buckingham, Buckinghamshire, Eng.: Open University Press, 1999).

46. Seneca, *The Workes of Lucius Annaeus Seneca,* trans. Thomas Lodge (London, 1614), p. 482. All further quotations from Seneca refer to Lodge's translation.

47. Cokayne, *Experiencing Old Age in Ancient Rome,* p. 88.

48. Thomas Wilson, *The Arte of Rhetorique,* ed. Thomas J. Derrick (New York: Garland, 1982), pp. 415–16.

49. Lemnius, *Touchstones of Complexions,* pp. 29r–v. For a curious suggestion of a "national" constitution, moreover, see Harrison's *Description of England,* where the author takes past English physicians to task for prescribing "outlandish [foreign] drugs," when indigenous ones would have better served, "sith God in nature hath so disposed His creatures that the most needful are the most plentiful and serving for such general diseases as our constitution most commonly is affected withal" (p. 268).

50. Andreas Laurentius, *Discourse of the Preservation of the Sight; Of Melancholike Diseases; Of Rheumes, and Of Old Age,* trans. Richard Surphlet (London, 1599), pp. 173–4 and 177.

51. See Lotario dei Segni (Pope Innocent III), *De miseria condicionis humane,* ed. and trans. Robert E. Lewis (Athens: University of Georgia Press, 1978), esp. pp. 106–9 on old age. For an extended and thoughtful treatment of medieval perspectives on senescence, see Shahar's book, *Growing Old in the Middle Ages,* whose subtitle— *"Winter clothes us in shadow and pain"*—aptly characterizes period sentiment. Regarding national cultural and literary attitudes to old age, Alicia K. Nitecki has pointed out English adherence to a conventional "view that exposes man's fear and repugnance in the face of aging, that treats the aged as grotesques, as vehicles of metaphor rather than as characters. It is this same view that the period's greatest poet, Chaucer, explores and enlarges but does not radically alter or obliterate" ("Figures of Old Age in Fourteenth-Century English Literature," in *Aging and the Aged in Medieval Europe,* ed. Michael M. Sheehan [Toronto: Pontifical Institute, 1990], p. 116). See also George R. Coffmann, "Old Age from Horace to Chaucer: Some Literary Affinities and Adventures of an Idea," *Speculum* 9 (1934): 249–77.

52. Minois, *History of Old Age,* p. 305.

53. Petrarch, book 8, letter 2, in *Letters of Old Age: Rerum senilium libri I–XVIII,* 2 vols., trans. Aldo S. Bernardo, Saul Levin, and Reta A. Bernardo (Baltimore: Johns Hopkins University Press, 1992), 1:278–79 and 275. In the same letter, he spurns an admirer's pity for his advanced years with the charge, "do not weep because I am not young; weep because I once was" (p. 273). Later, in *Seniles* 17.2, he again hails the "health of the mind" as age's attribute, even as he remarks on the purported commonality of octogenarians and nonagenarians in his day (2:646 and 651). The poet would even take his patron, Cardinal Giovanni Colonna, gently to task for complaining about the many discomforts his early old age has brought, invoking Cicero's *De senectute* as the last word on the subject, and uses the opportunity to interpolate a tribute to his own paternal great grandfather Gattius, who lived to the age of a hundred and four and enjoyed a wide-ranging authority that dignified his later years. Petrarch, bk. 6, letter 3, in *Letters on Familiar Matters: Rerum familiarium libri I–XXIV,* trans. Aldo S. Bernardo, 3 vols. (Albany: SUNY Press, 1975–85), 1:301–4.

54. Petrarch, *Remedies for Fortune Fair and Foul,* trans. Conrad H. Rawski, 5 vols. (Bloomington: Indiana University Press, 1991), 1:14 and 17.

55. Ibid., 3:195 (2.83.195).

56. Gabriele Zerbi, *Gerontocomia: On the Care of the Aged,* trans. L. R. Lind (Philadelphia: American Philosophical Society, 1988), pp. 50 and 304. Zerbi links *"senes"* etymologically with *nesciant,* suggesting a breakdown of knowledge itself, and "decrepit" with *crepitum* or "creaking" (pp. 31–32).

In his treatise *De pueris instituendis,* Erasmus likewise displays the presumed disgust that old age will inspire in youth. Arguing that the best teacher simultaneously should adopt a "fatherly attitude" toward his pupils and "must, as it were, become a child again and thus win the affection of his students," he remarks how "it is foolish to entrust one's children to old, nearly decrepit men for their first education. Such men are truly children; their stammering speech is real and not pretended. I prefer a teacher who is of an age when his vigour is in its prime, an age which does not repel his pupils and allows him to assume any role" (trans. Beert C. Verstraete in *Collected Works of Erasmus,* vol. 26, ed. Kelly Sowards [Toronto: University of Toronto Press, 1985], p. 334).

57. Robert Finlay, "The Venetian Republic as a Gerontocracy: Age and Politics in the Renaissance," *Journal of Medieval and Renaissance Studies* 8 (1978): 172. There, a member of the patrician class could hope to enter the circle of governing power by only following an extensive *cursus honorum,* when he had joined the *vecchi* or "old men." Finlay quotes Girolamo Priuli as stating that "A doge who remains in office for a long time tends to bore the city and will be hated by everybody."

58. Minois declares flatly that, for Castiglione, "the courtier was in every way the opposite of the greybeard," and that the courtly circle he imagined "demonstrated their profound disdain for old age" (pp. 256 and 259). Taunton echoes and elaborates on this opinion: the elder's effort to participate in such characteristic activities as courtship, athletic or military displays, or even poetry writing "betrays a gross breech of court etiquette" and so leaves the aging courtier "in an impossible position: behaviour by which courtly grace is defined is no longer available to him, yet not to perform these acts is to forfeit his courtly self and function . . . [B]y very definition, there is no such thing as an old courtier" (p. 76).

59. Baldassare Castiglione, *The Book of the Courtier,* trans. Sir Thomas Hoby (London: David Nutt, 1900), p. 1. All further in-text citations refer to this edition. Although Hoby's conspicuous emphasis on *The Courtier'*s applicability to youth in part has to do with the youthful age of his own patron, Lord Henry Hastings, the translator fully appreciated the premium Castiglione placed upon the youthfulness of his idealized subject and its dialogic exponents. Hoby notes how "none, but a noble yonge Gentleman, and trayned up all his life time in Court, and of worthie qualities, is meete to receive and enterteine so worthy a Courtier" and hopes that Hastings's model will prompt "other yonge and Courtly Gentlemen" not to "shonn hys company" (p. 6). Hoby claims that his own translation effort was inspired by "the continual requestes and often perswasions of many yong gentlemen" (p. 10). It clearly spoke to its target audience: as Peter Burke recalls, the translation continued to be reprinted throughout Elizabeth's reign, in 1577, 1588, and 1603; *The Fortunes of the Courtier: The European Reception of Castiglione's Cortegiano* (University Park: Pennsylvania State University Press, 1995), p. 64.

60. As Marina Beer has observed, Castiglione conjures the arguments Cicero marshals in his *De senectute* here only to turn them inside out. See her "Le Maschere del Tempo nel *Cortegiano,*" in *La Corte e il "Cortegiano" I: La Scena del Testo,* ed. Carlo Ossola (Rome: Bulzoni, 1980), p. 208.

61. While it is true enough that, as Richard A. Lanham has so insightfully argued, "in *The Courtier* folly is almost cherished," the folly of old age appears to find little sympathy there; *The Motives of Eloquence: Literary Rhetoric in the Renaissance* (New Haven: Yale University Press, 1976), p. 159. See also Frank Whigham's interesting reflection on the hypocrisies of

courtly condemnation of *cosmesis* in his *Ambition and Privilege: The Social Tropes of Eliza-bethan Courtesy Theory* (Berkeley: University of California Press, 1984), esp. pp. 116–17 and his extended note, pp. 223–24. While the protest against cosmetics was most extensively directed against women, it might (as *Il Cortegiano* illustrates) just as easily be turned against the old.

62. Stephen D. Kolsky, "Old Men in a New World: Morello da Ortona in the *Cortegia-no*," *Italica* 75 (1998): 343. Although Kolsky has pointed out how "Morello da Ortona is the anti-Cato who transgresses all the advice that the Roman gave to his young listeners," he also discerns that "Morello cannot simply be described as a figure of fun, despite the laugh-ter at his expense," since "the first three books of the *Cortegiano* might be read as a series of exclusions for older men, prohibiting them from taking part in various court activities" (337, 332, and 334). Even Bembo qualifies his definition of age, "taking not withstanding this name Olde, not for the age at the pittes brinke, nor when the canelles of the body be so feble, that the soule can not through them worke her feates, but when knowlage in us is in his right strength" (p. 346). Compare Steven Marx's claim that Bembo's Neoplatonism serves as "a means to transcend and thereby eliminate the antinomy of youth and age, pleasure, and wisdom" ("'Fortunate Senex': The Pastoral of Old Age," *Studies in English Literature* 25 [1985]: 42).

63. In that regard, we may retrospectively hear an even more bittersweet note in the author's lament over the early demise of too many of his courtly models. As Maria Theresa Ricci observes, Castiglione's "project of creating a model character to be aspired to . . . leads him to despise, or rather, fear certain aspects of real life: old age, for example, which he himself cannot evade." She goes on to conclude that, "Despite the author's attempt to re-habilitate it in his last book, age remains all the same totally unbecoming to the courtier. It is in effect an impediment to the 'art of living,' in as much as the spirit of an elderly person is no longer compatible with a good many pleasurable things, and can therefore no longer savour them" ("Old Age in Castiglione's *The Book of the Courtier*," in Campbell, *Growing Old in Early Modern Europe*, p. 70).

64. Thomas, "Age and Authority in Early Modern England," 205.

65. Ibid., 207 and 243.

66. Ibid., 244. Smith concurs that, if "early modern Englishmen looked upon old age as simply another stage in life, one of the seven through which all persons must pass," they nonetheless conceived old age "as something entirely different, a reversal of all the previous stages" (125). Lawrence Stone likewise generalizes that "old age had previously been highly respected as a stage of life's progression, during which weakening physical powers were compensated for by the accumulation of wisdom and dignity; it now came to be seen as a period of decay in all faculties, as the biological organism approached death . . . Thus the old did not merely lose power as the patriarchs of the lineage, they also lost respect" (*The Family, Sex and Marriage in England 1500–1800* [New York: Harper, 1977], p. 403). See also Gilbert's article, and Janet Roebuck, "When Does 'Old Age' Begin?: The Evolution of the English Definition," *Journal of Social History* 12 (1979): 416–28.

67. Sir Thomas Wyatt, *The Complete Poems*, ed. R. A. Rebholz (New Haven: Yale Uni-versity Press, 1978), p. 74.

68. *The Mirror for Magistrates*, ed. Lily B. Campbell (New York: Barnes and Noble, 1938), pp. 302 and 308, lines 115 and 330–36. Further quotes from the *Mirror*, cited by line numbers, refer to this edition.

69. Cicero, *Of Old Age*, fol. ‡iv. All further quotations, hereafter cited in the text, refer to Newton's translation of 1569. Apart from these translations, the Latin text would see no fewer than six separate editions in the period from 1584 to 1604. All citations from the Latin original I interpolate refer to *Cato maior de senectute*, ed. J. G. F. Powell (Cambridge: Cambridge University Press, 1988).

70. For a brief reflection on Newton's address to Paulet as an instance of "complex appro-

priation of text for specific social engineering," which "ensures that the idealising rhetoric of old age in the original percolates into the politics of aging in his own day" see Taunton, *Fictions of Old Age*, pp. 7–8. Newton's revised text appeared in *Fowre Severall Treatises of M. Tullius Cicero* (London, 1577).

71. Aristotle, *Rhetoric*, in *Complete Works: The Revised Oxford Translation*, ed. Jonathan Barnes, 2 vols. (Princeton: Princeton University Press, 1984), 2:2214–15. The orator Isocrates—whose *Panathenaicus*, composed in his ninety-fourth year, Cato invokes—proclaims likewise in that very speech that, despite his gifts and celebrity, he is "not content to live on these terms"; rather, he confesses, "my old age is so morose and captious and discontented that I have oftentimes before this found fault with my nature, which no other man has contemned, and have deplored my fortune, although I have had no complaint against it other than that the philosophy which I have chosen to pursue has been the object of unfortunate and unscrupulous attacks" (Isocrates, *Discourses, Orations, and Letters*, 3 vols., trans. George Norlin [Cambridge: Harvard University Press, 1928–29], 2:377–79).

72. In her celebrated but contentious study *The Coming of Age* (1972), Simone de Beauvoir pilloried the Latin author for what she perceived as an elitist conservatism that distorts his commentary and prevents an audience from taking his smug claims seriously (de Beauvoir, *The Coming of Age*, trans. Patrick O'Brian [New York: Putnam, 1972], pp. 118–20). The social historian M. I. Finley likewise finds Cicero's survey disappointingly "disingenuous" ("The Elderly in Classical Antiquity," 1981, repr. in *Old Age in Greek and Latin Literature*, ed. Thomas M. Falkner and Judith de Luce [Albany: SUNY Press, 1989], p. 15). Though Minois regards the tract as "a beautiful piece of writing," he also acknowledges that, in all likelihood, "Cicero could only convince the converted, the old men already happy to be such," of the rewards of old age: "The others, by far the most numerous, would not be affected at all by his rhetoric" (p. 111).

73. Thane, *Old Age in English History*, pp. 40 and 43.

74. John Hendricks, "Cicero and Social Gerontology: Context and Interpretation of a Classic," *Journal of Aging Studies* 7 (1993): 339; Tim G. Parkin, "Aging in Antiquity: Status and Participation," in Paul Johnson and Pat Thane, eds., *Old Age from Antiquity to Post-Modernity* (London: Routledge, 1998), p. 25.

75. Dean Rodeheaver, "Psychological Adaptation and Virtue: Geropsychological Perspectives on Cicero's *De Senectute*," *Journal of Aging Studies* 7 (1993): 358.

76. "But I do prescribe ordres unto the Senate," Cato declares to his young auditors, "and shew to them what things in mine opinion are most expedient to be done, and geeve certaine informacion to them beforehand, how they maye make warre upon the spightful *Carthaginians*, whose cancard harts have a great while wished & contrived our confusion, whose malicious stomaks I shall never cease to feare, until I know perfectlye, that their proude Citye is distroyed, ruynated and utterly subverted" (fol. 11v–12).

77. Plutarch, *Morals*, trans. Philemon Holland (London, 1603), p. 384. Following Cicero's lead, Plutarch even more emphatically insists that ongoing activity in public service is crucial to the senior members of society, who otherwise will swiftly experience the attrition and rapid desiccation of their capabilities and hence of their very identities. Since ability rather than chronological age determines one's right to occupy positions of authority, it is only natural that the elder should remain in place for as long as is physically possible. Insisting "the white head and gray beard (which some laugh and make good game at) . . . beare witnesse of long experience, and adde unto them a reputation and authoritie" (p. 391), Plutarch works to translate the signs of physical aging collectively as "honourable tokens of their right to command, and of their preeminence above others" (p. 391). But his telling assumption that society instinctually finds these very signs of age risible makes the elder's need to assert himself, and thereby to overcome these prejudices, all the more pressing.

78. Small, *The Long Life*, pp. 5 and 6.

79. Kiernan Ryan, "*King Lear:* A Retrospect, 1980–2000," *Shakespeare Survey* 55 (2002): 10.

80. Thane, "Social Histories of Old Age and Aging," 106.

81. In addition to Woodward's work, see esp. William Kerrigan, "Life's Iamb: The Scansion of Late Creativity in the Culture of the Renaissance," in Woodward and Schwartz, *Memory and Desire*, pp. 168–91; and Gordon McMullan, *Shakespeare and the Idea of Late Writing* (Cambridge: Cambridge University Press, 2007).

2. Elizabeth I's Politics of Longevity

1. The last full decade of Elizabeth I's reign would "witness the dying off of an establishment, of an 'old gang,'" as R. B. Wernham remarks, in whose place "a younger group was coming to the fore, young men who had grown up in the prospering Protestant 1570s and 1580s"; *The Making of Elizabethan Foreign Policy, 1558–1603* (Berkeley: University of California Press, 1980), p. 83. If their advent reduced the late Elizabethan court to "a sordid and self-seeking playpen for overgrown and ill-tempered children," in Christopher Haigh's delightfully dismissive characterization (*Elizabeth I,* 2nd ed. [New York: Longman, 1998], p. 108), they regarded themselves as more victimized than spoiled.

2. Feria, quoted in Carolly Erickson, *The First Elizabeth* (New York: Summit Books, 1983), p. 174. On the factional and generational strife attending Essex's emergence at court, see esp. Paul E. J. Hammer: "The advanced age of many key officers and Elizabeth's own unwillingness to introduce fresh blood had already made her government sclerotic" (*The Polarisation of Elizabethan Politics: The Political Career of Robert Devereux, 2nd Earl of Essex, 1585–1597* [Cambridge: Cambridge University Press, 1999], p. 390).

3. William Camden, *The Historie of the Most Renowned and Victorious Princesse Elizabeth, Late Queene of England* (London, 1630), 4:221 and 224.

4. Writing in the year of her death, John Clapham remarks how Elizabeth's life "had been drawn out to such a length as she outreigned two emperors of Germany, four French kings, eight bishops of Rome, surpassing in number of years all her predecessors, two only excepted, and in felicity of government excelling them all without exception" (*Elizabeth of England: Certain Observations Concerning the Life and Reign of Queen Elizabeth,* ed. Evelyn Plummer Read and Conyers Read [Philadelphia: University of Pennsylvania Press, 1951], p. 101). In a compelling assessment of Elizabeth's "consciousness of herself as a survivor," Mary Beth Rose explores the queen's reorientation of a masculine ethic of killing or dying well toward what she calls a "heroics of endurance"; *Gender and Heroism in Early Modern English Literature* (Chicago: University of Chicago Press, 2002), pp. 38 and 54.

5. See, for example, the essays in Julia Walker (ed.), *Dissing Elizabeth: Negative Representations of Gloriana* (Durham, N.C.: Duke University Press, 1998), and Haigh, *Elizabeth I,* p. 172.

6. Camden, *Historie,* 4:222.

7. On this, see Marie Villeponteaux, "'Not as women wonted be': Spenser's Amazon Queen," in Walker, *Dissing Elizabeth,* p. 210, and Marie Axton's *The Queen's Two Bodies: Drama and the Elizabethan Succession* (London: Royal Historical Society, 1977). In *"The Heart and Stomach of a King": Elizabeth I and the Politics of Sex and Power* (Philadelphia: University of Pennsylvania Press, 1994), Carole Levin cogently unpacks the implications of the fact that, "for all of the use of male as well as female images, for all the doubling that occurred, Elizabeth existed in a female body" (p. 146).

8. Susan Frye, *Elizabeth I: The Competition for Representation* (New York: Oxford University Press, 1993), p. 100. In their study of the "afterlife" the queen came to know in later centuries, Michael Dobson and Nicola J. Watson discuss how Victorian depictions of her in old age grew so common that "Kingsley could observe ruefully in 1859 that 'it is much

now-a-days to find any one who believes that Queen Elizabeth was ever young, or who does not talk of her as if she was born about seventy years of age covered with rouge and wrinkles' " (*England's Elizabeth: An Afterlife in Fame and Fantasy* [Oxford: Oxford University Press, 2002], p. 158).

9. Frye, *Elizabeth I,* p. 98.

10. Leah Marcus, "Erasing the Stigma of Daughterhood: Mary I, Elizabeth I, and Henry VIII," in Lynda E. Boose and Betty S. Flowers (eds.), *Daughters and Fathers* (Baltimore: Johns Hopkins University Press, 1989), p. 415. Compare Patrick Collinson's observation that "Elizabeth gambled on the unlikely chance of living to the age that she did, outliving the problems which loomed so large in the fifteen-seventies and eighties" ("Elizabeth I and the Verdicts of History," *Historical Research* 76 [2003]: 491).

11. Rob Content, "Fair Is Fowle: Interpreting Anti-Elizabethan Composite Portraiture," in Walker, *Dissing Elizabeth,* p. 230; see also Erickson, *The First Elizabeth,* p. 207. As Anne Somerset reminds us, Elizabeth was "fortunate in her longevity" which enabled her to see policy through—a luxury her royal siblings, their reigns cut short, never knew (*Elizabeth I* [New York: Knopf, 1991], p. 571). If Frederick Chamberlin's 1922 thesis regarding Elizabeth's congenital infirmities does not persuade us of her weak constitution, his extensive documentation captures contemporary nervousness about the queen's alleged frailty; see his *The Private Character of Queen Elizabeth* (New York: Dodd, Mead, 1922). Only in the early 1580s, however, as the threat of Mary Stuart grew even more intense, did it become illegal to cast nativities or pursue prophecies of the queen's lifespan. See the statute 23 Elizabeth c. 2, in G. W. Prothero, *Select Statutes and Other Constitutional Documents Illustrative of the Reigns of Elizabeth and James I,* 4th ed. (1913; repr., Westport, Conn.: Greenwood Press, 1983), pp. 77–80; and William Compton, *A Most Exact and New Inventorie of All the Goods, Excellencies, and Memorable Actions Worthy Any General or Particular Knowledge, from the First Daies of the Conquerer to the Last Daies of Queene Elizabeth* (London, 1608), p. O3.

12. Letter to the Count of Hannau, cited in James M. Osborn, *Young Philip Sidney: 1572–1577* (New Haven: Yale University Press, 1972), p. 309. The Latin original can be found in Sidney's *Works,* ed. Albert Feuillerat, 4 vols. (1912; repr., Cambridge: Cambridge University Press, 1968), 3:103. Contrast this with the letter of March 24, 1586 (3:166).

13. De Quadra to Philip, quoted in Chamberlin, *Private Character of Elizabeth I,* p. 54.

14. Elizabeth I, *Collected Works,* ed. Leah S. Marcus, Janel Mueller, and Mary Beth Rose (Chicago: University of Chicago Press, 2000), pp. 138–39 and 141. The Latin text comes from *Autograph Compositions and Foreign Language Originals,* ed. Janel Mueller and Leah S. Marcus (Chicago: University of Chicago Press, 2003), p. 118. All quotations from Elizabeth's works, cited hereafter as *CW* and *AC,* refer to these editions. A convivial speech at Cambridge University the following year reaffirms her vitality: "For my age is not yet senile, nor have I reigned for such a long time; so may I, before I pay my debt to nature (if Atropos does not sever the thread of life more quickly than I hope), do some famous and noteworthy work" (*CW,* 88). In a subsequent prayerbook published at decade's end, the queen beseeches divine protection for all princes so "constituted" (que tu as constituez en ce mesme depré de prééminence [*CW,* 147; *AC,* 132]), expresses gratitude for being lifted above "weak, timid, and delicate" feminine nature as a "vigorous, brave, and strong" figure (*CW,* 157), and closes with a ventriloquizing of her subjects in a prayer for her own "long life with health of the body, peace, prosperity, and magnificence" (*CW,* 161). In the wake of a second possible bout with smallpox in 1572, Elizabeth boasted to the earl of Shrewsbury, "there is no beholder would believe that ever I had been touched by such a malady," and encourages her Parliament in 1576 that "God will not in such haste cut off my days but that, according to your own desert and my desire, I may provide some good way for your security" (*CW,* 213 and 170–71).

15. She goes on to close her parliament of 1567 with the question, "But do you think that either I am unmindful of your surety by succession, wherein is all my care, considering I

know myself to be mortal?" (*CW,* 108), and almost a decade later in 1576 offers parliament the mock-confirmation "I know I am but mortal, which good lesson Mr. Speaker in his third division of a virtuous person's properties required me with reason to remember" (*CW,* 170).

16. Sir John Harington, *Nugae Antiquae,* 2 vols. (1804; repr., New York: AMS Press, 1966), 1:116. All quotations cited hereafter as *Nugae* refer to this edition.

17. William Harrison, *The Description of England,* ed. Georges Edelen (Ithaca, N.Y.: Cornell University Press, 1968), p. 449.

18. Erin J. Campbell, "'Unenduring' Beauty: Gender and Old Age in Early Modern Art and Aesthetics," in *Growing Old in Early Modern Europe: Cultural Representations,* ed. Erin J. Campbell (Aldershot, Hampshire, Eng.: Ashgate, 2006), p. 159.

19. Amy M. Froide, "Old Maids: The Lifecycle of Single Women in Early Modern England," in Lynn Botelho and Pat Thane (eds.), *Women and Ageing in British Society since 1500* (Harlow, Essex, Eng.: Longman/Pearson, 2001), pp. 89–90.

20. Lynn Botelho, "Old Age and Menopause in Rural Women Early Modern Suffolk," in Botelho and Thane, *Women and Ageing,* p. 53. See also Sara Mendelson and Patricia Crawford, *Women in Early Modern England 1550–1720* (Oxford: Clarendon Press, 1998), esp. pp. 184–94; and Aki C. L. Beam, "'Should I as Yet Call you Old?': Testing the Boundaries of Female Old Age in Early Modern England," in Campbell, *Growing Old in Early Modern Europe,* pp. 95–116.

21. On this tradition, see Mary D. Garrard, *Artemisia Gentileschi: The Image of the Female Hero in Italian Baroque Art* (Princeton: Princeton University Press, 1989), p. 144.

22. As early as 1563, her council had circulated a draft of a proclamation "to prohibit all manner of other persons to draw, paint, grave, or portray her majesty's personage or visage for a time until, by some perfect patron or example, the same may be by others followed"; *Tudor Royal Proclamations,* ed. Paul L. Hughes and James F. Larkin, 3 vols. (New Haven: Yale University Press, 1969), 2:240. On the "Mask of Youth," see esp. Roy Strong, *Gloriana: The Portraits of Queen Elizabeth* (New York: Thames and Hudson, 1987), pp. 147–51. As Haigh summarizes, "There appears to have been some official decision in about 1594 that Elizabeth should be pictured as eternally youthful, presumably to prevent fears for the future . . . In 1596, the Privy Council ordered officials to seek out and destroy all unseemly portraits, which were said to have caused the Queen great offence: the object of the campaign seems to have been the elimination of the image of Elizabeth as an old woman" (pp. 153–54). Hanna Betts proposes that crises of the 1590s "were exacerbated by indications of the queen's growing decrepitude" as "Elizabeth's increasingly garish attempts to simulate her former appearance . . . became the living emblem of her exhausted government" ("'The Image of this Queene so quaynt': The Pornographic Blazon 1588–1603," in Walker, *Dissing Elizabeth,* p. 169). Strong, Walker, and Louis Adrian Montrose delineate the propagandistic manipulation of the queen's image along similar lines. See Strong's *The Cult of Elizabeth: Elizabethan Portraiture and Pageantry* (Berkeley: University of California Press, 1977); Walker's "Bones of Contention: Posthumous Images of Elizabeth and Stuart Politics," in her *Dissing Elizabeth,* pp. 252–76, esp. p. 264; and Montrose's "Idols of the Queen: Policy, Gender, and the Picturing of Elizabeth I," *Representations* 68 (1999): 108–61.

23. Ben Jonson, *Conversations with William Drummond,* in *Ben Jonson,* ed. C. H. Herford and Percy and Evelyn Simpson, 11 vols. (Oxford: Clarendon Press, 1925–63), 1:141–42. We need to be equally skeptical of the queen's purported credulity in her dealings with Cornelius Lannoy, a Dutch alchemist imprisoned for his failure to transmute base metals, whose efforts to discover an "elixir of perpetual youth" she is said to have sponsored around 1570. See Erickson, *The First Elizabeth,* p. 261.

24. For the fullest exploration of this dynamic, see Frye, *Elizabeth I.*

25. I adopt the generic term, once more, from Margaret Morganroth Gullette's anatomy

of ageist discourse in her *Aged by Culture* (Chicago: University of Chicago Press, 2004), esp. pp. 132–37.

26. Erickson, *The First Elizabeth*, p. 192.

27. Reported in Chamberlin, *Private Character of Queen Elizabeth*, p. 58.

28. Conyers Read, *Lord Burghley and Queen Elizabeth* (New York: Knopf, 1960), p. 210. Burghley goes on to note that it might actually be more to the queen's physical detriment should she remain single, which would risk leaving her "subject to such dolours and infirmities as all physicians do usually impute to womankind for lack of marriage" (p. 211).

29. Sir Ralph Sadler, *The State Papers and Letters of Ralph Sadler,* ed. Arthur Clifford, 2 vols. (Edinburgh: Constable, 1809), 2:573.

30. Quoted in *The Letters of Queen Elizabeth I,* ed. G. B. Harrison (New York: Funk and Wagnalls, 1935), p. 149.

31. John Stubbs, *John Stubbs's* Gaping Gulf *with Letters and Other Relevant Documents,* ed. Lloyd E. Berry (Charlottesville: University Press of Virginia, 1968), p. 9. Subsequent quotes from the *Gaping Gulf* refer to this edition.

32. John King and Ilona Bell both underline the way in which Stubbs's direct engagement with Elizabeth's "body natural" implicitly comes to approach "mockery of the legal fiction of the queen's 'two bodies,' " emphasizing how "the male body politic was only as strong as the queen's female body natural" (King, "Queen Elizabeth I: Representations of the Virgin Queen," *Renaissance Quarterly* 43 [1990]: 50; Ilona Bell, " 'Souereaigne Lord of lordly Lady of this Land': Elizabeth, Stubbs, and the *Gaping Gulf,*" in Walker, *Dissing Elizabeth*, p. 109).

33. Susan Doran, *Monarchy and Matrimony: The Courtships of Elizabeth I* (London: Routledge, 1996), p. 166. Although we have no definitive date for Singleton's birth, the fact that he was perhaps publishing as early as 1525 sets his age in 1579 as the early seventies, at least.

34. Although Marcus, Mueller, and Rose transpose the vowels in *vielles* to arrive at *veilles* ("those on night watch"), the original French, into which Harrison had inserted the additional "i" to arrive at *vieilles,* sets up an arresting precedent for the more explicitly pejorative, self-pitying caricature she offers in the later missive cited below.

35. Harrison, *Letters,* p. 142–43.

36. Elizabeth's original French reads "La paouure vieille qui vous honore autant (l'ose dire) que quelques leune garse que trouuerez lamais" (*AC,* 157).

37. Read, *Lord Burghley and Queen Elizabeth,* p. 271.

38. See Ilona Bell's discussion of Elizabeth's more synthetic approach to her Petrarchan model in this poem, in her *Elizabethan Women and the Poetry of Courtship* (Cambridge: Cambridge University Press, 1998), pp. 109–13.

39. Leicester Bradner (ed.), *The Poems of Queen Elizabeth I* (Providence: Brown University Press, 1964), pp. 75–76. Grouping the piece among "Poems of Doubtful Authorship," Bradner characterizes Elizabeth as a writer whose manner "is more old-fashioned and heavy-handed," and so claims the poem is simply too good for her talents. Less parochial in their views about the queen's artistic range, Marcus, Mueller, and Rose reconfirm its authenticity; see their note in *CW,* 303.

40. George Puttenham, *The Art of English Poesy,* ed. Frank Whigham and Wayne A. Rebhorn (Ithaca, N.Y.: Cornell University Press, 2007), pp. 351–52. In the second book of his *Passions of the Mind in General* (1601), Thomas Wright gives a chapter to "Importunity of Passion," where he notes how "Inordinate Passions either prevent reason or are stirred up by a corrupt judgement, and therefore neither observe time nor place but upon every occasion would be leaping into action, importuning execution" (*The Passions of the Mind in General,* ed. William Webster Newbold [New York: Garland, 1986], p. 144).

41. Jennifer Summit offers insight into the representative dialogic character of "The doubt of future foes" in " 'The Arte of a Ladies Penne': Elizabeth I and the Poetics of Queenship,"

English Literary Renaissance 26 (1996): 395–422. For Elizabeth's reformulation of received Petrarchan convention, see Bell's *Elizabethan Women.*

42. On Harington's contact with Elizabeth in the Tower, and the manuscript's likely transmission at this time, see Ruth Hughey, *John Harington of Stepney, Tudor Gentleman: His Life and Works* (Columbus: Ohio State University Press, 1971), pp. 45–50.

43. All quotation from Wyatt's poems refers to *Tottel's Miscellany (1557–1587),* ed. Hyder Edward Rollins, 2 vols. (Cambridge: Harvard University Press, 1966).

44. Barbara Estrin delineates how Wyatt here "triply spoils the woman: first, he effaces her idealized self; then he cancels her reproductive self; finally, in stillness, he dries up her desiring self." In so doing, Estrin argues, he lays bare the profound rancor lurking behind the staid reverence for Petrarchism's cruel mistress; *Laura: Uncovering Gender and Genre in Wyatt, Donne, and Marvell* (Durham, N.C.: Duke University Press, 1994), p. 98.

45. Michel de Montaigne, *The Essayes,* trans. John Florio, 3 vols. (London: Oxford University Press, 1904–6), 3:35 and 36.

46. Hammer, *Polarisation of Elizabethan Politics,* p. 92. The Genoese ambassador writing to Philip in the Armada's aftermath may likewise have been pandering to his addressee's wishes when on November 5, 1588 he wrote: "The Queen is much aged and spent, and is very melancholy. Her intimates say that this is caused by the death of the earl of Leicester; but it is very evident that it is rather the fear she underwent and the burden she has upon her" (quoted in Chamberlin, *Private Character of Elizabeth I,* p. 69).

47. For a fuller reflection on this, see Erickson, *The First Elizabeth,* p. 357. Sadler reported in September 1584 that the Scottish queen "uttred her grief of her long imprisonment, having spent her yeres from 24 to past 40, and by combre and impotency become old in body" (2:389). She was not above writing directly to Elizabeth around that time how the countess of Shrewsbury had related "About four or five years ago" that "coming to lose your monthly period, you would very soon die" (quoted in Chamberlin, *Private Character of Elizabeth I,* p. 68). Up to the time of his dismissal in April 1585, Sadler himself had relentlessly pleaded his own old age in his appeals to be excused from his nerve-wracking duties as Mary's keeper (2:424, 461, 496, and 539).

48. Interestingly, the speech's published version would mute some of these expressions in favor of a pragmatic acknowledgment of the hazards of sudden, violent death. See *CW,* 193.

49. See John Guy, "The 1590s: The Second Reign of Elizabeth I?" in *The Reign of Elizabeth I: Court and Culture in the Last Decade,* ed. John Guy (Cambridge: Cambridge University Press, 1995), pp. 1–19.

50. In Haigh's view, "Elizabeth had failed to develop a new role: the aged actress looked foolish as she continued to play the part which had once made her famous"; she "had nothing new to offer—she was certainly not going to appear as grandmother of the nation" (*Elizabeth I,* p. 172).

51. By way of contrast, her acquiescence to Sir Henry Lee's elaborate 1590 retirement performance confirms her more balanced acceptance of the need for elder members of her court to curtail their duties. Lee was the man chiefly responsible for the institution of the November 17 Accession Day tilts that ran annually at least from 1575 on. See George Peele's poetic account, *Polyhymnia,* in *Works,* ed. A. H. Bullen, 2 vols. (1888; repr., Port Washington, N.Y.: Kenniket Press, 1966), 2:286–302; and William Segar, *Honor Military and Civill* (London, 1602), pp. 198–200. The poem that Lee crafts for the occasion, "My golden locks time hath to silver turnd," offers a remarkable vision of resignation and "progress" by dignified age.

52. I quote from the copy published only after the queen's death: Anthony Rudd, *A Sermon Preached at Richmond before Queene Elizabeth of famous memorie, upon the 28. of March, 1596* (London, 1603), pp. 30 and 53.

53. John Manningham, *The Diary of John Manningham of the Middle Temple, 1602–1603,*

ed. Robert Parker Sorlien (Hanover, N.H.: University Press of New England, 1976), p. 194.

54. Only her prose version of Marguerite de Navarre's devotional poem *Le Miroir de l'âme pécheresse*, completed at age eleven as a gift for her stepmother, Katherine Parr, and appropriated by the reformer John Bale, saw publication in her lifetime. See Shell's introduction to his edition of the Marguerite translation, *Elizabeth's Glass* (Lincoln: University of Nebraska Press, 1993), pp. 3–73.

55. *Elizabeth I: Translations, 1544–1589*, ed. Janel Mueller and Joshua Scodel (Chicago: University of Chicago Press, 2009), p. 452. All further quotes from Elizabeth's translations refer to this edition and its companion, *Elizabeth I: Translations, 1592–1598*, ed. Janel Mueller and Joshua Scodel (Chicago: University of Chicago Press, 2009). For the sake of consistency, I quote from the modernized versions that the editors supply.

56. Bradner observes that "the same mistake of translating *Corus* as the east wind which is found in Elizabeth's Boethius (IV.v.13) [of 1593] occurs here at line 74" (*Poems*, p. 80). Marcus and Scodel "favor a date in or after 1589" (*Translations, 1592–1598*, p. 443).

57. Camden, *Historie*, 4:51.

58. *Queen Elizabeth's Englishings of Boethius, Plutarch and Horace*, ed. Caroline Pemberton (EETS 1899; repr., Millwood, N.Y.: Kraus, 1975), pp. ix–x.

59. For an alternative reading of the political motivations of Elizabeth's Boethius, see Lysbeth Benkert, "Translation as Image-Making: Elizabeth I's Translation of Boethius's *Consolation of Philosophy*," *Early Modern Literary Studies* 6.3 (2001): 2.1–20, http://purl.oclc.org/emls/06–3/benkboet.htm.

60. John Bale, the publisher of Elizabeth's Marguerite translation, had himself recorded Boethius among Alfred's literary accomplishments in his *Illustrium Maioris Britanniae scriptorium* (1549), fol. 66.

61. The queen signed her letter of protest to Henry "Your most assured sister, if it be after the old fashion [*la Vielle mode*]; with the new I have nothing to do" (*CW*, 371; *AC*, 166).

62. Ernst Robert Curtius, *European Literature and the Latin Middle Ages*, trans. Willard R. Trask (Princeton: Princeton University Press, 1953), p. 102. Curtius discusses Philosophia in the context of a tradition of female figures combining old age and youth, unusually prevalent among both Christian and pagan authors in late antiquity.

63. *Horace His* arte of Poetrie, pistles, *and Satyrs Englished* (London, 1567), p. *vi.

64. Although Marcus and Scodel feel that the translation's final twenty lines "read as if they were left for revising" (*Translations, 1592–1598*, p. 457), we know the project was not merely abandoned. Her amanuensis's postscript, appended to the autograph manuscript, reports delivery of a fair copy of "Her Ma[jes]ties translation of a peece of Horace *de arte poetica* written with her own hand, and copied by me for her Ma[jes]tie the iiiith of November 1598. and at that day I delyvered it unto her own handes" (*Queen Elizabeth's Englishings*, p. 149), suggesting this was as far as she intended to go.

65. "The Queen was sixty-five when she did this version, and she probably scorned to use eyeglasses" (*Poems*, p. 86).

66. Louis Montrose, *The Subject of Elizabeth: Authority, Gender, and Representation* (Chicago: University of Chicago Press, 2006), p. 213.

67. André Hurault, Sieur de Maisse, *A Journal of All That Was Accomplished*, trans. and ed. G. B. Harrison and R. A. Jones (Bloomsbury: Nonesuch, 1931), p. 59. All further quotations from the *Journal* refer to this translation. Since the modern manuscript copy of de Maisse's journal from which the translators worked proved unavailable from the Bibliothèque Nationale, I rely upon Lucien Anatole Prevost-Paradol's *Élisabeth et Henri IV (1595–1598): Ambassade de Hurault de Maisse* (Paris, 1855) for the French, which I cite hereafter wherever available. De Maisse describes Elizabeth's hand as "Plus grande que la mienne de trois grands diogts. Elle l'a eue fort belle, elle est maintenant fort maigre, mais le teint en est fort beau" (Prevost-Paradol, p. 173).

68. Carole Levin, "'We Princes, I Tell You, Are Set on Stages': Elizabeth I and Dramatic Self-Representation," in S. P. Cerasano and Marion Wynne-Davies (eds.), *Readings in Renaissance Women's Drama: Criticism, History, and Performance 1594–1998* (London: Routledge, 1998), p. 114.

69. For Forman's diary entry, see A. L. Rowse, *The Casebooks of Simon Forman: Sex and Society in Shakespeare's Age* (London: Pan Books, 1976), p. 31. See also Louis Adrian Montrose, "'Shaping Fantasies': Figurations of Gender and Power in Elizabethan Culture," *Representations* 2 (1983): 61–94. For discussions of both the Forman and Portmort episodes, see esp. the final chapters of Levin's *Heart and Stomach of a King*, pp. 121–72.

70. "Chose que vous osteroit toute creance de voz ministres qui vous ont abusé le doute par tant de louange de ce que quand vous serez l'oculaire iuge vous ne trouuerez nullement responder au demy de qui vous font a croyre qui me feront vne disgrace en cuydant m'advancer le respect" (*AC,* 167).

71. R. B. Wernham, *The Return of the Armadas: The Last Years of the Elizabethan War Against Spain, 1595–1603* (Oxford: Clarendon Press, 1994), p. 212. "Clearly someone was fooling someone," the historian wryly goes on to observe (p. 213).

72. "Elle avait le devant de sa robe en manteau ouvert et luy voyoit-on toute la gorge et assez bas et souvent, comme si elle eust en trop chaud, elle eslargissoit avec les mains le devant dudict manteau . . . sa gorge se montre assez ridée, autant que (la laissoit veoir) le carcan qu'elle portoit au col, mais plus bas elle a encore la charnure fort blanche et fort déliée autant que l'on eust peu veoir" (Prevost-Paradol, *Élisabeth et Henri IV,* p. 151).

73. "Un robe dessous de damas blanc, ceinte et ouverte devant, aussy bien que sa chemise, tellement qu'elle ouvrait souvent cette robe et luy voyait-on tout l'estomac jusques au nombril . . . elle a cette façon qu'en rehaussant la teste elle met les deux mains à sa robe et l'entrouvre, tellement qu'on luy veoit tout l'estomac" (ibid., p. 155).

74. It appears to inform, for instance, Paul Johnson's description of the queen's allegedly slattern retirement: "Decorated like a Christmas-tree to keep up the image of regality in public, in private she often did not bother at all, and hardly concealed from her ministers that she was an old lady, still very much in control, but increasingly inclined to dwell in the past" (*Elizabeth I* [New York: Holt, Rinehart, and Winston, 1974], p. 375). Stephany Fotanone's reading of the episode as evidence "that Elizabeth continued to attempt an alluring and captivating appeal, despite her age" represents a contrasting standard attribution of the behavior to vain dotage, as if the monarch had bought into the Petrarchan flattery that had prevailed since the 1580s ("'My Most Seeming Virtuous Queen': Gertrude and the Manifestation of Aging Sexuality in Early Modern England," *Washington College Review* 2002 [wc-review.washcoll.edu/2002/fontanone.html]). Erickson likewise finds "an air of the macabre" about the de Maisse meetings, imagining the queen as "a lively, clacking skeleton whose energetic jerkiness belied her wrinkled cheeks and bare gums" (*The First Elizabeth,* p. 385). For Betts, the diary entries exemplify one more instance of Elizabeth's "increasingly garish attempts to simulate her former appearance," intimating "a sense in which the royal physique contained its own satire during this period" ("'Image of this Queene,'" pp. 169 and 176).

75. Lisa Jardine, *Reading Shakespeare Historically* (London: Routledge, 1996), pp. 21–25. In the notes to her argument, Jardine oddly looks to deny some of the spectacle altogether, ascribing our false impression of the queen's exhibitionism to the modern translators' misconstruction of de Maisse's entries (pp. 163–64). Her assertion that "'Gorge' here surely means 'throat' rather than 'bosom'" fails adequately to account for de Maisse's startled reaction—which we cannot attribute merely to "Catholic" prudery—as she seems to acknowledge in her qualifiers, "but it is clear that de Maisse is disturbed by the gestures of revealing," and that "one would still want to take note of Hurault de Maisse's difficulty with the breach of decorum" (p. 164, nn. 13, 14, and 16). Prevost-Paradol himself aligns the description with Paul Hentzner's observation of the queen's uncovered "bosom" (cited in n. 78 below), p. 124.

76. See Michael C. Schoenfeldt's study of "inner" bodily regimen and self-dominion in his *Bodies and Selves in Early Modern England: Physiology and Inwardness in Spenser, Shakespeare, Herbert, and Milton* (Cambridge: Cambridge University Press, 1999), esp. pp. 24–33, and Elizabeth D. Harvey's fresh reflections on the way in which skin came to signify "a more complex border between inside and outside, one that emphasizes the shifting, dynamic relation between the two"; "The Touching Organ: Allegory, Anatomy, and the Renaissance Skin Envelope," in Elizabeth D. Harvey (ed.), *Sensible Flesh: On Touch in Early Modern Culture* (Philadelphia: University of Pennsylvania Press, 2003), p. 85.

77. Stephen Cohen, "(Post)modern Elizabeth: Gender, Politics, and the Emergence of Modern Subjectivity," in Hugh Grady (ed.), *Shakespeare and Modernity: Early Modern to Millennium* (London: Routledge, 2000), pp. 26–27.

78. Apart from the famous observation of Paul Hentzner, the German visitor to London who in 1598 had diagnosed Elizabeth's black teeth as "a defect the English seem subject to, from their too great use of sugar" (John Nichols, ed., *The Progresses and Public Processions of Queen Elizabeth*, 3 vols. [1823; repr., New York: Burt Franklin, n.d.], 3:424), Elizabeth's dental discomforts had even more practical consequences for de Maisse, whose initial conference was delayed by the "cold in her teeth [un catarre sur les dentes]" that she suffered (*Journal* 18; Prevost-Paradol, *Élisabeth et Henri IV,* 149).

79. G. B. Harrison (ed.), *The Elizabethan Journals,* 2 vols. (New York: Doubleday, 1965), 1:482.

80. "[E]t me compta là-dessus un compte d'un sien trésorier des finances qui disoit que c'étoit la force d'amour qui faisoit faire cela au roy d'Espagne et que c'étoit un dangereux amour" (Prevost-Paradol, *Élisabeth et Henri IV,* p. 123).

81. In her "The Myth of Elizabeth at Tilbury," *Sixteenth Century Journal* 23 (1992): 95–114, Susan Frye challenges the authenticity of the sole surviving account by Dr. Lionel Sharp, published long after the event. Elizabeth's current editors, Marcus, Mueller, and Rose, maintain its place within the canon: see *CW,* 325, n.1.

82. "The Queenes visiting of the Campe at *Tilsburie* with her entertainment there" and "A joyful new Ballad," in Francis Oscar Mann (ed.), *The Works of Thomas Deloney* (Oxford: Clarendon, 1967), pp. 478 and 473.

83. Wernham, *Return of the Armadas,* pp. 211 and 190.

84. Again, see Hentzner's observation that in her progress Elizabeth's "bosom was uncovered, as all the English ladies have it till they marry" (Nichols, *Progresses and Public Processions,* 3:424).

85. King, "Queen Elizabeth I," 32.

86. "Qu'elle avoit affaire à de grandes et diverses humeurs, et à des peuples, lesquels si bien faisoient grande demonstration de l'aimer, que néantmoins étoient légers et inconstants, et qu'elle devoit craindre toute chose" (Prevost-Paradol, *Élisabeth et Henri IV,* p. 87).

87. " 'Je ne pense point mourir de sitôt, monsieur l'ambassadeur, et ne suis pas si vieille que l'on pense.' . . . [E]lle se faisait tort d'appeler si souvent de ce nom di vieille et, Dieu merci, sa disposition était telle qu'elle n'avait aucune raison de s'appeler ainsi . . . Et à la vérité, hors le visage qui se montre vieil et les dents, il n'est possible de voir une si belle et si vigoureuse disposition, tant de l'esprit que du corps" (ibid., p. 186).

88. Penry Williams suggests that "at least from a distance Elizabeth's physical appearance, aided by her dresses and jewels, may well have matched her representation in portraits. Even so, there was some anxiety about her age and approaching death"; *The Later Tudors: England 1547–1603* (Oxford: Oxford University Press, 1995), p. 328. Somerset concurs: "though physically vigorous and mentally alert, her appearance was that of an old woman," something she offset by dressing "with an exhibitionism and splendour that was calculated to take the breath away" (*Elizabeth I,* p. 556).

89. Sir Arthur Collins (ed.), *Letters and Memorials of State,* 2 vols. (1746; repr., New York: AMS Press, 1973), 2:114 and 131. All further citations refer to this edition.

90. Frye translates the motto as "[I prefer] death to being consigned to obscurity (literally, burial)" (*Elizabeth I,* p. 99), but its literal significance seems more appropriate to the circumstance.

91. Around this time, the Scottish ambassador Belitreis records that "she had been furious with Hunsdon when the latter imprudently protested that it was unwise for 'one of her years' to ride horseback all the way from Hampton Court to Nonsuch.' 'My years?' she replied. 'Maids! To your horses quickly.' She refused to speak to Hunsdon for the next two days." She allegedly "lengthened her summer progress, 'by reason of an intercepted letter, wherein the giving over of long voyages was noted to be a sign of age' " (quoted in Johnson, *Elizabeth I,* p. 427).

92. *The Anonymous Life of William Cecil, Lord Burghley,* ed. Alan G. R. Smith (Lewiston, Maine: Edwin Mellen Press, 1990), p. 103.

93. See Sir Robert Sidney's letter to Harington, where he reports in 1600 that the queen "doth wax weak since the late troubles, and Burleigh's death doth often draw tears from her goodly cheeks." Sir John Harington, *Letters and Epigrams,* ed. Norman Egbert McClure (Philadelphia: University of Pennsylvania Press, 1930), p. 389.

94. Arthur Freeman (ed.), "Essex to Stella: Two Letters from the Earl of Essex to Penelope Rich," *English Literary Renaissance* 3 (1973). Freeman places the undated letter "between the Cadiz expedition and the Irish fiasco (1596–99)."

95. Walter Bourchier Devereux, *Lives and Letters of the Devereux, Earls of Essex, in the Reigns of Elizabeth, James I, and Charles I,* 2 vols. (London: John Murray, 1853), 2:131. Subsequent citations from the letters refer to this edition.

96. Henry Cuffe, *The Differences of the Ages of Mans Life: Together with the Originall causes, Progresse, and End thereof* (London, 1607), p. 121.

97. Somerset, *Elizabeth I,* p. 534; Wallace MacCaffrey, *Elizabeth I: War and Politics, 1588– 1603* (Princeton: Princeton University Press, 1992), p. 573.

98. Johnson denies that Essex's betrayal and fall "had any profound emotional effect on Elizabeth," correctly observing that "Her last years were, in fact, ones of considerable accomplishment, of recovery from the dark period of economic distress which lasted from the mid-1590s until the end of the decade" (*Elizabeth I,* p. 412).

99. Hentzner, in Nichols, *Progresses and Public Processions,* 3:424; Thomas Platter, *Thomas Platter's Travels in England 1599,* trans. Clare Williams (London: Jonathan Cape, 1937), p. 192.

100. Harrison, *Letters,* pp. 278–79.

101. Quoted in Somerset, *Elizabeth I,* p. 554.

102. Harington, *Letters and Epigrams,* pp. 96–97.

103. *The Chamberlain Letters: A Selection of the Letters of John Chamberlain concerning Life in England from 1597 to 1626,* ed. Elizabeth McClure Thomson (n.p.: Capricorn, 1966), p. 22.

104. Nichols, *Progresses and Public Processions,* 3:603; Manningham, *Diary,* pp. 207–8.

105. Jennifer Woodward, *The Theatre of Death: The Ritual Management of Royal Funerals in Renaissance England, 1570–1625* (Woodbridge, Suffolk, Eng.: Boydell Press, 1997), p. 109.

106. Quoted in Anthony Harvey and Richard Mortimer (eds.), *The Funeral Effigies of Westminster Abbey* (Woodbridge, Suffolk, Eng.: Boydell Press, 1994), p. 156.

3. Out to Pasture: The Bucolic Elder in Spenser, Sidney, and Their Heirs

1. Marsilio Ficino, *Three Books on Life,* trans. Carol V. Kaske and John R. Clark (Binghamton, N.Y.: Medieval and Renaissance Texts and Studies, 1989), pp. 189 and 201.

2. Thomas G. Rosenmeyer, *The Green Cabinet: Theocritus and the European Pastoral Lyric* (Berkeley: University of California Press, 1969), pp. 56 and 59.

3. Steven Marx, "'Fortunate Senex,': The Pastoral of Old Age," *Studies in English Literature* 25 (1985): 22 and 41. Grouping the youth–age opposition that he treats together with "those conceptual polarities, like body and soul or nature and art, that Renaissance writers thought *with* as much as they thought *about*," however, the closest Marx comes to addressing the experience of victimization and objectification to which I attend is in his passing reference to the "satiric and moral strain" he construes as "a response to the old person's treatment by a society that considers the aged as expendable" (37).

4. George Puttenham, *The Art of English Poesy*, ed. Frank Whigham and Wayne A. Rebhorn (Ithaca, N.Y.: Cornell University Press, 2007), p. 128. Puttenham denied "that the eclogue should be the first and most ancient form of artificial poesy," in favor of a more deliberated genesis, "under the veil of homely persons and in rude speeches to insinuate and glance at greater matters, and such as perchance had not been safe to have been disclosed in any other sort" (pp. 127–28).

5. Sir Philip Sidney, *The Countess of Pembroke's Arcadia (The New Arcadia)*, ed. Victor Skretkowicz (Oxford: Clarendon Press, 1987), p. 23. All further quotations from the *New Arcadia*, hereafter cited as *NA* in the text, refer to this edition.

6. Jacopo Sannazaro, *Arcadia and Piscatorial Eclogues*, trans. Ralph Nash (Detroit: Wayne State University Press, 1966), pp. 63–64. Subsequent quotations from Sannazaro refer to this translation. Later in the narrative, when Opico is gratuitously presented with "a most delicate staff of wild pear wood"—a prize in the funerary games he was obliged to sit out—the old man observes ambiguously, "So great are the privileges of age, my son, that we are compelled to obey them, whether we will or whether we will it not," and immediately launches into a nostalgic recollection of his athletic prowess of younger days. He closes with the somber note, "You, then, whose ages permit it, exert yourselves in youthful contests; Time and Nature lay other laws on me" (pp. 127–28).

7. William J. Kennedy, *Jacopo Sannazaro and the Uses of Pastoral* (Hanover, N.H.: University Press of New England, 1983), p. 124.

8. When Nemesianus's old shepherd Tityrus reverses the invitation and charges his young companion to sing an elegy in memory of his fellow *senex* Meliboeus, the boy celebrates the deceased elder's kindly sponsorship of youth with the supreme compliment that their company bewailed his passing no less than they would have "if churlish death had carried you off in your prime [*si florentes mors invida carperet annos*]." Nemesianus, Eclogue 1.47, in *Minor Latin Poets*, trans. J. Wright Duff and Arnold M. Duff (Cambridge: Harvard University Press, 1978), with minor adjustments.

9. "O Meliboeus, a god provides us with this leisure [*O Meliboee, deus nobis haec otia fecit*]," Tityrus proclaims, and later recalls his journey to Rome, where "I saw that youth [*illum vidi iuvenem*]"; Virgil, Eclogue 1.6.42, trans. H. R. Fairclough (Cambridge: Harvard University Press, 1978). Michael O'Loughlin regards this reliance upon external agencies as the key feature distinguishing pastoral from epic; see his *The Garlands of Repose: The Literary Celebration of Civic and Retired Leisure; The Traditions of Homer and Vergil, Horace and Montaigne* (Chicago: University of Chicago Press, 1978).

10. When Mantuan's younger speaker Fulica indicts youthful folly, his elderly companion Cornix consoles that (in George Turbervile's translation) "We Countrie men are Sottes / and Fooles of e[v]rie age"; *The Eglogs of the Poet B. Mantuan Carmelitan* (London, 1567), p. 53v. When Googe's young shepherd Daphnes solicits the old Amintas to sing because "many a saged saw lies hid / within thine aged breast," the elder shapes a cautionary song about love's hazards, funded by the harsher experiences he met with in his own early years (19–20). His versified counsel leaves more than a hint of understanding that physical limitation informs some of his now conservative stance: "And thus an end: I wearied am, / my wind is old and faint, / Such matters I do leave to such / as finer far can paint" (157–60); citations refer to Barnabe Googe, *Eclogues, Epitaphs, and Sonnets*, ed. Judith M. Kennedy (Toronto: University of Toronto Press, 1989).

11. *Sera animum que cura subit? Brevis ecce iuvente / Flos cecidit. Tunc tempus erat! Iam discere turpe est / Quod pulcrum didicisse foret* (Petrarch, *Bucolicum Carmen* 4.64–66, trans. Thomas G. Bergin [New Haven: Yale University Press, 1974]; subsequent quotations from Petrarch's pastoral verse refer to this translation). While the transparent topical allegories of Petrarch's collection direct its speakers' characterizations, the work offers a generally darker portrayal of senescence throughout; from Eclogue 5's image of Rome as a helpless elderly matron, to the sixth eclogue's caricature of Pope Clement VI as an indolent, aged sensualist, to Eclogue 8's grasping father-figure Ganymede, the overall outlook is perhaps best summed up in the lines "But little / Long life avails a man. We always seek out what will hurt us" (9.38–39; *Quid vivere longum / Fert homini? Nec desinimus nocitura precari*).

12. Helen Small, *The Long Life* (New York: Oxford University Press, 2007), p. 11.

13. Kathleen Woodward, "Against Wisdom: The Social Politics of Anger and Aging," *Journal of Aging Studies* 17 (2003): 56. This in turn helps justify, in Woodward's view, "the disengagement theory of aging—that older people 'naturally' withdraw from their social roles so as to make their ultimate disappearance—death—less difficult for the smooth functioning of society" (63).

14. For a splendid assessment of the relationship between anger and artistry in late life, see William Kerrigan, "Life's Iamb: The Scansion of Late Creativity in the Culture of the Renaissance," in *Memory and Desire: Aging—Literature—Psychoanalysis*, ed. Kathleen Woodward and Murray M. Schwartz (Bloomington: Indiana University Press, 1986), pp. 168–91.

15. *Spenser's Minor Poems*, ed. Ernest de Selincourt (Oxford: Clarendon Press, 1910), p. 3. All quotations from *The Shepheardes Calender* refer to this edition: I cite prose excerpts parenthetically by page number, verse passages by corresponding line numbers.

16. Harry Berger Jr., *Revisionary Play: Studies in the Spenserian Dynamics* (Berkeley: University of California Press, 1988), p. 288. Patrick Cullen likewise sees "the psychological power struggle between age and youth" as representative of "the balance-in-opposition of the natural year"; *Spenser, Marvell, and Renaissance Pastoral* (Cambridge: Harvard University Press, 1970), pp. 34 and 41.

17. See R. L. Renwick's comment that "The reverence due to age and station may seem a strange theme for the innovating poet, but it is in line with Spenser's ideals and character"; quoted in *The Works of Edmund Spenser: A Variorum Edition*, ed. Edwin Greenlaw et al., 11 vols. (Baltimore: Johns Hopkins University Press, 1943), 7:254.

18. *The Miscellaneous Prose of Sir Philip Sidney*, ed. Katherine Duncan-Jones and Jan Van Dorsten (Oxford: Clarendon Press, 1973), p. 112. See also Richard Halpern's chapter "Margins and Marginality: *The Shepheardes Calender* and the Politics of Interpretation," in his *The Poetics of Primitive Accumulation: English Renaissance Culture and the Genealogy of Capital* (Ithaca, N.Y.: Cornell University Press, 1991), pp. 176–214.

19. On the way Spenser notoriously leaves indeterminate just how much time passes, literally and symbolically, over the *Calender*'s course, see for instance Gary M. Bouchard, "'Stayed Steps': Colin Clout's Slow Hastening into Riper Years," *Studies in Iconography* 15 (1993): 197–214.

20. Even Berger's brilliant reading is inflected by a transparent distaste for the character, whose bitter resentment of youth he traces "not simply [to] ethical disapproval but nostalgia for pleasures he is deprived of by age" (p. 398). Berger adopts a skeptical view of "Spenserian gerontology" generally, regarding Colin "less as Spenser's mouthpiece than as his target," whose "December" senescence serves to expose the limitations of a "paradise principle" that "engenders the inability to accept aging, engenders hatred of one's aging body and the desire to recover old delights in some new form" (pp. 385 and 441). Lynn Staley Johnson provides an equally harsh reading of Thenot, whose attack only reveals "the depths of his own envy for the younger shepherds," whose "real purpose . . . is revenge," and

whose fable "reveals him as the spiteful, contentious, slanderous, and vengeful member of the debate"; *The Shepheardes Calender: An Introduction* (University Park: Pennsylvania State University Press, 1990), pp. 66, 67, and 70. As my argument makes clear, I do not share their sense of Thenot's cynical motives.

21. Berger, *Revisionary Play*, p. 396. More facetiously, Berger later refers to the "magical rejuvenation" we need to posit if we regard the character featured in "Februarie," "Aprill," and "November" as the same person (p. 428).

22. *The Kalender of Shepherdes*, ed. Oskar Sommer, 3 vols. (London: Kegan Paul, Trench, Trübner, 1892), 3:155.

23. E. K.'s attitude itself faces significant qualification in the period, which had often come to associate an older generation, not with divine agelessness, but with the heresies of the "old" Catholic faith. See especially John N. King, "Spenser's *Shepheardes Calender* and Protestant Pastoral Satire, in *Renaissance Genres*, ed. Barbara Kiefer Lewalski (Cambridge: Harvard University Press, 1986), p. 390.

24. Cullen, *Spenser, Marvell, and Renaissance Pastoral*, p. 37. Berger (again) extends this, remarking that the "obvious aphoristic truth" that Cullen concedes to Thenot's *sententiae* "may only seem true because it sounds obvious and aphoristic" (p. 424).

25. Louis S. Friedland, for instance, points out that "For this turn of the 'oracion' Spenser had no model known to us, so that it must be regarded as his own invention, a fresh version of the age-old fable"; "Spenser's Fable of 'The Oake and the Brere,'" *Shakespeare Association Bulletin* 16 (1941): 56.

26. In the Aesopian original, and in Avianus's and Breton's reiterations, it is the tree's strength and magnificence that are at issue rather than its age, though Plutarch makes the application in his advisory that the aged politician not be "like unto old runt-trees or dodils, which repining as it were at others, doe manifestly hinder and take away the spring and growth of yoong poles and plants which come up under them, or grow neere under them" (Plutarch, *Morals*, trans. Philemon Holland [London, 1603], p. 399). For the other versions, see *Caxton's Aesop*, ed. R. T. Lenaghan (Cambridge: Harvard University Press, 1967), pp. 135–36; Avianus, Fable 16 (*Minor Latin Poets*, trans. J. Wight Duff and Arnold M. Duff [Cambridge: Harvard University Press, 1978], pp. 706–7); and Nicholas Breton, *Poems*, ed. Jean Robertson (Liverpool: Liverpool University Press, 1952), pp. 58–59. See also Spenser's later *Ruines of Time* (1591), where the poet laments how virtue is now despised "Of him, that first was raisde for vertuous parts, / And now broad spreading like an aged tree, / Lets none shoot up, that nigh him planted bee" (451–53).

27. See Renwick's ironic reading of these lines, cited in the *Variorum:* "it seems clear that they are spoken from the cynical point of view of the Briar, or of an observer who voices his sympathy, after the English manner, in apparent cynicism: this 'holy eld' business is all nonsense; anyone who believes in it will only come to grief; nobody respects 'honourable old age' nowadays!" (7:265).

28. Sidney's "troublesome relationship with authority" is a staple of the biographical and critical commentary of the past thirty years: see especially Richard C. McCoy, *Sir Philip Sidney: Rebellion in Arcadia* (New Brunswick, N.J.: Rutgers University Press, 1979); James M. Osborn, *Young Philip Sidney: 1572–1577* (New Haven: Yale University Press, 1972); and Katherine Duncan-Jones, *Sir Philip Sidney: Courtier Poet* (New Haven: Yale University Press, 1991).

29. Duncan-Jones, *Sir Philip Sidney*, p. 23.

30. Letter of January 30, 1580, *The Correspondence of Sir Philip Sidney and Hubert Languet*, trans. Steuart A. Pears (London, 1845), p. 170. Neil L. Rudenstine finds the letters' concerns refracted in much of Sidney's poetic fiction: "'youthful ardour' and rashness confront the often tedious wisdom of old age; young truants argue with stern moralists in a set of dialogues which articulate some of the main tensions discovered in Sidney's correspondence"; *Sidney's Poetic Development* (Cambridge: Harvard University Press, 1967), p. 35.

31. Sir Philip Sidney, *The Countess of Pembroke's Arcadia (The Old Arcadia)*, ed. Jean Robertson (Oxford: Clarendon Press, 1973), p. 3. All further quotations from the *Old Arcadia*, cited in the text as *OA*, refer to this edition. Although Sidney's secretary, Edmund Molyneux, records that the work was undertaken first in 1577, Robertson suggests that "evidence points to the composition of the bulk of the story when he was at Wilton and Ivy Church from March to August 1580" (p. xvi). See her commentary on pp. xv–xix, which also notes Sidney's possible contact with Spenser at Leicester House in the year of the *Calender*'s publication.

32. The *New Arcadia* places him at "nigh threescore years" at the time of his marriage to Gynecia, who has borne him two daughters, Pamela and Philoclea, now aged seventeen and sixteen respectively; see *NA*, 317, and *OA*, 5.

33. See Christopher Martin, "Misdoubting His Estate: Dynastic Anxiety in Sidney's *Arcadia*," *English Literary Renaissance* 18 (1988): 369–88.

34. Theocritus, *Idylls and Epigrams,* trans. Daryl Hine (New York: Atheneum, 1982), p. 18.

35. Judith Haber, *Pastoral and the Poetics of Self-Contradiction: Theocritus to Marvell* (Cambridge: Cambridge University Press, 1994), p. 25.

36. Rudenstine, *Sidney's Poetic Development*, pp. 114 and 37. For fuller evaluations of Philisides's role, see ibid., 106–14, and Edward Berry, *The Making of Sir Philip Sidney* (Toronto: University of Toronto Press, 1998), pp. 63–101.

37. Haber, *Pastoral and the Poetics of Self-Contradiction*, p. 58. For my own contrasting view of the important corrective function that the eclogic interludes serve, see Martin, "Misdoubting His Estate," 383–85.

38. Rudenstine, *Sidney's Poetic Development*, p. 38; McCoy, *Sir Philip Sidney*, pp. 47, 152, and 78. More recently, Gavin Alexander writes off Geron as an "old crock"; *Writing After Sidney: The Literary Response to Sir Philip Sidney, 1586–1640* (Oxford: Oxford University Press, 2006), p. 11.

39. Robert E. Stillman, *Sidney's Poetic Justice:* The Old Arcadia, *Its Eclogues, and Renaissance Pastoral Traditions* (Lewisburg, Pa.: Bucknell University Press, 1986), p. 112.

40. For accounts of the manuscripts' fortunes after Sidney's death, see Robertson's and Skretkowicz's accounts in their introductions, and H. R. Woudhuysen's superb synthetic discussion in *Sir Philip Sidney and the Circulation of Manuscripts, 1558–1640* (Oxford: Clarendon Press, 1996), pp. 299–355.

41. Quoted from *The Poems of Sir Philip Sidney*, ed. William A. Ringler, Jr. (Oxford: Clarendon Press, 1962), p. 248.

42. See, for instance, the description of how Pyrocles' father, Euarchus, had inherited a kingdom afflicted by a combination of "old men long nuzzled in corruption" and a younger generation "very fault-finding but very faulty," which he proceeds to set in order (*NA*, 160); the destructive competitive love of Plangus's father, "though he were already stepped into the winter of his age," for his son's mistress (*NA*, 216); and the characterization of Dido's grasping father, Chremes, as "a drivelling old fellow, lean, shaking both of head and hands—already half earth, and yet then most greedy of earth" (*NA*, 245).

43. Woudhuysen, *Sir Philip Sidney and the Circulation of Manuscripts*, p. 300. See also Robertson's edition of the *Old Arcadia*, pp. xxxvii–xl.

44. Henry Chettle, *Englands Mourning Garment* (London, 1603), pp. E1 and C2.

45. Thomas Lodge, *Complete Works,* 4 vols. (New York: Russell and Russell, 1963), 1:4. All quotations from Lodge, cited hereafter in the text, refer to this edition, which paginates each of Lodge's individual works separately.

46. See Robertson's *OA* introduction, pp. xxxvii–xxxviii. For a more recent assessment of Lodge's possible access to the *Arcadia* manuscript, see Woudhuysen, *Sir Philip Sidney and the Circulation of Manuscripts,* pp. 302–3.

47. Sukanta Chaudhuri, *Renaissance Pastoral and its English Developments* (Oxford: Clarendon Press, 1989), p. 203.

48. Ibid., p. 228.

49. *The Works of Michael Drayton,* ed. J. William Hebel, 5 vols. (Oxford: Shakespeare Head Press, 1961), 1:50. All further quotations from Drayton, cited hereafter in the text, refer to this edition.

50. Francis Sabie, *Pans Pipe* (London, 1595), p. A2. All further quotations, cited parenthetically, refer to this edition.

51. Richard Barnfield, *Poems 1594–1598,* ed. Edward Arber (Westminster: Constable, 1896), p. 6. All further in-text quotations from Barnfield refer to this edition.

52. Marx, " 'Fortunate Senex,' " 21.

4. Sexuality and Senescence in Late Elizabethan Poetry: "Old Strange Thinges"

1. Geffrey Whitney, *A Choice of Emblemes* (London, 1586), pp. 132–33.

2. Thomas Campion, *A Booke of Ayres* (1601), quoted from *Campion's Works,* ed. Percival Vivian (Oxford: Clarendon Press, 1909), p. 6.

3. All quotations from Donne refer to the corresponding volumes of *The Variorum Edition of the Poetry of John Donne,* ed. Gary Stringer et al., vol. 8: *The Epigrams, Epithalamions, Epitaphs, Inscriptions, and Miscellaneous Poems* (Bloomington: Indiana University Press, 1995); and vol. 2: *The Elegies* (Bloomington: Indiana University Press, 2000).

4. See, for instance, Thomas Nashe's caricature of the antiquarian in his *Pierce Penniless* of 1592: "A thousand gewgaws and toys have they in their chambers, which they heap up together with infinite expense and are made believe of them that sell them that they are rare and precious things . . . It argueth a very rusty wit so to dote on wormeaten eld"; *Selected Works,* ed. Stanley Wells (Cambridge: Harvard University Press, 1964), p. 44. Everard Guilpin's *Skialetheia* (1598) offers a similar picture of the "foppery / The Antiquary would perswade us to" in his Satire 1.136–42; *Skialetheia, or A Shadowe of Truth, in Certaine Epigrams and Satyres,* ed. D. Allen Carroll (Chapel Hill: University of North Carolina Press, 1974), p. 67.

5. See esp. Anne Ferry's chapter in *All in War with Time: Love Poetry of Shakespeare, Donne, Jonson, Marvell* (Cambridge: Harvard University Press, 1975), pp. 67–125; and John Carey's sequence of chapters—"Bodies," "Change," "Death"—in his *John Donne: Life, Mind and Art* (London: Faber, 1981), pp. 131–230.

6. *The Passionate Pilgrime,* reprinted in the variorum edition of Shakespeare's *Poems,* ed. Hyder Edward Rollins (Philadelphia: J. B. Lippincott, 1938), p. 290. All quotations from Jaggard's text refer to this edition.

7. As Leslie Fiedler observes, premodern thinking "assumes that sexual desire and phallic potency (however unseemly they may be in the aged) never cease as long as life lasts. Consequently, what is presented as problematical is the propriety rather than the possibility of sex in the shadow of death." This contrasts with a more "modern" outlook, where "the propriety of concupiscence at an advanced age is taken for granted, while its possibility is assumed to be . . . doubtful in the extreme"; "More Images of Eros and Old Age," in Kathleen Woodward and Murray M. Schwartz (eds.), *Memory and Desire: Aging—Literature—Psychoanalysis* (Bloomington: Indiana University Press, 1986), pp. 48–49.

8. For fuller discussions of this tradition, see especially George R. Coffman, "Old Age from Horace to Chaucer: Some Literary Affinities and Adventures of an Idea," *Speculum* 9 (1934): 249–77; and Shulamith Shahar, *Growing Old in the Middle Ages: "Winter clothes us in shadow and pain,"* trans. Yael Lotan (London: Routledge, 1997), passim.

9. See, for instance, *Odes* 1.25 and 4.13. The even more virulent Epode 8 grounds Tim G. Parkin's claim that in classical lyric "The stereotyped old woman is, in sum, a disgusting, haggard, stinking, toothless, and sex-crazed *fellatrix.*" *Old Age in the Roman World: A Cultural and Social History* (Baltimore: Johns Hopkins University Press, 2003), p. 86.

10. Cathy Yandell, "Carpe Diem, Poetic Immortality, and the Gendered Ideology of Time," *Renaissance Women Writers: French Texts/American Contexts,* ed. Anne R. Larsen and Colette H. Winn (Detroit: Wayne State University Press, 1994), p. 122.

11. All quotes refer to *The Elegies of Maximianus,* ed. Richard Webster (Princeton: The Princeton Press, 1900), and to L. R. Lind's translation, published together with his rendition of Gabriele Zerbi's *Gerontocomia: On the Care of the Aged* (Philadelphia: American Philosophical Society, 1988). Surviving under Gallus's name, Maximianus's work lived beyond its circulation as a popular medieval school text into the Renaissance, reprinted throughout the sixteenth century. On the Gallus attribution and the elegies' influence on sixteenth-century English poetry, see Webster's edition of Maximianus, pp. 15–16 and 59.

12. Karen Cokayne, *Experiencing Old Age in Ancient Rome* (London: Routledge, 2003), p. 82.

13. See *The Greek Anthology* 5. 13, 48, 62, and 258, and 282; Parkin, *Old Age in the Roman World,* pp. 86–87.

14. Stella Achilleos, "Youth, Old Age, and Male Self-Fashioning: The Appropriation of the Anacreontic Figure of the Old Man by Jonson and his 'Sons,'" in Erin Campbell (ed.), *Growing Old in Early Modern Europe: Cultural Representations* (Aldershot: Ashgate, 2006), pp. 40–41. See also Patricia A. Rosenmeyer's extended discussion of old age's role in the poems in her *The Poetics of Imitation: Anacreon and the Anacreontic Tradition* (Cambridge: Cambridge University Press, 1992), pp. 57–62.

15. Giovanni Gioviano Pontano, *Baiae,* trans. Rodney G. Dennis (Cambridge: Harvard University Press, 2006), pp. 120–21.

16. Sir Thomas Wyatt, *The Complete Poems,* ed. R. A. Rebholz (New Haven: Yale University Press, 1978), pp. 74 and 145.

17. *Poems and Dramas of Fulke Greville, First Lord Brooke,* ed. Geoffrey Bullough, 2 vols. (New York: Oxford University Press, 1945), 1:83.

18. *The Works of Michael Drayton,* ed. J. William Hebel, 5 vols. (Oxford: Shakespeare Head Press, 1961), 2:314.

19. See Vaux's "The aged lover renounceth love," in *Tottel's Miscellany (1557–1587),* ed. Hyder Edward Rollins, rev. ed., 2 vols. (Cambridge: Harvard University Press, 1966), 1:165–66. In "Beyng asked the occasion of his white head, he aunswereth thus," Vaux again catalogues the bitter life experiences that age embodies, only to express "joye" that the years have brought him to a more pious sobriety; see *The Paradise of Dainty Devices (1576–1606),* ed. Hyder Edward Rollins (Cambridge: Harvard University Press, 1927), pp. 52–54. Kevin P. Laam finds in Gascoigne's works an invocation of old age "as a malleable fiction," wherein the aged physique professes its crippled inadequacies as "a spark of defiance from the poet who has been unduly harried past his prime": "The body broken down by experience, by singular virtue of its experience, is arguably the most qualified to piece itself back together"; "Aging the Lover: The *Poesies* of George Gascoigne," in Campbell, *Growing Old in Early Modern Europe,* pp. 78 and 82. I find the evidence he summons in the "Anatomye" and "The Divorce of a Lover" too thin to support his provocative claims. The poet's cagey manipulations of the theme adhere too closely to more conventional dismissal of old age's pathetic decrepitude—the "feeble heads" and "crooked croanes" that represent senescence—to break free of gerontophobic orthodoxies.

20. *The Autobiography of Thomas Whythorne,* ed. James M. Osborn (Oxford: Clarendon Press, 1961), p. 20. All further quotations from the work, cited hereafter in the text, refer to this edition. Where the difficulties of Whythorne's eccentric "new Orthografye" obscures the sense, I have silently normalized the spelling.

21. All quotations refer to *The Poems of Sir Walter Ralegh: A Historical Edition,* ed. Michael Rudick (Tempe: Arizona Center for Medieval and Renaissance Studies, 1999).

22. Stephen J. Greenblatt, *Sir Walter Ralegh: The Renaissance Man and His Roles* (New Haven: Yale University Press, 1973), p. 193n36.

23. On the development of this convention, see Elkin Calhoun Wilson, *England's Eliza* (Cambridge: Harvard University Press, 1939), pp. 273–320.

24. "[T]he poet does not encourage us to look *through* his image to the substantial reality behind it—the reality of the aging Elizabeth—but to know and pay tribute to the qualities that inhere in the figure of Diana into whom the queen has been transformed: perfect beauty and virtue, supreme power, and, above all, the mastery of time and mutability" (*Sir Walter Ralegh*, p. 66).

25. Laurent Joubert, *Popular Errors*, trans. Gregory David de Rocher (Tuscaloosa: University of Alabama Press, 1989), p. 120.

26. On the connection between Ralegh's poem and the earlier Walsingham ballads, see Helen Hackett, *Virgin Mother, Maiden Queen: Elizabeth I and the Cult of the Virgin Mary* (New York: St. Martin's Press, 1995): "since it seems that pilgrimage-ballads, and specifically Walsingham-ballads, were associated with both forsaken love and worldly mutability, it is easy to see why the form appealed to [Ralegh]" (p. 160).

27. Since the holograph survives in Ralegh's fair copy, most readers suspect that the poem in its entirety comprised no more than the passages we have, and that the titular twenty-two (or more) "boockes" intend only to convey the speaker's larger-than-life grief. On this, see Greenblatt: "Ralegh may simply have used the grandiose titles to create the aura of an immensely long poem, suggesting to the queen—and to himself, perhaps—an almost boundless suffering immortalized in verse" (*Sir Walter Ralegh*, p. 62).

28. See Marion Campbell's passing remark on the atypical way that age is invoked in the poem, where "pastoral references return perfunctorily at the end . . . as attempts are made [unsuccessfully] to present old age and immanent death in traditional pastoral terms as an incorporation into the landscape"; "Inscribing Imperfection: Sir Walter Ralegh and the Elizabethan Court," *English Literary Renaissance* 20 (1990): 240.

29. Robert E. Stillman, "'Words cannot knytt': Language and Desire in Ralegh's *The Ocean to Cynthia*," *Studies in English Literature* 27 (1987): 46.

30. Quoted in Greenblatt, *Sir Walter Ralegh*, p. 76.

31. See the commentary in her edition of Ralegh's *Selected Poetry and Prose* (London: Athlone Press, 1965), p. 210.

32. On this, see the entry for "Thanatos" in *The Oxford Classical Dictionary*, ed. N. G. L. Hammond and H. H. Scullard, 2nd ed. (Oxford: Clarendon Press, 1970), p. 1050.

33. Colin Burrow, "Editing the Sonnets," *A Companion to Shakespeare's Sonnets*, ed. Michael Schoenfeldt (Maldon, Mass.: Blackwell, 2007), p. 147. See also John Roe's note to the sonnet in his updated edition of *The Poems* (Cambridge: Cambridge University Press, 2006): "some of the readings make poor sense in the *PP* version[;] . . . they present a simpler, less interesting version of the theme and reduce the imaginative wordplay of 1609" (p. 246).

34. Arthur F. Marotti, "Shakespeare's Sonnets as Literary Property," *Soliciting Interpretation: Literary Theory and Seventeenth-Century English Poetry*, ed. Elizabeth D. Harvey and Katherine Eisaman Maus (Chicago: University of Chicago Press, 1994), p. 151. Roe once more concurs, with an even more striking rationale: "The fear of ageing and loss of sexual attractiveness are the poem's twin themes, but they preoccupy the lover rather than his mistress, who in the 1609 version is accused of dishonesty or infidelity . . . towards him, not of trying to appear younger than she is. Growing old is conventionally what women fear, and so it would be natural for a memorial transcriber to assume that the mistress is as worried by this as the speaker; the result not only confuses the issue but reduces its complexity" (p. 246).

35. All citations refer to *Shakespeare's Sonnets*, ed. Stephen Booth (New Haven: Yale University Press, 1977).

36. John Klause, "Shakespeare's *Sonnets*: Age in Love and the Goring of Thoughts," *Studies in Philology* 80 (1983): 305–6.

37. Ibid., 317.

38. Ibid., 309.

39. Dympna Callaghan, "Confounded by Winter: Speeding Time in Shakespeare's Sonnets," in Schoenfeldt, *A Companion to Shakespeare's Sonnets,* pp. 104 and 108.

40. Though included in the Quarto, the poem was marginalized to the point where its authenticity came into question. Its critical rehabilitation as an integral part of the volume begins with John Kerrigan's *The Sonnets and A Lover's Complaint* (Harmondsworth: Penguin, 1986); see esp. pp. 12–18 of his Introduction. For more recent evaluations, see *Critical Essays on Shakespeare's* A Lover's Complaint: *Suffering Ecstasy,* ed. Shirley Sharon-Zisser (Aldershot, Hampshire, Eng.: Ashgate, 2006). All citations from the *Complaint* refer to Roe's New Cambridge edition of *The Poems.*

41. As Lisa Fraenkel has recently elaborated, the seducer draws his power precisely from his "unruliness," a vice proudly aligned with his very age: "It is the rudeness that is authorized, not the youth; . . . the authorizing agent becomes its own authorized object"; *Reading Shakespeare's Will: The Theology of Figure from Augustine to the Sonnets* (New York: Columbia University Press, 2002), p. 191.

42. For a stimulating historicist discussion that touches on the matter of age in the poem—aligning its narrative with Sir Henry Lee's courtship of Anne Vavasour following her seduction and abandonment by Edward de Vere, earl of Oxford—see Ilona Bell, "Shakespeare's Exculpatory Complaint," in Sharon-Zisser, *Critical Essays,* pp. 91–107.

43. As I have discussed elsewhere, Shakespeare's persona at this initial stage of the sequence emerges as a spokesman for larger societal prejudices to which he presumes his addressee subscribes. See "And Men's Eyes: Shakespeare's Politic Lover," in Christopher Martin, *Policy in Love: Lyric and Public in Ovid, Petrarch and Shakespeare* (Pittsburgh: Duquesne University Press, 1994), pp. 130–91.

44. See, for instance, Christopher Ricks, "Lies," *Critical Inquiry* 2 (1975): 121–42.

45. In a provocative effort to recast the sequence's "dark lady," Ilona Bell has argued that 138's consummation is denied in the surrounding poems and therefore remains more a misogynistic wish fulfillment on the part of the would-be seducer/poet. While her reading effectively challenges many critical presumptions, this suggestion seems less persuasive given the poet's casual, openly sexual claims to her elsewhere, as in 151. See Ilona Bell, "Rethinking Shakespeare's Dark Lady," in Schoenfeldt, *A Companion to Shakespeare's Sonnets,* pp. 293–313.

46. Joel Fineman, *Shakespeare's Perjured Eye: The Invention of Poetic Subjectivity in the Sonnets* (Berkeley: University of California Press, 1986), p. 165.

47. For a survey of efforts to date the poem, see the Variorum *Elegies,* pp. 836–41. I follow those who place "The Autumnall" amid Donne's Elizabethan elegies, although questions about precise dating do not significantly affect my reading.

48. Cf. J. L. Austin's observation about how "the average excuse gets us only out of the fire into the frying pan," quoted in Margaret W. Ferguson, *Trials of Desire: Renaissance Defenses of Poetry* (New Haven: Yale University Press, 1983), p. 139.

49. On Donnean paradox generally, see Rosalie L. Colie's *Paradoxia Epidemica: The Renaissance Tradition of Paradox* (Princeton: Princeton University Press, 1966), pp. 96–141.

50. *Paradoxes and Problems,* ed. Helen Peters (Oxford: Clarendon, 1980), pp. 4–6.

51. Mary Alice Greller, "Donne's 'The Autumnall': An Analysis," *Literatur in Wissenschaft und Unterricht* 9 (1975): 7.

52. Even Arthur Marotti, our most formidable advocate for the "coterie" setting of Donne's oeuvre, disputes the Herbert connection: "the evidence for this social context is weak," he concludes, and further notes that the poem "lacks the signs of direct or indirect complimentary purpose"; *John Donne, Coterie Poet* (Madison: University of Wisconsin Press, 1986), p. 52. For a history of the Herbert association, see the Variorum *Elegies,* pp. 280–82, 288, and 836–41. The titles ascribed to the elegy in several manuscript groups take Herbert

as the intended subject, a presumption that Walton authorized in his *Life of Donne* (1670). Since the late nineteenth century, the linkage has troubled efforts to date the poem. From at least 1933 on, such commentators as Alec Brown, Roger Bennett, Alan Armstrong, John Carey, and John Shawcross anticipated Marotti's dismissal of the biographical reading.

53. Alan Armstrong, "The Apprenticeship of John Donne: Ovid and the Elegies," *ELH* 44 (1977): 438.

54. Heather Dubrow, "Donne's Elegies and the Ugly Beauty Tradition," in *Donne and the Resources of Kind,* ed. A. D. Cousins and Damian Grace (Madison, Wisc.: Fairleigh Dickinson University Press, 2002), pp. 60–61.

55. Henry Cuffe, *The Differences of the Ages of Mans Life* (London, 1607), pp. 119–20.

56. On this, see E. E. Duncan-Jones, "Donne's Praise of Autumnal Beauty: Greek Sources," *Modern Language Review* 56 (1961): 213–15.

57. Cited in Robert Jütte, "Aging and Body Image in the Sixteenth Century: Hermann Weinsberg's (1518–97) Perception of the Aging Body," *European History Quarterly* 18 (1988): 261.

58. Elizabeth D. Harvey, "The Touching Organ: Allegory, Anatomy, and the Renaissance Skin Envelope," in *Sensible Flesh: On Touch in Early Modern Culture,* ed. Elizabeth D. Harvey (Philadelphia: University of Pennsylvania Press, 2003), p. 85.

59. On this, see Steven R. Smith's "Death, Dying, and the Elderly in Seventeenth-Century England," *Aging and the Elderly: Humanist Perspectives in Gerontology,* ed. Stuart F. Spickler et al. (Atlantic Highlands, N.J.: Humanities Press, 1978), pp. 205–19.

60. Erasmus, *Collected Works: Poems,* trans. Clarence H. Miller, ed. Harry Vredeveld (Toronto: University of Toronto Press, 1993), p. 15.

61. Carey, *John Donne,* p. 199.

62. *England's Helicon 1600, 1614,* ed. Edward Hyder Rollins, 2 vols. (Cambridge: Harvard University Press, 1935), 1:110–11.

5. "Confin'd to Exhibition": *King Lear* through the Spectacles of Age

1. Theognis, *Elegies* 271–78, trans. Dorothea Wender (Harmondsworth: Penguin, 1973), p. 106. The Greek text can be found in the Loeb *Elegy and Iambus,* trans. J. M. Edmunds, 2 vols. (Cambridge: Harvard University Press, 1968), 1:260.

2. All citations from *King Lear* refer to the "conflated" text of the play in the Riverside edition, although I note distinctions between the Quarto and Folio versions where relevant.

3. William C. Carroll, *Fat King, Lean Beggar: Representations of Poverty in the Age of Shakespeare* (Ithaca, N.Y.: Cornell University Press, 1996), p. 185.

4. *The Paradise of Dainty Devices (1576–1606),* ed. Hyder Edward Rollins (Cambridge: Harvard University Press, 1927), p. 111.

5. The tendency is long-standing. Eighty years ago, for example, Lily B. Campbell devoted practically all of a chapter promisingly titled "*King Lear:* A Tragedy of Wrath in Old Age" to the rage that Lear in fact shares with many younger figures in the plays, only incidentally aligning this with the propensity to anger that Aristotle had stereotyped onto the elderly; *Shakespeare's Tragic Heroes: Slaves of Passion* (New York: Barnes and Noble, 1930), pp. 175–207. More recently, William O. Scott displays a similar inclination in his "Contrasts of Love and Affection: Lear, Old Age, and Kingship," *Shakespeare Survey* 55 (2002): 36–42, delving insightfully into the political and social legalities subtending Lear's resignation at the expense of a detailed treatment of what these have to say about his self-conception as the superannuated figurehead of the realm he has long governed.

Among the handful of studies training their attention more exclusively on Lear's constitutional psychology, many become too prescriptive or clinically reductive to do the character's idiosyncrasies full justice. For Kirk Combe and Kenneth Schnader, Lear serves as a case study of the "Frail Elder" (in contrast to Prospero's "Well Elder") who demonstrates "that old age may be fraught with suffering and particularly that the clash of insensitive youth with frail age is deadly"; "Shakespeare Teaching Geriatrics: Lear and Prospero as Case Studies in Aged Heterogeneity," *Aging and Identity: A Humanities Perspective*, ed. Sara Munson Deats and Lagretta Tallent Lenker (Westport, Conn.: Praeger, 1999), p. 44. Despite the appearance of more pointed recent analyses like those of Lyell Asher ("Lateness in *King Lear*," *Yale Journal of Criticism* 13 [2000]: 209–28), Gordon McMullan (*Shakespeare and the Idea of Late Writing: Authorship in the Proximity of Death* [Cambridge: Cambridge University Press, 2007], esp. pp. 294–313), and Anthony Ellis (*Old Age, Masculinity, and Early Modern Drama* [Farnham, Surrey, Eng.: Ashgate, 2009]), Helen Small's summary assessment that "Remarkably little of the vast literature on *King Lear* . . . says much or anything about old age" obtains (*The Long Life*, p. 5).

    6. On Pantalone, see especially Ellis, *Old Age*, pp. 115–35. While Ellis draws upon the synopses offered in Flaminio Scala's *Il teatro delle favole rappresentative* (Venice, 1611) to advance the interesting case that commedia dell'arte's "mocking treatments of Pantalone (the ones the genre is most famous for) actually buttress, by negative example, his more sober, domestically responsible incarnation" (p. 116), the prevailing "derogatory portrait of old age" remained most influential in broader theatrical channels at least throughout the 1500s.

    7. *Gammer Gurtons Nedle*, 3.3.17 and 47, in *Chief Pre-Shakespearean Dramas*, ed. Joseph Quincy Adams (Boston: Houghton Mifflin, 1924).

    8. John Lyly, *Mother Bombie*, 2.3.96–98, in *Complete Works*, ed. R. Warwick Bond, 3 vols. (Oxford: Clarendon Press, 1902). All further in-text citations from Lyly's works refer to this edition.

    9. On the work's dating and provenance, see Leslie Mahin Oliver, "John Foxe and the Drama *New Custom*," *Huntington Library Quarterly* 10 (1947): 407–10.

    10. Anthony Esler, *The Aspiring Mind of the Elizabethan Younger Generation* (Durham, N.C.: Duke University Press, 1966), p. 73.

    11. Henry Smith, *The Sermons* (London, 1593), p. 464. All further in-text citations from Smith refer to this edition.

    12. *A new Enterlude . . . entitled new Custome* (N.p., 1573), p. Aii. All further in-text citations from the play refer to this edition.

    13. Herbert S. Donow, "To Everything There Is a Season: Some Shakespearean Models of Normal and Anomalous Aging," *The Gerontologist* 32 (1992): 736.

    14. Ellis, *Old Age, Masculinity, And Early Modern Drama*, p. 57.

    15. See Curtis Perry, *The Making of Jacobean Culture: James I and the Renegotiation of Elizabethan Literary Practice* (Cambridge: Cambridge University Press, 1997), esp. pp. 153–87.

    16. Okes set Lloyd's text in mid-October of 1607, and its run overlaps the Quarto *Lear*'s late December printing. See Peter W. M. Blayney, *The Texts of* King Lear *and Their Origins* (Cambridge: Cambridge University Press, 1982), pp. 78–80.

    17. Lodowick Lloyd, *Linceus Spectacles* (London, 1607), p. 14. All further in-text citations from Lloyd refer to this edition.

    18. On this scene generally, see esp. Edward L. Rocklin's commentary in "The Smell of Mortality: Performing Torture in *King Lear* 3.7," in Jeffrey Kahan (ed.), *King Lear: New Critical Essays* (New York: Routledge, 2008), pp. 297–325.

    19. Citation refers to the text included in vol. 7 of Geoffrey Bullough (ed.), *Narrative and Dramatic Sources of Shakespeare*, 8 vols. (London: Routledge, 1957–75).

    20. On the centrality of vision and the gaze in Shakespeare's play, see Philip Armstrong's psychoanalytic reading, "Uncanny Spectacles: Psychoanalysis and the texts of *King Lear*," *Textual Practice* 8 (1994): 414–34; and Pascale Aebischer's gender-focused approach in *Shakespeare's Violated Bodies: Stage and Screen Performance* (Cambridge: Cambridge University Press, 2004), pp. 151–89.

    21. If *King Lear*'s opening scene seems like "actually the last scene of some other play," as

John Barton avers (quoted in Asher, "Lateness in *King Lear*," 213), this perhaps has something to do with the confluence of sources that I remark here.

22. On Shakespeare's "omissions" from his source generally, see Jean R. Brink, "What Does Shakespeare Leave Out of *King Lear*," in Kahan, *King Lear*, pp. 208–30.

23. Northrop Frye, *Northrop Frye on Shakespeare* (New Haven: Yale University Press, 1988), p. 103; John W. Draper, "The Old Age of King Lear," *Journal of English and Germanic Philology* 39 (1940): 531. Along with alleging Lear's waning mental competence, readings frequently assail the king's irresponsibility: see, for example, Campbell's contention that he "is divesting himself of cares which he no longer wishes to carry" and does so "not in the interest of the recipients of his benefits but because he seeks release from duties that are burdensome" (*Shakespeare's Tragic Heroes*, p. 183); James P. Driscoll's claim that Lear primarily "seeks an opportunity to frolic in old age" and "renders himself ridiculous by yearning to enact anew mythic patterns appropriate only for an impetuous young hero on a quest for ego independence" ("The Vision of *King Lear*," *Shakespeare Studies* 10 [1977]: 166–67); William F. Zak's construction of the king as "a holiday-licensed lord of misrule" (*Sovereign Shame: A Study of* King Lear [Lewisburg, Pa.: Bucknell University Press, 1984], p. 121); and Emily Wilson's notion that "He wants to keep for himself only the things that seem to weigh nothing" (*Mocked with Death: Tragic Overliving from Sophocles to Milton* [Baltimore: Johns Hopkins University Press, 2004], p. 120). Others detect even deeper pathological turns behind his actions: see esp. Harry Berger Jr.'s discussion of the way Lear's "darker purpose moves him to aggression against others; the darkest purpose moves him to aggression against himself" (*Making Trifles of Terrors: Redistributing Complicities in Shakespeare*, ed. Peter Erickson [Stanford: Stanford University Press, 1997], p. 34). On Lear's character in performance, see the thumbnail sketch in Kahan's "Introduction," *King Lear*, pp. 48–50.

24. For a developed example of this "alternative" assessment, see esp. Harry V. Jaffa's classic "The Limits of Politics: *King Lear*, Act I, scene i," in Allan Bloom and Harry V. Jaffa, *Shakespeare's Politics* (New York: Basic Books, 1964), pp. 113–45. Richard Strier examines the opening scene and its consequences in terms of "a set of spontaneous bad decisions on Lear's part supervening on a plan that might well have been workable"; "Faithful Servants: Shakespeare's Praise of Disobedience," in *The Historical Renaissance: New Essays on Tudor and Stuart Literature and Culture*, ed. Heather Dubrow and Richard Strier (Chicago: University of Chicago Press, 1988), p. 112. Scott addresses "indications that commoners in Shakespeare's time . . . sometimes arranged for themselves a more modest legal version of Lear's attempt to secure his final years while shaking off the cares of age" ("Contrasts of Love and Affection," 36). Richard Halperin treats "Lear's division of the kingdom" as "a wager of sorts, or even an experiment, to see if the signs of royal power can outlast their material base" and "an act of aggressive generosity that cannot be matched, which reduces everyone else to the inferior and passive position of recipient"; *The Poetics of Primitive Accumulation: English Renaissance Culture and the Genealogy of Capital* (Ithaca, N.Y.: Cornell University Press, 1991), pp. 233 and 249. The scene's terrible consequences are, from this perspective, the result of failed strategy, not incompetence or senility.

25. *The Civile Conversation of M. Steeven Guazzo*, trans. George Pettie and Bartholomew Young, 2 vols. (London: Constable and Co., 1925), 2:65. Subsequent in-text citation refers to this edition.

26. In his introduction to the play in *The Norton Shakespeare*, Stephen Greenblatt comments on the ceremony's "theatrical" character: "Since the shares have already been apportioned, Lear evidently wants his daughters to engage in a competition for his bounty without having to endure any of the actual consequences of such a competition; he wants, that is, to produce in them something like the effect of theater, where emotions run high and their practical effects are negligible." *The Norton Shakespeare*, ed. Stephen J. Greenblatt et al. (New York: Norton, 1997), p. 2310.

27. Sara Munson Deats, "The Dialectic of Aging in Shakespeare's *King Lear* and *The Tempest*," in *Aging and Identity: A Humanities Perspective,* ed. Sara Munson Deats and Lagretta Tallent Lenker (Westport, Conn.: Praeger, 1999), p. 25. Likewise, see Carolyn Asp's contention that the play "depicts the futile efforts of an aging patriarch to elude death" ("'The Clamor of Eros': Freud, Aging, and *King Lear,*" in Woodward and Schwartz, *Memory and Desire: Aging—Literature—Psychoanalysis,* ed. Kathleen Woodward and Murray M. Schwartz [Bloomington: Indiana University Press, 1986], p. 197); and James L. Calderwood's more programmatic claim that Lear "liberates himself from the cares of kingly office, but he refuses to liberate his daughters from caring for him," and in so doing denies death in "an act of giving that is also an act of taking" (*Shakespeare and the Denial of Death* [Amherst: University of Massachusetts Press, 1987], p. 136).

28. Nina Taunton, *Fictions of Old Age in Early Modern Literature and Culture* (New York: Routledge, 2007), p. 72. I depart from Taunton's general reading of the play as a critique of Lear's "refusal to behave in the manner fitting to old men" and her notion that, "though he pays lip service to his own advanced years he does not regard his retirement as such, because he still intends to hold the reins of power, and he intends his twice-yearly visitations to his daughters to be conducted in the costly and burdensome manner of a reigning monarch, like Elizabeth's near-ruinous visitations upon her courtiers' country estates" (pp. 71–72).

29. Paul W. Kahn, *Law and Love: The Trials of* King Lear (New Haven: Yale University Press, 2000), p. 28.

30. Kent's actual age, despite the disarming precision of his declaration to Lear, "I have years on my back forty-eight" (1.4.38–39) when (in disguise) he sues to Lear for preferment, has long proved a source of critical controversy, as others in the play perceive him as significantly older. Small makes the reasonable suggestion that he is likely "pitching his age down to secure employment with Lear" (*The Long Life,* p. 74); I concur, and regard him, along with Gloucester, as a senior representative of the older generation in Shakespeare's cast.

31. On the efficacy of the daughters' claims, see Asher's remarks, "Lateness in *King Lear,*" 212–13. As R. A. Foakes rightly contends, Kent's deliberately confrontational challenge, "What wouldst thou do, old man?" loses its point if the king is already regarded as "no more than an 'old man'"; "King Lear: Monarch or Senior Citizen?" in *Elizabethan Theater: Essays in Honor of S. Schoenbaum,* ed. R. B. Parker and S. P. Zitner (Newark: University of Delaware Press, 1996), p. 273. Most recently, see Maurice Charney's assessment of the sisters' "acerbic and loveless remarks" here, which "provide a chilling commentary on the scene we have just witnessed"; *Wrinkled Deep in Time: Aging in Shakespeare* (New York: Columbia University Press, 2009), pp. 12–13.

32. For a brief but useful reflection on Lear as an example of what clinical gerontologists term "anomalous aging" and the social costs commonly associated with this experience, see Herbert S. Donow, "'To Everything There Is a Season': Some Shakespearean models of Normal and Anomalous Aging," *The Gerontologist* 32 (1992): 733–38. Anomalous aging takes place when "nonconforming characters defy expectations, disturbing their fellow characters in the process, because they won't fit some procrustean mold." Lear certainly matches this description, as "his plans for retirement—proposing to trail his huge retinue in monthly odysseys from the northern reaches of Albany hundreds of miles to Cornwall and back—hardly bespeak a course of senescent reflection" (733, 735–36).

33. As Marion D. Perret observes, "Lear, stripped of power, still tries to command, while Gloucester, stripped of capability, still tries to serve"; "*Lear's* Good Old Man," *Shakespeare Studies* 17 (1985): 97.

34. For the notion that a "Darker ambiguity shadows Edgar's design" as "he promises a cure of despair, but withholds the obvious remedy," see Marvin Rosenberg, *The Masks of King Lear* (Berkeley: University of California Press, 1972), p. 266.

35. See again Halperin on the "hopeless idealism" of Lear's initial gesture (*Poetics of Primitive Accumulation,* p. 233), and Laurel Porter's contention that "it is not age, but an unin-

formed view of the ambitious and avaricious people around them which takes both Lear and Kent off guard"; "King Lear and the Crisis of Retirement," *Aging in Literature,* ed. Laurel Porter and Laurence M. Porter (Troy, Mich.: International Book Publishers, 1984), p. 65.

36. Small, *The Long Life,* p. 84.

37. As Ewan Fernie points out, it is Lear's "unique distinction among tragic heroes . . . that he dies pointing away from himself, at somebody else"; *Shame in Shakespeare* (London: Routledge, 2002), p. 207.

38. See, for instance, Drew Milne's conclusion, "The final breaking of Lear's body reveals not the breaking of a weak heart, but of a tragically strong heart which will not weep"; "What Becomes of the Broken-Hearted: *King Lear* and the Dissociation of Sensibility," *Shakespeare Survey* 55 (2002): 62.

39. For a synopsis of the scholarship and bibliography, along with a survey of the powerful counterarguments, see Kiernan Ryan, "*King Lear:* A Retrospect, 1980–2000," *Shakespeare Survey* 55 (2002): 2–3.

40. McMullan, *Shakespeare and the Idea of Late Writing,* pp. 306 and 313.

Epilogue: Figures of Retire

1. Simone de Beauvoir, *The Coming of Age,* trans. Patrick O'Brian (New York: Putnam's, 1972), p. 290.

2. For an excellent survey and critique of Beauvoir's position, see Helen Small's *The Long Life* (New York: Oxford University Press, 2007), pp. 11–15. "To persist in a view of ourselves as 'not yet really old' [in Beauvoir's outlook] will be bad faith (the cardinal error for existentialists): going on believing in something about ourselves in the face of clear counter-evidence . . . And yet it is apparent that for Beauvoir it is almost impossible for the old person *not* to live in bad faith. Bad faith is the only way to keep going" (p. 14).

3. Anthony Ellis, *Old Age, Masculinity, and Early Modern Drama* (Farnham, Surrey, Eng.: Ashgate, 2009), p. 164.

4. George Puttenham, *The Art of English Poesy,* ed. Frank Whigham and Wayne A. Rebhorn (Ithaca, N.Y.: Cornell University Press, 2007), p. 384.

5. As Pat Thane observes, "Sixty was long the age at which law or custom permitted withdrawal from public activities on grounds of old age"; "Social Histories of Old Age and Aging," *Journal of Social History* 37 (2003): 97. Keith Thomas likewise points out that, although "So long as a man was capable [in the period], he could go on for as long as he liked," still "the idea of retirement as such was familiar"; "Age and Authority in Early Modern England," *Proceedings of the British Academy* 62 (1976): 236. See also Joel T. Rosenthal, "Retirement and the Life Cycle in Fifteenth-Century England," in Michael M. Sheehan (ed.), *Aging and the Aged in Medieval Europe* (Toronto: Pontifical Institute of Mediaeval Studies, 1990), pp. 173–88, for an assessment of the extent to which "retirement, at least in limited quantity and quality, as an institutional approach and as a personal solution," in fact existed on the threshold of early modernity (p. 175).

6. Thane, "Social Histories," 94.

7. Citation from *A Poetical Rhapsody,* ed. Hyder Edward Rollins, 2 vols. (Cambridge: Harvard University Press, 1931), 1:50. All further quotations from the poem, referenced parenthetically by page number, refer to this edition.

8. *The Essayes of Michael Lord of Montaigne,* trans. John Florio, 3 vols. (London: Oxford University Press, 1904–6), 3:21. All further in-text citations from Montaigne refer to this edition.

9. Homer, *The Odyssey,* trans. Richmond Lattimore (New York: Harper, 1975), bk. 18, line 74. For the full text of Lucian's "Heracles," see the Loeb edition of the works, trans. A. M. Harmon, 8 vols. (Cambridge: Harvard University Press, 1979), 1:63–71.

Index

Achilleos, Stella, 105, 206n14

Actes and Monuments (Foxe), 32

Aebischer, Pascale, 210n20

Aesop, 76, 203n26

Alciato, Andrea, 100, 178

Alençon, François de Valois, duc de (suitor to Elizabeth I), 24–25, 31, 34–38, 42

Alexander, Gavin, 204n38

Anacreontea, 105

Anatomy of Melancholy (Burton),177

Arcadia (Sannazaro), 66–68, 201n6

Arcadia (Sidney), 25, 27, 63, 65–66, 68, 79–91, 93, 95, 100–101, 150–53, 177, 180, 204n31, 204n42

Aristotle (*Rhetoric*), vii, 19, 26, 29, 191n71

Armstrong, Alan, 126, 209n53

Armstrong, Philip, 210n20

Art of English Poesy (Puttenham), 36, 38, 66, 177–79, 182, 184, 195n40, 201n4

Arte of Rhetorique (Wilson), 13, 188n48

Ascham, Roger, 44

Asher, Lyle, 174, 210n5, 212n31

Asp, Carolyn, 212n27

As You Like It (Shakespeare), 3, 64, 91, 124, 144, 146, 149

Ausonius, 105

Austin, J. L., 208n48

Avianus, 76, 203n26

Axton, Marie, 192n7

Bacon, Sir Francis (*Historia vitae & mortis*), 177

Baiae (Pontano), 105

Barnfield, Richard, 65, 97–100

Beam, Aki C. L., 194n20

Beauvoir, Simone de (*The Coming of Age*), 176, 180, 191n72, 213n2

Beer, Marina, 189n60

Bell, Ilona, 195n32, 195n38, 196n41, 208n42, 208n45

Benkert, Lysbeth, 197n59

Berger, Harry, Jr., 25, 68–70, 202n16, 202–3n20, 203n21, 203n24, 211n23

Berry, Edward, 204n36

Betts, Hanna, 194n22, 198n74

Biggs, Simon, 188n45

Blayney, Peter W. M., 210n16

Boethius (*De consolatione philosophiae*), 25, 45–47

Botelho, Lynn, 6, 7, 33, 177, 194n20

Bouchard, Gary M., 202n19

Braden, Gordon, 186n23

Bradner, Leicester, 48, 195n39, 197n56

Breton, Nicholas, 76, 203n26

Brink, Jean R., 211n22

Bucolicum carmen (Petrarch), 67–68, 202n11

Burghley. *See* Cecil, William, Lord Burghley

Burke, Peter, 189n59

Burrow, Colin, 114, 207n33

Burrow, J. A., 185n8
Burton, Robert (*Anatomy of Melancholy*), 177

Calderwood, James L., 212n27
Callaghan, Dympna, 116, 208n39
Camden, William, 30, 45–46, 146, 192n3
Campbell, Erin J., 7, 33, 186n27, 194n18
Campbell, Lily B., 209n5, 211n23
Campbell, Marion, 207n28
Campion, Thomas, 100–101
Carey, Henry, First Baron Hunsdon, 43
Carey, John, 133, 205n5
Carey, Sir Robert, 62
Carroll, William C., 138, 209n3
Castiglione, Baldassare (*The Courtier*), 15–17, 189nn58–60, 189n63
Caxton, William, 18
Cecil, William, Lord Burghley, 35, 43, 52, 54, 59–60, 195n28
Chamberlain, John, 62
Chamberlin, Frederick, 193n11
Charney, Maurice, 7, 187n28, 212n31
Chaudhuri, Sukanta, 95, 204n47
Chettle, Henry, 91
Chew, Samuel C., 185n8
Cicero, 94; *De senectute*, 6, 10–11, 14, 18–24, 61, 180, 187n42, 188n53, 190n69, 191n72, 191nn76–77
Civile Conversation (Guazzo), 153–54
Clapham, John, 192n4
Coffmann, George R., 188n51, 205n8
Cohen, Stephen, 53, 199n77
Cokayne, Karen, 10, 11, 104, 186n21
Colie, Rosalie L., 208n49
Colin Clouts Come Home Againe (Spenser), 110
Collinson, Patrick, 193n10
Colte, John, 62
Combe, Kirk, 209n5
The Coming of Age (de Beauvoir), 176, 180, 191n72, 213n2
Compton, William, 193n11
"Concerning olde Age," in *A Poetical Rapsody*, 181–82
constitution, as physical state, 2–4, 8–9, 11–14, 22, 24, 27, 31–32, 62, 68, 136, 139,

143, 159, 163, 165, 167, 176–78, 183
Content, Rob, 193n11
The Courtier (Castiglione), 15–17, 189nn58–60, 189n63
Crawford, Patricia, 194n20
Cuffe, Henry, 60, 128
Cullen, Patrick, 202n16
Curtius, Ernst Robert, 47, 197n62

Deats, Sara Munson, 212n27
De consolatione philosophiae (Boethius), 25, 45–47
Defence of Poetry (Sidney), 69
Deloney, Thomas, 56
de Maisse. *See* Hurault, André, Sieur de Maisse
De senectute (Cicero), 6, 10–11, 14, 18–24, 61, 180, 187n42, 188n53, 190n69, 191n72, 191nn76–77
Devereux, Robert, Second Earl of Essex, 25, 30–31, 42, 50, 59–61, 192n2, 200n98
Discoverie of a Gaping Gulf (Stubbs), 35–36, 38, 195nn31–32
Dobson, Michael, 192n8
Doctor Faustus (Marlowe), 141
Donne, John, 29, 107; "Antiquary" (Epigram 1), 101–2; "The Autumnall," 26, 103, 125–35, 208n47, 208n52; Holy Sonnet 11, 133; "That old Men are more Fantastique then younge" (paradox), 126
Donow, Herbert S., 145, 210n13, 212n32
Drant, Thomas, 47
Draper, John W., 211n23
Drayton, Michael, 65, 95–97, 106
Driscoll, James P., 211n23
Dubrow, Heather, 127, 209n54
Dudley, Robert, Earl of Leicester, 43, 55, 60, 196n46
Duncan-Jones, E. E., 209n56
Duncan-Jones, Katherine, 79, 203n28
Duran, Susan, 195n33

Edward VI, 5, 53–54
Elizabeth I, 2, 8, 30–63 passim, 79, 103, 108, 112, 141, 146, 172–77, 180, 192n4, 192nn7–8, 193nn10–11, 196n46, 198n74, 199n78 and 88, 200n91, 200n98,

207n24; and de Maisse embassy, 25, 48–58; funeral effigy of, 62; letters, 32, 36, 50–51, 53, 61, 195n34, 195n36, 195n39, 197n61; marriage negotiations, 24, 32, 34–36, 42; and "Mask of Youth" convention, 33–34, 54, 62, 194n22; poetry, 24, 36–42, 195n39; prayers, 32, 193n14; and Shakespeare, 26–27, 172–75; speeches, 25, 32, 42–43, 50, 55–56, 61–62, 193–94nn14–15; translations, 25, 44–48, 197n54, 197n56, 197n59, 197nn64–65

Ellis, Anthony, 7, 145, 177, 187n28, 210n6
Erasmus, Desiderius, 5, 132, 189n56
Erickson, Carolly, 192n2, 193n11, 194n24, 196n47, 198n74
Esler, Anthony, 2, 185nn3–5
Essex. See Devereux, Robert, Second Earl of Essex
Estrin, Barbara, 196n44

Fernie, Ewan, 213n37
Ferry, Anne, 205n5
Ficino, Marsilio, 64
Fiedler, Leslie, 9, 187n35, 205n7
Fineman, Joel, 123, 208n46
Finlay, Robert, 15, 189n57
Finley, M. I., 191n72
Florio, John (translator of Montaigne), 182–83
Foakes, R. A., 212n31
Fontanone, Stephany, 198n74
Fortescue, Thomas, 3, 4, 13, 14, 185n7
Foxe, John (Actes and Monuments), 32
Fraenkel, Lisa, 208n41
Freedman, Richard, 185n2
Friedland, Louis S., 203n25
Froide, Amy M., 33, 194n19
Frye, Northrop, 153, 211n23
Frye, Susan, 30–31, 192n8, 194n24, 199n81, 200n90
Fulwood, William (A Spectacle for Perjurers broadside), 147–48

Gammer Gurtons Nedle, 140
Garrard, Mary D., 194n21
Gascoigne, George, 106, 206n19
generational conflict: dramatic representa-
tion of, 140–45, 150, 154–63, 172, 176; at the Elizabethan court, 2, 30, 60–61, 79, 146, 192nn1–2; and pastoral, 64–65, 67–68, 70–90, 96–97, 201n3, 201n6, 201n8, 201n10, 202n20; and Protestant ideology, 142–44, 203n23
gerontophobia, 1, 8, 15, 18, 26, 29, 33, 48, 70, 83, 85, 87, 94, 103, 116, 118–20, 122–23, 126–27, 132, 134–36, 140, 143–44, 157, 165, 169, 177, 180, 185n2
Gilbert, Creighton, 5, 6, 186n17
Googe, Barnabe, 67, 201n10
Gorges, Sir Arthur, 112
Greek Anthology, 105, 128
Greenblatt, Stephen J., 107–8, 207n24, 207n27, 211n26
Greller, Mary Alice, 126, 208n51
Greville, Fulke, First Lord Brooke, 62, 106, 135
Guazzo, Stefano (Civile Conversation), 153–54
Guilpin, Everard, 205n4
Gullette, Margaret Morganroth, 1, 9, 185n2, 187n38
Guy, John, 43, 196n49

Haber, Judith, 83, 85, 204n35
Haigh, Christopher, 192n1, 194n22, 196n50
Halpern, Richard, 202n18, 211n24, 212n35
Hammer, Paul E. J., 192n2
Harington, Sir John, 32, 44, 59, 62, 194n16
Harington, Sir John, the elder, 38, 196n42
Harrison, William, and Holinshed's Chronicle, 4, 13, 32, 186n9, 188n49
Harvey, Elizabeth D., 129, 199n76
Hatton, Sir Christopher, 43, 60
Hazan, Haim, 9, 187n37
Hendricks, John, 191n74
Henry III (King of France), 34
Henry IV (King of France), 45–46, 49–51, 56–58
Henry IV plays (Shakespeare), 144–45
Henry VIII (Shakespeare), 174–75
Hentzner, Paul, 61, 198n75, 199n78, 199n84
Hepworth, Mike, 188n45
Herbert, Lady Magdalen, 125–26

Hercules Oetaeus (Seneca), 44–45
Heywood, John, 107
Heywood, Thomas, 146, 177
Hicks, Greg, 139
Historia vitae & mortis (Bacon),177
Hoby, Sir Thomas, translator of Castiglione, 15, 18, 189n59
Hockey, Jenny, 10, 187n40
Homer, *Odyssey,* 110, 184
Horace, 47–48, 57, 103, 205n9
Howard, Henry, First Earl of Northampton, 35
Howes, John, 5
Hughey, Ruth, 196n42
Hurault, André, Sieur de Maisse (French ambassador to Elizabeth I), 25, 31, 48–58, 61, 198n75, 199n78

Innocent III, Pope, 14, 188n51
Isocrates, 191n71

Jaffa, Harry F., 211n24
Jaggard, William, and *The Passionate Pilgrime,* 102, 114–15, 135
James, Allison, 10, 187n40
James VI and I, 42, 50, 61–62, 146
Jardine, Lisa, 52, 198n75
Jenkins, Richard, 10, 187n40
Johnson, Lynn Staley, 202n20
Johnson, Paul, 198n74, 200n98
Jonson, Ben, 33, 135, 194n23
Joubert, Laurent, 8, 9, 14, 108–9, 187nn32–33
Juvenal, 103

Kahn, Paul W., 154, 212n29
Kalender of Shepherdes, 71
Kendall, Timothe, 1, 3, 124, 185n1
Kennedy, William J., 67, 201n7
Kerrigan, William, 28, 186n23, 192n81, 202n14
King, John, 57, 195n32, 203n23
King Lear (Shakespeare), 8, 9, 26–29, 90, 137–76 passim, 180, 209–10n5, 210n16, 211nn23–24, 211n26, 212nn27–28, 212nn30–35, 213nn37–39
Klause, John, 115, 120, 207n36

Knollys, Sir Francis, the elder, 43
Kolsky, Stephen D., 17, 190n62

Laam, Kevin P., 206n19
Lambarde, William, 61
Languet, Hubert, 79, 85, 88, 203n30
Lanham, Richard A., 189n61
Lannoy, Cornelius, 194n23
Laslett, Peter, 186nn11–12
Latham, Agnes, 113, 207n31
Laurentius, Andreas, 13–14, 188n50
Lee, Sir Henry, 196n51, 208n42
Lemnius, Levinus, 13, 17, 185n6
Letters of Old Age (Petrarch), 14, 188n53
Letters on Familiar Matters (Petrarch), 188n53
Levin, Carole, 49, 192n7, 198nn68–69
life stages, early modern subdivisions of, 3–4, 8–9, 13–14, 32–33, 71, 187n33
Linceus Spectacles (Lloyd), 147, 172
Lloyd, Lodowick (*Linceus Spectacles*), 147, 172
Lodge, Thomas, 11, 65, 91–95, 97, 144, 204n46
A Lover's Complaint (Shakespeare), 114, 116–18, 208nn40–42
Lucian, 178–79, 184
Lyly, John, 140–41, 147, 149

MacCaffrey, Wallace, 200n97
"Maidens choice twixt Age and Youth," in *The Passionate Pilgrime,* 102
Manningham, John, 44, 62, 196n53
Mantuan, 67, 201n10
Marcus, Leah, 31, 193n10
Marlowe, Christopher (*Doctor Faustus*), 141
Marotti, Arthur, 115, 207n34, 208n52
Martin, Christopher, 80–81, 204n33, 204n37, 208n43
Marx, Steven, 65, 98, 190n62, 201n3
Mary I, 38, 53
Mary Stuart, Queen of Scots, 36, 38, 41–43, 196n47
Maximianus, 26, 103–4, 206n11
McCoy, Richard, 85–86, 203n28
McMullan, Gordon, 28, 173, 192n81
Mendelson, Sara, 194n20

Merry Wives of Windsor (Shakespeare), 145–46
Mexia, Pedro, 3
Middleton, Thomas, 177
Mildmay, Sir Walter, 43
Milne, Drew, 213n38
Minois, Georges, 6, 14, 186n25, 189n58, 191n72
Mirror for Magistrates, 17–18, 150, 190n68
Montaigne, Michel de, 42, 182–84
Montrose, Louis Adrian, 48, 194n22, 197n66, 198n69

Nashe, Thomas, 205n4
Nemesianus, 67, 201n8
New Custome (interlude), 141–43, 145
Newton, Thomas: translator of Cicero, 18, 22, 187n42, 191n70; translator of Lemnius, 13, 17, 185n6
Nitecki, Alicia K., 188n51

oak and briar fable, 75–78, 203nn25–26
Ocean to Scinthia (Ralegh), 110–14, 120, 207nn27–28
Odyssey (Homer), 110, 184
Okes, Nicholas, 147, 210n16
old age: classical conceptions of, 10–13, 19–24, 29; in contemporary cultural scholarship, 5–8, 10, 28, 185n2, 186n22, 187n38; early modern definitions of, 1–9, 13–18, 28; and early modern demography, 4–5, 185n5; and sexuality, 8–9, 16–17, 24, 26, 80–83, 98–110, 114–36, 187n32, 205n7, 207n34; and women, 32–33, 103, 205n8, 207n34
"Olde *Melibeus* Song, courting his Nimph," in *Englands Helicon,* 135–36
Old Law, 177
The Old, Old Very Old Man (Taylor), 177
Oliver, Leslie Mahin, 210n9
O'Loughlin, Michael, 201n9
Osborn, James M., 193n12
Ottaway, Susannah R., 7, 177, 186n21
Ovid, 49, 83, 105

Pantalone (stock character in commedia dell'arte), 140, 210n6

Paradise of Daintie Devices (Whetstone), 138
Parkin, Tim, 19, 105, 186n21, 191n74, 205n9
pastoral: in humanist literary hierarchy, 66; as locus of retirement, 63; place of elder in, 64–68, 70–79, 181–82
Paulet, Sir Amyas, 34
Paulet, William, 18
Perret, Marion D., 212n33
Perry, Curtis, 146, 173, 210n15
Petrarch: *Bucolicum carmen,* 67–68, 202n11; *Letters of Old Age,* 14, 188n53; *Letters on Familiar Matters,* 188n53; *Remedies for Fortune Foul and Fair,* 14–15, 189n54
Philip II (King of Spain), 55
Plato, *Republic,* 19
Plautus, 103
Plutarch, 23, 47, 76, 180, 191n77, 203n26
Pontano, Giovanni Gioviano (*Baiae*), 105
Porter, Laurel, 212n35
Portmort, Thomas, 50
Puckering, Sir John, 43
puer senex figure, 69, 142, 144
Puttenham, George (*Art of English Poesy*), 36, 38, 66, 177–79, 182, 184, 195n40, 201n4

Ralegh, Sir Walter, 26, 29, 38, 60, 103; "Epitaph on Sidney," 108; "Farewell to the Court," 109; "Nature that washt her hands in milke," 107; "Nymphs reply," 107–8; *Ocean to Scinthia,* 110–14, 120, 207nn27–28; "Praysed be *Dianaes* faire and harmelesse light," 108; "Walsingham," 109–10, 112, 119, 207n26
Read, Conyers, 195n28
Remedies for Fortune Foul and Fair (Petrarch), 14–15, 189n54
Renwick, R. L., 202n17, 203n27
Republic (Plato), 19
Rhetoric (Aristotle), vii, 19, 26, 29, 191n71
Ricci, Theresa, 190n63
Rich, Penelope, 60
Ricks, Christopher, 208n44
Rocklin, Edward L., 210n18
Rodheaver, Dean, 20, 191n75
Roe, John, 207nn33–34

Roebuck, Janet, 190n66
Rose, Mary Beth, 192n4
Rosenberg, Marvin, 212n34
Rosenmeyer, Patricia A., 206n14
Rosenmeyer, Thomas G., 65, 200n2
Rosenthal, Joel T., 213n5
Rowley, Thomas, 177
Rowse, A. L., 50
Rudd, Anthony, Bishop, 43–44, 196n52
Rudenstine, Neil, 84–85, 203n30, 204n36
Ruines of Time (Spenser), 203n26
Ryan, Kiernan, 28, 192n79, 213n39

Sabie, Francis, 65, 97
Sackville, Sir Thomas, 17–18
Sadler, Sir Ralph, 35, 195n29, 196n47
Sannazaro, Jacopo (*Arcadia*), 66–68, 201n6
Schnader, Kenneth, 209n5
Schoenfeldt, Michael C., 10, 187n41, 199n76
Scott, William O., 209n5, 211n24
Seneca, 188n46; Epistle 12, 12–13, 130; Epistle 121, 11; *Hercules Oetaeus*, 44–45
senex amans tradition, 103, 123, 136
Shahar, Shulamith, 10, 186n21, 188n51
Shakespeare, William: *As You Like It*, 3, 64, 91, 124, 144, 146, 149; *Henry IV* plays, 144–45; *Henry VIII*, 174–75; *King Lear*, 8, 9, 26–29, 90, 137–76 passim, 180, 209–10n5, 210n16, 211nn23–24, 211n26, 212nn27–28, 212nn30–35, 213nn37–39; *A Lover's Complaint*, 114, 116–18, 208nn40–42; *Merry Wives of Windsor*, 145–46; *Sonnets*, 114–16, 118–25, 207nn33–34, 208n43, 208n45
Sheafe, Thomas (*Vindiciæ Senectutis*), 177
Shell, Marc, 44, 197n54
Shepheardes Calender (Spenser), 8, 25, 63, 65, 68–79, 85, 90–91, 93, 95, 110, 177, 180, 182
Sidney, Mary, 89
Sidney, Sir Philip, 5, 29, 32, 108, 203n28, 203n30; *Arcadia*, 25, 27, 63, 65–66, 68, 79–91, 93, 95, 100–101, 150–53, 177, 180, 204n31, 204n42; *Defence of Poetry*, 69; and *King Lear*, 90, 150–53, 164

Sidney, Sir Robert, 59, 200n93
Singleton, Hugh, 35, 195n33
Small, Helen, 6, 28, 68, 166, 186n22, 210n5, 212n30, 213n2
Smith, Henry, 142–43
Smith, Steven R., 5, 187n13, 190n66, 209n59
Sohm, Philip, 7, 187n28, 188n45
Somerset, Anne, 193n11, 199n88
Songes and Sonettes (Tottel), 38–39
Sonnets (Shakespeare), 114–16, 118–25, 207nn33–34, 208n43, 208n45
A Spectacle for Perjurers (broadside), 147–48
Spenser, Edmund, 29; *Colin Clouts Come Home Againe*, 110; *Ruines of Time*, 203n26; *Shepheardes Calender*, 8, 25, 63, 65, 68–79, 85, 90–91, 93, 95, 110, 177, 180, 182
Stancroft, William, Archbishop, 177
Stillman, Robert, 86, 112, 204n39, 207n29
Stone, Lawrence, 190n66
Strier, Richard, 211n24
Strong, Roy, 194n22
Stubbs, John (*Discoverie of a Gaping Gulf*), 35–36, 38, 195nn31–32
Summit, Jennifer, 195n41
Surphlet, Richard (translator of Laurentius), 13

Tague, Ingrid H., 7
Tate, Nahum, 139
Taunton, Nina, 7, 8, 187n30, 189n58, 191n70, 212n28
Taylor, John (*The Old, Old Very Old Man*), 177
Terence, 103
Thane, Pat, 4–6, 9, 19, 28, 180, 185n5, 186n19, 213n5
Theocritus, 83
Theognis, 137
Thomas, Keith, 6, 17, 28, 186n24, 213n5
Topcliffe, Richard, 50
Tottel, Richard, *Songes and Sonettes*, 38–39
Troyansky, David G., 186n21
True Chronicle Historie of King Leir, 146, 150, 153, 211n22

Vaux, Sir Thomas, Second Baron Vaux,
106, 206n19
Vertue, George, 62
Villeponteaux, Marie, 192n7
Vindiciæ Senectutis (Sheafe), 177
Virgil, 67, 110, 201n9
vituperatio senectute tradition, 103, 205n8

Walker, Julia, 192n5, 194n22
Walsingham, Sir Francis, 35, 43, 60
Watson, Nicola J., 192n8
Wernham, R. B., 192n1, 198n71
Whetstone, George (*Paradise of Daintie
Devices)*, 138
Whigham, Frank, 190n61
White, Rowland, 59–60
Whitney, Geffrey, 100–101
Williams, Penry, 199n88
Wilson, Elkin Calhoun, 207n23

Wilson, Emily, 211n23
Wilson, Thomas (*Arte of Rhetorique*), 13,
188n48
Woodward, Jennifer, 200n105
Woodward, Kathleen, 28, 68, 185n2,
186n21, 202n13
Woudhuysen, W. R., 90, 204n40
Wright, Thomas, 195n40
Wrightson, Keith, 186n12
Wyatt, Sir Thomas, the elder, 17, 24,
38–40, 106–7, 190n67, 196n44
Wyatt-Brown, Anne, 6, 186n20
Wythorne, Thomas, 106–7

Yandell, Cathy, 103, 206n10

Zak, William F., 211n23
Zerbi, Gabriele, 15, 189n56

After completing his PhD at the University of Virginia in 1986 and spending a year as visiting assistant professor at Kenyon College, CHRISTOPHER MARTIN joined the English Department at Boston University in 1987, where he has served as NEH Distinguished Teaching Professor, and specializes in the literature and culture of early modern Europe. In addition to two previous books—*Policy in Love: Lyric and Public in Ovid, Petrarch and Shakespeare* (1994) and *Ovid in English* (1998)—he has published articles in such journals as *English Literary Renaissance, Early Modern Women, John Donne Journal, Spenser Studies, Shakespeare Quarterly, Sidney Journal, Essays in Criticism*, and *Illinois Classical Studies*. He lives with his wife Lydia in Quincy, Massachusetts.